Class Acts

Teachers Reflect on Their Own Classroom Practice

Edited by

IRENE HALL

CAROLYN H. CAMPBELL

EDWARD J. MIECH

Reprint Series No. 29
Harvard Educational Review

Library of Congress Catalog Card Number 96-78839

ISBN 0-916690-31-8

Harvard Educational Review
6 Appian Way
Gutman Library Suite 349
Cambridge, MA 02138

Cover Design: David Ford
Editorial Production: Dody Riggs
Typesetting: Sheila Walsh

Contents

CONTENTS

Foreword

VIVIAN GUSSIN PALEY

What compels some of us periodically to turn our classrooms inside out, pulling apart the status quo in order to test yet another notion we cannot get off our minds? Annie Dillard thinks she knows why, and, though she is describing writers, not teachers, she comes pretty close to pinning it down.

In *The Writing Life* she states:

> Why do you never find anything written about that idiosyncratic thought you avert to, about your fascination with something no one else understands? Because it is up to you. There is something you find interesting for a reason hard to explain. It is hard to explain because you have never read it on any page; there you begin. You were made and set here to give voice to this, your own astonishment.[1]

Such a sense of wonder is no small thing. The exhilaration of it all keeps Dillard and other writers at their desks for hours on end, as if their lives depend on finding the perfect sentence with which to convey each detail of this astonishment.

Imagine these same feelings transposed into a teacher's classroom life. Suddenly the day is infused with new highs and lows of purpose and perplexity, as the stubborn habits of a lifetime compete with a determined resolve to follow the "idiosyncratic thought," no matter where it leads.

When teachers stumble onto "something no one else understands" and begin to replace the plot and motivation of familiar school scenarios with a story no one has heard before, it is a heady experience. And not always a welcome one. The old ways step on fewer conventional beliefs and practices and will seldom drive a person to the writing table after a full day of teaching.

White Teacher, my first book, came about in just such a way, though I tried to avoid paths of inquiry in which it would necessarily be my own behavior that would be examined and found wanting. The idiosyncratic thoughts that both astonished and disheartened me concerned the possibility that I did not view every child in the same favorable light. Having made the awful discovery that my expectations for Black children might be lower than those I held for White children, my fate was sealed. I would forever after be searching for the truth behind this and all other carefully hidden cover-ups that surrounded me in the classroom.

---

[1] Annie Dillard, *The Writing Life* (New York: Harper & Row, 1989), pp. 67–68.

Since these subjects were seldom openly discussed, I would have to become my own best witness, watching for the predetermined, unequal judgments levied upon children who did not look, speak, or move in accord with my own shadow. Once entered, the avenue of self-disclosure is inescapable; the further one wanders, the more evidence is to be found.

Whatever were the circumstances of the new narratives in the books that followed, my original focus leaped out from every corner, always ready to astonish me. Obviously there was still a great distance to go toward creating classrooms in which every person's story becomes a necessary and equal part of the communal legend.

The teachers who describe their findings in *Class Acts* have been overtaken by their own unexpected disclosures; something is going on in their classrooms that they must study closely and ponder grandly. As their teaching and studying ride tandem on a road suddenly filled with bumps and potholes, it becomes clear that talk will not be enough. The process of self–examination underlying any significant alteration of classroom behavior and belief — when we ourselves are the teachers — must finally reach the pages of our daily journal. There is no other way to listen to ourselves think.

In the stories included here, each teacher has stumbled upon a uniquely different matter of concern. *Stumbled* is the way it happens. A child or parent says something disturbing, or a line in a book points accusingly in our direction, and the ground beneath us begins to tremble. Lessons go wrong, reliable connections are obscured, safe relationships appear to crumble, and the walls close in. The time is ripe for astonishment.

Annie Dillard, who so beautifully evokes the ordinary and extraordinary in her own life, would, I think, find much to write about if she were a classroom teacher. The continual unfolding of young lives in the minutiae of daily events provide those of us fortunate enough to be both stage director and audience an endless supply of conflicts, characters, and continuities for our stories. We are in the enviable position of watching a multitude of dramas pass across the same stage while we imagine ways to engage the actors and sweeten the outcome.

Having come upon a vision of a better world, we place our dreams directly into action. This is the way of teachers. And, even if we decide to join Ms. Dillard's company of writers, there will always be a difference. We may learn to simulate in writing the dilemmas, discoveries, and departures that no one else understands in the way we do, but we are bidden to return the next day or the next year, stage center front, and try everything out again. The script is always ready to be rewritten, with a new cast of characters in place, and we ourselves are never the same.

Schoolteachers cannot escape this continual rethinking of interpretations and postulations; our students will not sit still long enough for definitive portraits and our wishes often supersede the actual event. Never can we say, "There, it's done, I've explained it all."

In the more than twenty years since I began to write about my classroom, I have met increasing numbers of teachers who are writing about theirs. I must warn them that the activity is addictive. The habit of asking one's own questions and then reorganizing the classroom in order to search for answers is irresistible.

Nor can the "What will happen if we . . . ?" be kept the private domain of the teacher. Children are quick to perceive that school has become a place where people learn to move with the flow of their own questions. It is an intellectually and emotionally charged drama and the children become our primary colleagues. Together we examine and act out each line of the script, building our narrative from the ground up, always trying to determine who we are and what we are learning.

Since we are creating a story no one has ever heard before, there is no way of knowing where the next turn in the plot will appear. Each day we throw out our net, ready to be astonished by what we catch, for it is in the unfamiliar, the unheralded, and the unexpected that we find our unique teaching and writing voices.

"But there is always so much else to do," a student teacher tells me. "Why make it such a roundabout process? I mean, besides the fact that it's really fun to teach this way." She pauses, "Or is that the point?"

We smile at each other; she has found me out.

Introduction

Sometimes a single first-person reflection by a teacher on his or her own teaching is worth a hundred academic treatises on how to join educational theory and practice. In this remarkable collection of articles, primary and secondary school teachers delve deeply into the vital and complex worlds of their classrooms as they struggle to gain a better understanding of their students, themselves, and the act of teaching. Driven by curiosity and the desire to improve their practice, these teachers show how open-ended and concerted inquiry into the world of the classroom over time can blur traditional dichotomies between research and teaching, theory and practice, and teaching and learning in concrete ways that directly benefit students.

The contributors to *Class Acts* represent a diversity of backgrounds, subjects, grade levels, educational philosophies, pedagogical strategies, and teaching contexts. They share a common approach, however, in that they all take time to reflect on finding new ways to listen to students, to make sense of their own teaching, and to take risks to transform work and social relations in their classrooms. In reflecting on their own classroom practice and then sharing those reflections with a wider audience, these teachers offer an engaging model of classroom teaching that stands in stark contrast to the traditional pedagogy found in U.S. schools — a pedagogy that has changed relatively little over the past century.[1]

In the traditional pedagogical model, the teacher stands at the front of the classroom, students sit in straight rows facing the teacher, and the teacher "fills" the students with information. Metaphorically speaking, teachers are like pitchers of knowledge who pour information into empty vessels, their students. If these empty vessels are of roughly the same size and type, teachers can dispense their information with particular efficiency, so school policies promoting homogeneous grouping and tracking work in tandem with this model of classroom teaching. Within this traditional paradigm, instruction is teacher-centered, student learning is construed as a passive process of receiving information, and pedagogy is impersonal; the individuality of each student in the room has little or no influence on the content and form of the lessons presented by the teacher.[2]

---

[1] For a historical analysis of this subject, see Larry Cuban's *How Teachers Taught: Constancy and Change in America's Classrooms, 1890–1990* (New York: Teachers College Press, 1993).

[2] Paulo Freire refers to this traditional model of pedagogy as the "banking model" of education in *Pedagogy of the Oppressed*, 2nd ed. (London: Penguin, 1996). bell hooks also offers an extended critique of this model in her book *Teaching to Transgress* (New York: Routledge, 1994).

The contributors to *Class Acts* provide compelling visions of classroom teaching that are far richer and more dynamic than this traditional model. All emphasize the importance of listening to their students and learning from what they hear. These teachers see their students as much more than a faceless mass. Their classrooms become, rather, communities in which teacher and students are individuals who learn together and from one another.

Several examples from *Class Acts* help illustrate this point. In "Living with the Pendulum: The Complex World of Teaching," Jeanette Throne explains that when working with Matthew, a kindergarten student, she discovered that she "had to let Matthew teach me so I could learn how best to teach him. What I learned from Matthew enriched my teaching for all children" (p. 208). In "Arts as Epistemology: Enabling Children to Know What They Know," Karen Gallas describes how she built her science program around listening to her first graders: "Juan [a student] was teaching me once again a lesson that I seem to have to relearn each year: listen to the children. They will show you what they know and how they learn best, and often that way is not the teacher's way" (p. 94). In "Writing Workshop as Carnival: Reflections on an Alternative Learning Environment," Timothy Lensmire emphasizes the centrality of his students: "Students have something to say about who speaks and who is heard. We ignore what they are saying at our children's and our own peril" (p. 147).

This unfolding of students' perspectives and understandings takes place over time. Vivian Gussin Paley, who contributed the foreword to *Class Acts*, vividly described this aspect of teacher reflection in an article that appeared in the *Harvard Educational Review*: "Like a slow-motion Polaroid developing its images, piece by piece, over many months, the children's patterns of thought and speech need much time to be revealed."[3] This process of reflecting on one's own classroom naturally reveals that some efforts on the part of the teacher are less successful than others. In *Class Acts*, the authors discuss difficulties they encountered in practice and do not gloss over the bumps in the road in order to present a neat, sanitized, "brochure" version of their classrooms.

The pedagogical shift in viewing students as subjects rather than objects, and of conceptualizing teaching as a dynamic process of inquiry and discovery rather than as a static, technical task, has a long history. According to Michael Huberman, a well-known qualitative researcher in education, an early example of the theory of teacher research comes from Giambattista Vico, who proposed in the eighteenth century that "participants in an activity have a *direct acquaintance* or *sympathetic insight* into the phenomena under study, whereas outsiders are more like an audience."[4]

---

[3] Vivian Gussin Paley, "Listening to What the Children Say," *Harvard Educational Review*, 56, No. 2 (1986), 127.

[4] A. Michael Huberman, "Moving Mainstream: Taking a Closer Look at Teacher Research," *Language Arts*, 73, No. 2 (1996), 124.

The Temple School in Boston, founded in the mid-1800s by Bronson Alcott (father of Louisa May), Elizabeth Peabody, and Margaret Fuller, is an early example of teachers and students engaging in a classroom community of inquiry in the United States. These three educators based their school on the fundamental principles that schools should be places where teachers and students test their ideas and that the good teachers are those who ask good questions. Alice and John Dewey's Laboratory School at the University of Chicago is another prominent example of teacher research in the United States at the turn of the century. The school's purpose was, as its name implied, to experiment continually in order to discover the conditions under which children learned best. Unlike many teacher researchers today, whose work is often "done in the interstices, on stolen time,"[5] teachers at the Laboratory School were expected, as faculty members, to challenge accepted notions about teaching and learning, to reflect systematically both individually and collaboratively on their practice, and to write about their findings.

Current teacher research aims to contribute to knowledge about teaching and to move both its practice and its lessons from the private world of good teaching to the public world of debate, discussion, and learning. The introduction to *Class Acts* includes an article by Susan Lytle and Marilyn Cochran-Smith, entitled "Teacher Research as a Way of Knowing," to help readers understand how teacher inquiry relates to the broader context of education research on teaching. Lytle and Cochran-Smith discuss how teacher research can redefine and enrich a knowledge base for teaching, a knowledge base that in the past has privileged the work of university researchers, and argue that viewing teachers as knowers, and not merely as receptacles for others' knowledge, is critical to altering the cultures of both schools and universities.

The importance of this mode of inquiry into classroom practice takes on an additional note of urgency when considering the role of schools in a society that is increasingly diverse, and increasingly influenced by the "information age." In her 1996 presidential address at the annual meeting of the American Education Research Association, Linda Darling-Hammond identified the advancement of teaching not only as the issue of the decade, but as the problem of the next century:

> The problem of the next century will be "the advancement of teaching," and its resolution will depend on our ability to develop knowledge for a very different kind of teaching than what has been the norm for most of this century. If we want all students to actually learn in the way that new standards suggest and today's complex society demands, we will need to develop teaching that goes far beyond dispensing information, giving a test, and giving a grade. We will need to understand how to teach in ways that respond to students' diverse approaches to learning, that are structured to

---

[5] Huberman, "Moving Mainstream," p. 130.

take advantage of students' unique starting points, and that carefully scaffold work aimed at more proficient performances.[6]

Reflective teaching is at the heart of pedagogical change. In *Class Acts,* the authors are immersed in the day-to-day realities of teaching, work with and respect their students as individuals, and focus on the complexities and intricacies of their own classroom practice. These first-person reflections have much to teach us about the role of thoughtful practitioners in developing better models of pedagogy to foster the growth of all our children.

IRENE HALL
CAROLYN H. CAMPBELL
EDWARD J. MIECH
Editors

---

[6] Linda Darling-Hammond, "The Right to Learn and the Advancement of Teaching: Research, Policy, and Practice for Democratic Education," *Educational Researcher, 25,* No. 6 (1996), 7.

Teacher Research
as a Way of Knowing

SUSAN L. LYTLE

MARILYN COCHRAN-SMITH

Over the past several decades, there have been a variety of efforts to codify a knowledge base for teaching. Implicit in these efforts is a theory that privileges one source of knowledge, that of university researchers, over others. In this article, we argue that educators need to develop a different theory of knowledge for teaching, a different epistemology that regards inquiry by teachers themselves as a distinctive and important way of knowing about teaching. From this perspective, fundamental questions about knowing, knowers, and what can be known have different answers. Teachers are among those who have the authority to know — that is, to construct "capital K" knowledge about teaching, learning, and schooling. And what is worth knowing about teaching includes what teachers, who are researchers in their own classrooms, can know through their own systematic inquiry.

As we have argued previously (Cochran-Smith & Lytle, 1990), teacher researchers are uniquely positioned to provide a truly emic perspective that makes visible the ways students and teachers together construct knowledge. When teachers do research, they draw on interpretive frameworks built from their own histories and intellectual interests. Because their research process is embedded in practice, the relationship between knower and known is significantly altered. This obviates the necessity of "translating findings" in

This article appears with the permission of Teachers College Press. It is an adaptation of Chapter 3 in the book *Inside/Outside: Teacher Research and Knowledge*, edited by Susan L. Lytle and Marilyn Cochran-Smith, © Teachers College Press, Columbia University, 1993.

Harvard Educational Review Vol. 62 No. 4 Winter 1992, 447–474

the conventional sense, and moves teacher research toward praxis, or critical reflection on practice (Lather, 1986). Further, because teacher researchers often inquire with their students, students themselves are also empowered as knowers (Branscombe, Goswami, & Schwartz, 1992; Cone, 1990). With this different epistemology, teacher research, which is currently marginalized in the field, would contribute to a fundamental reconceptualization of the notion of knowledge for teaching. Through inquiry, teachers play a role in reinventing the conventions of interpretive social science, just as feminist researchers and critical ethnographers do by making problematic the relationships of researcher and researched, knowledge and authority, and subject and object (Crawford & Marecek, 1989; Noffke, 1990).

One way to illustrate the contrast we are suggesting between epistemologies of teaching is to examine a recent compilation of essays that represents the university-generated knowledge base. In 1989, the American Association of Colleges for Teacher Education (AACTE) released the charter edition of a volume intended to define the knowledge that beginning teachers should have and to close the gap between the "state of the art" and the "state of practice" in teaching. Entitled *Knowledge Base for the Beginning Teacher* (Reynolds, 1989), the volume begins with a statement of assumptions, each of which implicitly takes a position on ways of knowing about teaching:

1. What is known and worth knowing about teaching . . . should be related to the practical knowledge possessed by teachers of how and when to act in actual teaching situations.
2. Knowledge about teaching will never be absolute or complete. . . . Teachers should be prepared for a career in which they are continuously involved . . . in making adaptations in their work in accord with the changing knowledge base and their own teaching situations.
3. The knowledge base for teaching takes a variety of forms and is drawn from many disciplines and other sources, including research, inventions, tested practice (maxims), and value principles held by the community. . . . This knowledge base, when mastered, will provide teachers with a unique fund of knowledge. . . .
4. Teaching is a profession. Knowledgeable teachers are not technicians, but professionals, worthy and able to make reflective decisions or judgments and plans based on principled knowledge that is adapted to the particulars of their teaching situations, their students, their unique experiences, and their own special insights, self-knowledge, values, and commitments. They have a body of understandings, knowledge, skills, and dispositions: a set of constructs that can be invoked for the explanation of cognitive phenomena. . . . Professional judgment is required. Knowledge . . . enlarges the range and quality of discretionary judgments made by professional teachers in the performance of their complex work.
5. There is no single taxonomy or correct way of structuring the knowledge base for teaching. . . . The particular structure [of this volume] probably

will be revised in the future on the basis of added knowledge and improved professional insights. . . .

6. Although [this volume provides] a means for presenting a number of seemingly discrete areas of knowledge, the importance of the volume to teachers [is] the understanding of how professional knowledge is organized, validated, and used. (p. x)

By synthesizing and making accessible a wide range of important ideas about teaching, learning, and schooling, the volume provides a valuable resource for teacher education not only at the pre-service level, but across the developmental continuum. As Griffin (1989) underscores in the closing chapter, the contributors to the volume emphasize that knowledge for teaching is mutable and that theories, research, and practical wisdom all play influential roles in school programs.

While we do not wish to take issue with the ideas presented in the individual chapters of this volume — in fact, as teacher educators, we find them extremely valuable — we think it is important to question some of the assumptions about knowledge and teachers' roles in the creation and use of knowledge that frame the volume as a whole. Since Dewey's (1904) writings at the beginning of this century, scholars and researchers have devoted considerable attention to understanding the relationships of knowledge and teaching (Fenstermacher, 1986; Greene, 1973; Lortie, 1975; Shulman, 1986a,b, 1987). From various disciplinary perspectives and research paradigms, scholars have asked what it means to know about teaching — what can be known, how it can be known, who has the authority to know, and how knowledge can or should be used for theoretical and practical purposes. What the editors of the AACTE volume seem to be saying is that the knowledge that makes teaching a profession comes from authorities outside of the profession itself. What makes teachers professional is using this knowledge base in their daily practice. In the epistemology upon which this volume is based, then, teachers are knowledgeable in that they have "insights" as well as "knowledge, skills, and dispositions," which they call upon to explain phenomena and make judgments about practice. Teachers do not, however, participate in the *generation* of knowledge, or what the editors of the volume refer to as official, "principled," "discipline-based" knowledge.

Obviously we are *not* suggesting here that the knowledge contained in this volume or in other similar publications is of no use to teachers or teacher educators. To the contrary, we agree that there is a rich body of information generated by university researchers that ought to inform the practice of teaching, and that making that knowledge accessible for teachers' critical appraisal and adaptation is an essential endeavor. The epistemology embodied in these assumptions, however, is exclusionary and disenfranchising. It stipulates that knowing the knowledge base for teaching — what university researchers have discovered — is *the* privileged way to know about teaching. Knowing the knowledge base is, as the preface to the volume suggests, what "distinguishes more productive teachers from less productive ones" (Reynolds, 1989, p. ix).

Our aim in this article is to explore the contribution of teacher inquiry to a new theory of knowledge for teaching. This article is not an analysis of the forms and domains of teachers' knowledge, although this is an area that has yielded rich discussions in the field (e.g., Fenstermacher, 1986; Schön, 1983; Shulman, 1986b, 1987), nor is it merely a rhetorical argument in favor of teacher research as part of a growing popular movement. Furthermore, our question here is not, "Is teacher research research?" or even "What kind of research is teacher research?" Our intention is, rather, to contribute to the conversation about teaching and knowledge by arguing that research by teachers *is* a significant way of knowing about teaching. We argue that teacher research is a way of generating both *local knowledge* and *public knowledge* about teaching; that is, knowledge developed and used by teachers for themselves and their immediate communities, as well as knowledge useful to the larger school and university communities.

We have found it useful to define teacher research as systematic, intentional inquiry by teachers about their own school and classroom work (Cochran-Smith & Lytle, 1990). We base this definition in part on the work of Stenhouse (1985), who defines research in general as "systematic, self-critical enquiry," and in part on an ongoing survey of the literature of teacher writing. By systematic we refer primarily to ordered ways of gathering and recording information, documenting experiences inside and outside of classrooms, and making some kind of written record. Systematic also refers to ordered ways of recollecting, rethinking, and analyzing classroom events for which there may be only partial or unwritten records. By intentional we signal that teacher research is an activity that is planned rather than spontaneous, although we do not mean to suggest that important insights about teaching are only generated when planned. Our emphasis on intention is in keeping with Boomer's (1987) argument that "to learn deliberately is to research" and with Britton's (1987, p. 13) notion that "every lesson should be for the teacher an inquiry, some further discovery, a quiet form of research." By inquiry, we suggest that teacher research stems from or generates questions and reflects teachers' desires to make sense of their experiences — to adapt a learning stance or openness toward classroom life.

Many teachers have written about their work in forms that can be appropriately regarded as research (Lytle & Cochran-Smith, 1990). We have proposed four categories as a tentative typology of teacher research that acknowledges a wider range of teachers' writing as research. In the first, we include teachers' journals, published and unpublished. In the second category, we place both brief and book-length essays in which teachers analyze their own classrooms or schools and consider issues related to learners, curricula, and school organization. The third category includes accounts of teachers' oral inquiries and discussions, convened specifically for reflection and questioning. These are usually preserved in the form of written transcriptions or notes. Our final category includes small and larger scale classroom studies based on documentation and analysis procedures similar to those of university-based classroom research. In many respects, the forms of documentation in teacher research resemble the forms used in academic research, particularly standard forms of interpretive research. Field notes about classroom interactions, interviews with students and teachers, and classroom documents (e.g., students' writing and drawing, test scores, teachers' plans and handouts) are commonly collected by teacher researchers. In addition, teacher researchers often keep extensive journals and audiotape or videotape small and large group discussions, peer and teacher-student conferences, students' debates, role plays and dramatic productions, as well as their own classroom presentations. A strength of teacher research, like university-based qualitative research, is that it often entails multiple data sources that can be used to confirm and/or illuminate one another. (We discuss various forms and methods of teacher research in more detail in Cochran-Smith & Lytle, 1993).

In our analysis, we draw on a wide range of texts written by teachers — published and unpublished journals, essays, studies, and oral inquiries; accounts of teachers' groups that have appeared in national and local journals, newsletters, and booklets; and edited collections of teachers' work. We have selected examples from a range of K-12 grade levels and contexts, as well as from university settings. We quote at length from these texts because we think it is important to provide direct access to teachers' ways of explaining and representing relationships between inquiry and knowledge, rather than to filter teachers' perspectives and interpretations through our own. While we are drawing heavily on their texts, however, we do not presume to speak for teachers. Rather, this article represents our efforts to understand and present publicly what we are learning from teacher research from our own perspectives as university-based teacher educators and researchers.

TEACHER RESEARCH AND LOCAL KNOWLEDGE

In his volume of essays on interpretive anthropology, Geertz (1983) talks about the difficulties involved in representing emic, or insider, knowledge and meaning perspectives. He suggests that ultimately, anthropologists cannot really represent "local knowledge" — what native inhabitants see — but only what they see through; that is, their interpretive perspectives on their own experiences. Borrowing Geertz's term, we use *local knowledge* to signal both what teachers come to know about their own knowledge through teacher research and what communities of teacher researchers come to know when they build knowledge collaboratively.

Knowing One's Own Knowledge

We begin with the premise that, through their interactions, teachers and students together construct classroom life and the learning opportunities that are available (Bloome & Green, 1984; Erickson, 1986). It has been our experience as university-based teacher educators and researchers that teachers and students, regardless of stance or pedagogy, inevitably negotiate what counts as knowledge in the classroom, who can have knowledge, and how knowledge can be generated, challenged, and evaluated. We argue here that, through inquiry, teachers come to understand how this happens in their own classrooms and how their own interpretations of classroom events are shaped. To make the case that teacher inquiry is a way for teachers to know their own knowledge, we consider six examples that suggest some of the range and variation that occur in teacher researchers' topics, data collection strategies, interpretive perspectives, and modes of presentation.

— EXAMPLE ONE: BECOMING MEAN AND SENSITIVE

Prompted by the realization that there was a discrepancy between his intentions and what was going on in the classroom, Fecho (1989) began a study of teacher-student writing conferences. After viewing videotapes he had made in his classroom, Fecho was dissatisfied with what he saw:

> While some students were able to advance their own agendas and seek answers to their own questions, far too many students sat and waited for me to question, to figure out, and to change their writing. Although conferencing was successful in altering my relationships with the students, what occurred between us was still much too close to a teacher-centered classroom. . . . Provoked by these stimuli and supported by my colleagues . . . I resolved to take a more systematic look at my conferencing. Aside from the generic ethnographic question of, "What happens?" specifically, I was interested in what occurred in the conferences over the course of one school year — did the structure and work change or remain static? Did similarities and differences exist across conferences? Did the passing of time allow students to develop as conference participants? (pp. 3–4)

Although Fecho was intrigued by the arguments of academic researchers (e.g., Florio-Ruane, 1986; Michaels, Ulichney, & Watson-Gegeo, 1986) about the need to interrupt the replication in writing conferences of teachers' classroom dominance, in his work he did not simply implement the conferencing strategies one might derive from the literature. Rather, he set out to understand how face-to-face talk about writing functions and varies over time when a White teacher works with approximately thirty African American adolescents in an urban comprehensive high school. Fecho concluded the report of his research with these words:

> In one of our interviews, Geeman [a student] mentioned that our conferencing experience had led him to take second looks at the writing he did

for other classes. He liked the idea that he could be his own critic, that he could [in his words] be "mean and sensitive" to himself. I understood exactly what he meant. For myself, in the conference I had to be "mean" in order to resist my students' reliance on my expertise, but also "sensitive" to their needs and opinions. But looking at the phrase again, I realized that it also comments on my teacher research. As I find myself getting woozy watching tapes and reading transcripts, I know that I must continue looking for what the tapes may reveal, must continue to separate the real from the imagined, must continue seeing my practice with mean and sensitive eyes. For if I don't, who will? (pp. 20–21)

Although Fecho initiated and conducted the research, his students' inquiries brought unexpected insights into his own work. As he wrestled with the implications of sharing power, both he and his students came to view knowledge differently. They came to the similar realization that while those outside the particular context or setting can support, inform, challenge, and provide a context for learning, only learners themselves (whether teachers or students) can come to know, or assume responsibility for making meaning of, their work in the classroom.

— EXAMPLE TWO: BALANCING STRUCTURE AND FREEDOM

Like Fecho, Crouse (1990), a student teacher, wanted to explore classroom structures that would provide a predictable format for discussion but also create opportunities for students to take responsibility for their own ideas. Unlike Fecho, however, who had been teaching for more than a decade, Crouse was for the first time wrestling with ways to engage her third-grade students in active construction of knowledge as part of her report of a small-scale classroom study. In her research on literature study groups, Crouse drew on her reflective journal, daily lesson plans, field notes, and transcriptions of the group's interactions. Reflecting on her assumptions before beginning a unit on Roald Dahl's book, *Fantastic Mr. Fox*, Crouse wrote:

> In thinking about my literature study group before the unit began, I realized that a lot of my thoughts related to the issue of teacher-directed instruction versus child-centered education. I wanted the third graders in my group to discover and experience the wonderful world of *Fantastic Mr. Fox* on their own, but I wasn't sure how to do that without providing some sort of structure. I wanted to have a series of "grand conversations" à la Edelsky (1988), but I wasn't sure that I understood or agreed with this approach to literature in the classroom. I began to realize that I thought of teaching as the art of finding the right balance between providing a clear and cohesive structure that facilitates learning and giving children the freedom to construct knowledge themselves. Children need direction, as well as freedom of choice, and the teacher needs to be careful not to give too much of either. For me, this unit was going to be about, in part, playing with that balance. (p. 7)

It is clear that Crouse sees her classroom as a site of inquiry into children's learning, that she approaches the planning of a literature unit with central questions about the teacher's role. Within this larger agenda framed by issues around child-centeredness and teacher direction, Crouse also articulates a set of more specific questions about children's understanding of characterization, author's point of view, and how children's moral development is reflected in their responses to texts:

> During my discussions with [my cooperating teacher] about our plans for the unit on *Fantastic Mr. Fox*, I became interested in the presence of good characters who do bad things in Roald Dahl's books. I became interested in knowing what sense the children made of who was a good character and who was a bad character. More specifically, I wanted to know whether or not they could determine whose side Roald Dahl was on, and whether they viewed these good characters who did bad things as heroes. I was very curious to know, for example, how the children would feel about the fact that Mr. Fox stole from the farmers and did so in sneaky ways. Basically, I was interested developmentally in where children, age 8, are in terms of their moral development. (p. 9)

Crouse's questions do not take the form, "What works in my classroom?", but, rather, "What did the children understand? How can I learn with the children what is going on here?" Implicit in Crouse's account is a belief that children and teachers together construct the curriculum, and that the teacher can only come to know how to teach and how to learn from teaching by being attentive to their interactions. Like the more experienced teachers whose work we mention here, Crouse seems to regard knowledge generation as both the purpose of teaching and the subject of her own research.

— EXAMPLE THREE: THE MAKING OF HINDSIGHT

Like Crouse, Baum-Brunner (1993) also looked at literacy, but in this case, the focus was the writing workshops that occurred in her twelfth-grade classroom. When she analyzed the data — transcriptions of classroom interactions and multiple drafts of student writing — she had collected over the course of a semester, Baum-Brunner discovered that her assumptions about several of her students had been largely incorrect. Writing about the study in retrospect, Baum-Brunner reflected:

> As teacher, I taught this class, and consciously shaped it through my beliefs, training, choice of teaching techniques, [and] understanding of the genre. I even believed I understood consciously or intuitively most of what was occurring as I taught. Yet, by audiotaping the class and taking field notes at the time, and analyzing the interactions that had taken place, I realized I had *not*, in fact, accurately interpreted the interactions that had occurred. With the researcher's view, I saw that I had originally viewed as counter-

productive [one student's] imitation [of the language of others during workshop discussions]; later I saw that his imitative style [had] helped him rehearse a kind of talk he didn't know. Had I to do it over again, I would not have discouraged his imitative talk. Instead I would have accepted the imitation, perhaps even have encouraged him to imitate more. (p. 209)

Baum-Brunner not only observed stylistic differences among students' patterns of participation in the writer's workshop, she also expanded her interpretive framework — her notion of where to look and what to look at — in order to understand students' efforts to respond and revise their writing. As she points out, when teachers treat classroom occurrences as data, they see discrete and sometimes disparate events as parts of larger patterns of student behavior:

> The making of this insight was born out of my hindsight — my misjudgments and erroneous assumptions placed beside my view of the facts from another point in time. An outside researcher would have gotten a different . . . view. This hindsight was born out of my own experiences and . . . reflection about the feelings, assumptions, even myths that . . . shaped the teaching I did. Through analysis of disparities between [my original] feelings and [what I later realized] had occurred, I . . . created new pedagogy and theory about response and revision. (p. 209)

Rereading the texts of their classrooms allows teacher researchers to make visible their own characteristic ways of interpreting students' behavior and makes it possible for them to revisit and revise them.

— EXAMPLE FOUR: UNTRACKING ENGLISH

Cone (1990) and other high school English teachers had for several years experimented unsuccessfully with ways to make Advanced Placement English accessible to non-honors students and more minority students. In the spring of 1988, student teachers and master teachers were invited to the University of California at Berkeley for a private showing of *Stand and Deliver* and to meet Jaime Escalante, the Los Angeles calculus teacher whose phenomenal success teaching under-prepared students is dramatized in the film. After watching the film, teachers decided that what was wrong with their AP selection process was that they, rather than students, took full responsibility for selecting the class. In their words, they started that year to turn the AP selection process on its head. Later, in an essay reflecting on her year's experience with a program designed so that a wider range of students would qualify and succeed in the AP curriculum, Cone commented:

> For a long time I have been concerned about the damage done by academic ability grouping. I worried that schools label students and never allow them to get unlabeled or relabeled. As early as second grade, students are tested

for gifted. If they pass the test, they are tracked into gifted classes for the rest of their school years. Students who are not tested or who do not pass the test generally do not take honors classes. Ability grouping creates not only honors tracks: [it also creates] a two-tiered educational system of learners and nonlearners, an elite academic class, and an underclass that mirrors the social, racial, and economic underclass of our society as a whole. What would happen if the labels — "honors," "college prep," "average," "remedial" — came unglued? What would happen if students got to label themselves? What would happen if students got to choose the most academic class in the school if they wanted to — even if they weren't "gifted"?

Opening up AP English to all students who were willing to commit to a rigorous summer and year-long regimen of writing and reading allowed me to study first hand what does happen when students are given choices in their schooling. I discovered [that students] with combined SAT scores of 690 and 740 can learn with students with scores of 1290 and 1350; that students with SAT verbal scores of 460 and 490 can earn a 4 and a 5 on the national Advanced Placement English Language and Composition test; that students with SAT verbal scores of 290 and 380 can pass the University of California Subject A Exam. I discovered that gifted and nongifted students can discuss sophisticated literature with each other and can respond to each other's writing in ways that lead to thoughtful revision, and I discovered that giving them the chance to elect to work at the highest academic levels empowers them to see themselves as learners.

Opening up AP English also allowed me to see the kinds of changes I had to make as a teacher when students had accepted the challenge of a mixed-ability AP English class. Almost immediately, I saw that I had to move away from the front of the room, I had to turn classroom talk over to my students, I had to use writing to beget talk and talk to beget writing in ways that I had never used before. I had to give my students real choices about their education. Who did they want in their writing response group? How were they going to organize literary discussions? Which books were they going to read? Were they going to take the AP test? More than anything I had to learn how to shift the control of the class to my students in a way that suited my need for structure and their need to take control of their education. (pp. 27–28)

Cone was studying a complex and recursive set of interventions that took place over a full year as she and her students and colleagues constructed and reconstructed the curriculum. As a researcher, she explored the dynamic relationships that evolved among talk, writing, choice, changing roles, and student achievement. Cone's inquiry involved working with her students to renegotiate the meaning of student ability, construct new routes to textual understanding, and alter views about knowers and knowing in English classrooms. Like other teacher researchers, Cone diminished traditional distinctions between researcher and researched by making her agenda for the class public and by involving students in ongoing analysis of the data.

— EXAMPLE FIVE: THE MIDDLE GROUND

In an essay on teaching and knowledge, Howard (1989), an elementary school teacher, used detailed descriptions of student and teacher interactions to analyze the role of the teacher in creating the circumstances that make it possible for children to generate knowledge. Using what she calls "the middle ground" as a metaphor for the teacher's role, Howard explains how teachers mediate between children's interests and the broader world around them:

> I have to gauge the moment to set self-knowledge against other perspectives. I have to balance the child's need for privacy and time to put down roots against the broadening to be gained by a more public participation in the give-and-take of group activity. In a related way, I provide the lens between the "very now" and the "larger now" — the "now" we're living in at this time in our classroom, and the "now" of the past and future that expands around us. As the middle ground, I have to bridge all these states of being. It's hard to do. I am always aware of the connections I have failed to make — with children individually, between a child and the ideas he or she is pursuing, among the children as a group and their mutual interests, between the knowledge the children are making and both cultural and disciplinary knowledge.

In Howard's reflective essay, she presents an articulated view of knowledge as something "that arises between the inner impulses, interests, and qualities of the child and the physical and cultural world of which he or she is a part" (p. 229):

> My own limitations don't worry me the way they used to, because I have come to trust the vitality and thought of the children. I know I am doing a good job when some child says to me, equal to equal: "That's a good idea. . . ." Then I know the recognition I have given to the child's ideas has created a sense of equality; we are connected through our mutual pursuit of knowledge. We are, for the moment, colleagues in our respective pursuits. (p. 228)

With rich examples, Howard explores how knowledge arises in one classroom, how she works to give children room to make knowledge, and how she and the children construct knowledge together. In Howard's classroom, then, knowing one's own knowledge and the role one plays in generating knowledge with others is an explicit part of the curriculum.

— EXAMPLE SIX: RETHINKING RESISTANCE

Although worlds apart in one sense, Lewis (1989), a college teacher, is like Howard in that she analyzes the process of constructing knowledge with the students in her classroom — in this case an undergraduate sociology course for pre-service teachers, which was intended to raise questions about social relations from a critical perspective. In her essay, Lewis makes it clear that she is committed to feminist politics and pedagogy in the academy. In analyzing how students' responses to feminist theory emerged from conflicts between their own previous experiences and the discourse of the class, Lewis identified critical issues in a feminist pedagogy in part through analysis of her students' resistance. She both researched her own teaching and taught as a way of doing research — that is, her research informed her practice and her teaching functioned as an important site of inquiry for her larger project:

> I want to examine the potential basis of feminist teaching that does more than address the concerns of the already initiated. For me, the urgency of this issue arises from my own teaching. On the one hand, the often chilling stories of experiences women students share with me and each other in the context of our relations within the classroom point to their clear understanding of the politics of gender subordination: experiences that have affected them profoundly and yet which have no outlet for expression (often even understanding) within the confines of traditional academic practices.
>
> On the other hand, I hear that young woman who speaks to me in anger, who derides me for being the bearer of "bad news" and who wants to believe that our oppression/subordination is something we create in our own heads. It has been my experience that, for many women, working through and coming to a feminist perspective is not easy. This journey often generates anger and ultimately a politicization of every moment of our personal and public lives until we can come to grips with the positive political potential of our anger — an anger that is freed by the uncovering/unbinding of centuries of powerlessness and the denial of the conditions for speaking what we know, in terms circumscribed by our own desires and interests.
>
> Women don't need to be taught what we already know. . . . Nor do we need to be taught the language through which to speak what we know. Rather, we need to find ways of understanding what we are already saying and how we are saying it. (pp. 18–19)

Lewis's position is reminiscent of Berthoff's (1987) notion of teaching as "REsearching." Berthoff suggests that we do not need new information, but new ways to think about the information we already have:

> Educational research is nothing to our purpose, unless we formulate the questions; if the procedures by which answers are sought are not dialectic and dialogic, that is to say, if the questions and the answers are not continually REformulated by those who are working in the classroom, educational research is pointless. (pp. 29–30)

Classrooms with a feminist pedagogy, which explicitly make issues of knowledge, authority, and institutional hierarchies parts of the curriculum

(Ellsworth, 1989; Lather, 1991; Miller, 1987), provide strategic sites for understanding what it means for teachers to know their own knowledge through inquiry.

STANDING IN A DIFFERENT RELATION TO KNOWLEDGE

It is clear from their writings that these six teachers use inquiry as a way of knowing about teaching. Fecho (1989) examines what it means both to lead and to follow students. Crouse (1990) explores the delicate balance between structure and spontaneity in classroom talk. Baum-Brunner (1993) enlarges her understanding of the social nature of writing. Cone (1990) explores the consequences for achievement of empowering adolescents to make choices. Howard (1989) articulates a conceptual framework for students' and teachers' roles in constructing classroom knowledge. And Lewis (1989) demonstrates the inseparability of teaching and inquiry in the enactment of a critical pedagogy.

Teacher research is a powerful way for teachers to understand how they and their students construct and reconstruct the curriculum. By conducting inquiry on their own practices, teachers identify discrepancies between their theories of practice and their practices, between their own practices and those of others in their schools, and between their ongoing assumptions about what is going on in their classrooms and their more distanced and retrospective interpretations. Inquiry stimulates, intensifies, and illuminates changes in practice. Out of inquiry come analytic frameworks, as well as questions for further inquiry. Obviously one does not have to engage in teacher research in order to make decisions about or changes in classroom practice; teachers revise and reflect on their strategies regularly as part of the ongoing cycle of teaching (Paris, 1993; Schön, 1983). Neither is teacher research, in the sense we mean it, necessarily instrumental: it may involve deliberate change, but it may just as likely entail a deliberate attempt to make more visible what is already going on.

In contrast to the implication of the AACTE volume, then, what we argue here is that what "distinguishes more productive teachers" (Reynolds, 1989, p. ix) may *not* be mastery of a knowledge base; it may be, rather, standing in a different relationship not only to knowledge generated by university-based researchers in the field, but also to one's own knowledge and to one's students as knowers. Freire (1971) has argued that educators and their students are "knowing subjects," constantly learning from the process of teaching. For him, "education is a pedagogy of knowing" (p. 217). Knoblauch and Brannon (1988) have built on Freire's notion that teaching itself is a knowledge-generating process, suggesting that the defining characteristic of teacher researchers is their "knowledge of the making of knowledge" (p. 27). When we regard teaching as a process of generating knowledge with students, then we need to understand teacher research as a significant process of coming to know one's own knowledge and understanding how knowledge is constructed. There is a dynamic interaction among teachers' stances toward themselves as knowers, their students as knowers and learners, and their knowledge of disciplinary/subject matter (Lyons, 1990). From the texts of teacher research, we see that teachers have the legitimate authority to know about teaching. When teachers redefine their own relationships to knowledge about teaching and learning, they often begin to reconstruct their classrooms and to offer different invitations to their students to learn and know (Cochran-Smith & Lytle, 1990). When they change their relationships to knowledge, they may also realign their relationships to the brokers of knowledge and power in schools and universities.

Building Knowledge in the Community

We have defined intellectual communities of teacher researchers as networks of individuals who enter with other teachers into "a common search for meaning" in their work lives (Westerhoff, 1987) and who regard their research as part of larger efforts to transform teaching, learning, and schooling (Cochran-Smith & Lytle, 1993). In teacher-research communities, groups of teachers engage in joint construction of knowledge through reading, writing, and oral inquiry. For example, through conversation they make their tacit knowledge more visible (Polanyi, 1967), call into question assumptions about common practice (Giroux, 1984), and generate data that makes possible the consideration of alternatives. Some teacher-research groups regularly conduct oral inquiries, such as reflections on practice or descriptive reviews of students (Carini, 1986); literature studies (Edelsky, 1988); and doubting/believing discussions (Elbow, 1973). Other communities do not use oral inquiry formats, but they do talk in distinctive ways about their teaching. In addition, teacher-research communities use a wide range of texts, not all of which are published or disseminated, but which are essential to teachers' individual and collective gathering, recording, and analyzing data. Texts include teacher-researcher reports in the form of journals, essays, and studies, as well as selections from the extensive theoretical and research literatures in the fields related to teaching and learning. Texts used by teachers in their communities also include the written records of teachers' deliberations, informal writing used to facilitate the talk of these groups, transcripts of classroom interactions and interviews, notes made of classroom observations, as well as drafts of teachers' plans and work in progress.

Through inquiry, groups of teachers conjoin their understandings to create local knowledge in and for their own communities. Because teachers in different settings have diverse goals, activities, and ways of doing research, there is considerable variation in the knowledge constructed in different groups. We argue here that, just as the knowledge generated by individual teachers ought to count in an epistemology of teaching, so should the knowledge generated by particular communities of teachers.

To understand how teacher research is a way of knowing for the local community, we look in the next section at groups of teachers working together within a single institution, as well as at groups of teachers coming together from several institutions to form a community. Groups of teachers from one institution often use inquiry as a way to build curriculum. Phelps, the director of the Syracuse Writing Program, for example, describes the work of the community of university teachers involved in the freshman composition program:

> Teaching depends for its richness on a community of shared practice constituted through exchanges of talk and writing about curriculum. We are working actively to create such a sense of community among a mixed group (numbering close to 150) including full-time research faculty, part-time professional writing teachers, and graduate teaching assistants — largely young, inexperienced, and from disciplines other than composition. Our modes of interaction include "teacher talk" in weekly meetings of small groups, coteaching and mentoring arrangements, varied professional development activities, task forces and working groups on curriculum, and a remarkable amount of writing, including an in-house journal.
>
> The business of such a community is curriculum development as a form of knowledge-making. . . . Part of the work of the community is to make visible to itself (and to colleagues at the university) the ecology of curricular contexts in which any teaching decision is embedded, not merely abstractly, but as vivid, particular realities. This requires . . . practical investigations that go beyond classroom observations of one's own teaching to specify how actions fit together on the programmatic or institutional scale. . . . Through its talk, writing, inquiry, and action, members of the Writing Program are imagining and shaping its writing courses as a developmentally related sequence; translating the university curricula into a particularized range of writing, reading, thinking and learning tasks set for students; profiling the students themselves as unpredictably diverse and heterogeneous despite their apparent typicalities. . . . The Syracuse Writing Program, with its particular history of teaching practices and the heterogeneous composition of its thinkers and practitioners, presents both an extraordinarily difficult [and] complex context and a richly rewarding matrix for experiments and reflection on teachers' (and students') ways of knowing. (Phelps, 1991, pp. 866–867)

Explicit in Phelps's description is a definition of curriculum construction as community knowledge-building, accomplished through linking the specifics of classroom decisionmaking with the larger purposes of the institution. Thus the Syracuse teacher community uses inquiry into teachers' and students' ways of knowing to arrive at conjoined understandings that reflect the diversity of participants and contexts in university writing programs. Similarly, a group of faculty members at Michigan State University is involved in a process of reconstructing their teacher education curriculum by drawing on data collected by all those teaching different sections of an introductory course on teaching (Feiman-Nemser & Featherstone, 1992). Like the com-

15

munity at Syracuse, the Michigan group members share knowledge of particular classroom events in order to articulate a vision of the teacher education curriculum as a whole.

Moving back and forth between collaborative curriculum-building and data-gathering in individual classrooms occurs in teacher-researcher groups at all levels of the educational continuum. Colgan-Davis (1993), for example, describes a curriculum development project at Friends Select Lower School in Philadelphia, where a group of teachers met regularly over a year to build a curriculum that would meet the needs of diverse groups of learners:

> The unifying factor was that we all saw diversity in how our students learned and found this diversity a challenge. Some teachers who were originally attracted to Friends Select School because of its economic, cultural, and racial diversity found the differences in how children learn exciting, and came to the group to expand their skills in responding to children's needs. Others felt the school had lost sight of its mission, had accepted children who should not be in a private, academic school, and wanted the school to narrow its focus, clarify its standards, and begin to sift out those children whom they felt did not belong. Other teachers were mystified by how children learn, saw it as a "hidden act" and did not know how to respond when the student did not succeed. . . . (pp. 161–162)

Through a series of descriptions of students' work, reflections on key concepts, descriptive reviews, and analyses of other classroom data, the group explored its own values and assumptions about learners' appropriate behaviors and made specific recommendations for working with individual children in classrooms.

Using collaborative inquiry to design a curriculum that is responsive to diversity is also the goal of a group of Philadelphia Writing Project teachers who plan a yearly summer institute for adolescents participating in the school district's desegregation program. Their process, like the process of other groups involved in curriculum construction, allows for comparative interpretations of texts, students' work, and styles of teaching. Teachers jointly compose a set of readings that reflect their own diversities and those of their students, meet daily to write about their observations of students' oral and written interactions with multicultural literature, and analyze the variations that occur across classrooms in response to a common curriculum.

Developing curriculum through analysis of data is radically different from the process of curriculum development typically used by many schools and school districts. Often there are pre-established calendars and formal procedures for reviewing the curriculum in each subject area. These generally involve discussion of objectives and goals, as well as close examination and comparison of published materials. When curriculum construction is conceptualized as a process of inquiry and systematic consideration of data, however, it is qualitatively different from consideration of topics, books, or sequences of activities. When groups of teachers develop curriculum through inquiry, they use data from their own classrooms (e.g., students' work, actual lesson and unit plans, descriptions of individual learners, syllabi, texts, and teacher-made materials and assignments) to pose problems, sort out commonalities and differences in perspectives and values, and build instructional frameworks. Teacher groups involved in Charter Schools, such as Crossroads (Fecho, Pincus, & Hiller, 1990; Hiller, 1991), a school within Gratz High School in Philadelphia, intend to make curriculum construction based on observation, interviews, and collection of student work an ongoing dimension of their work.

Any time groups of teachers from the same institution come together to consider issues of curriculum and instruction, there is the potential for building knowledge for the local community. Self-studies for accreditation purposes, pupil support teams, supervisory sessions, and even department, faculty, and committee meetings could be reconceptualized as sites of inquiry, and their practices could be transformed to emphasize formulation of questions, data collection, analysis, and interpretation. This is similar to earlier propositions that schools and school systems have the potential to be centers for inquiry (Myers, 1985; Schaefer, 1967), and to recent calls for school-university partnerships wherein experienced and beginning teachers work together with university faculty in professional development schools (Holmes Group, 1990). And, of course, the notion that curriculum construction is a form of knowledge-making is an essential part of the history of teacher research. Stenhouse (1985) reminds us:

> Curriculum is the medium through which the teacher can learn his art. Curriculum is the medium through which the teacher can learn knowledge. Curriculum is the medium through which the teacher can learn about the nature of education. Curriculum is the medium through which the teacher can learn about the nature of knowledge. (p. 98)

In a certain sense, the typical curriculum committee and the teacher-research group seem worlds apart — it is difficult to imagine the shift from problem-solving to problem-posing, from quick closure to deeper exploration, and from making judgments to discovering relationships based on data. On the other hand, some of the contexts in which inquiry would be powerful already exist — particularly the new structural arrangements created as schools divide into teams, houses, and other smaller organizational units.

Rather than having a shared physical and institutional context, other teacher groups cross institutional boundaries and share a broad intellectual agenda. Teachers who have been associated with Patricia Carini, the Prospect School, and the North Dakota Study Group, for example, have organized a number of local communities, such as the Philadelphia Teachers Learning Cooperative, committed to the perspectives of progressive education in public schools. In *Speaking Out* (1986), a collection of Prospect Institute teachers' essays, Kanevsky and Traugh comment on the ways communities of teachers from different schools and school systems know about teaching:

> Our classrooms are complicated. . . . They generate lives of their own but they also include and respond to the lives people lead outside their walls. They are the setting for the exploration and implementation of ideas. They support the *having* of new ideas. . . . As teachers, we are temporarily immersed in this busy life, a part of what occurs. The question is: How do we lift our heads up out of the stream, which in its movement, carries us along, to see where we are going and look back at where we have been? And, if we are able to see, how do we keep track of what we see? How do we make sense of it and see the patterns in it?
>
> Taking advantage of the classroom's potential as a source of knowledge which will nurture and feed the quality of work done in that classroom requires special efforts and energy. However, the means we can use to pull what is important out of the vague, undifferentiated background of experience are readily available to us and indeed, they have long histories in the ordinary human effort to keep track and make sense of our work lives: conversations, journals, interviews, and stories are among the most useful of these modes. (p. 6)

The work of the Prospect community is based on a phenomenological view of knowledge and learning wherein teachers grapple with children's meanings as expressed in their projects and with the varied meanings that their colleagues find in children's work. To inform these investigations of children's learning over time, Carini and her colleagues at the Prospect School and the North Dakota Study Group have created a unique and extensive archive of drawing, writing, and other artifacts that functions as a resource for the wider community.

While the Teachers Learning Cooperative explores issues in urban education, teachers and administrators in the Biographic Literacy Profiles Project (Taylor, 1990) explore multiple literacies and alternative ways of assessing students' literacy development. They document children's literacy behaviors by writing descriptive biographic literacy profiles. In describing the work of the group, which grew out of her case studies on alternative modes for assessing literacy, Taylor shows how the group's process became a way of knowing about teaching:

> At the second institute that took place, . . . teachers and administrators who had been participating in the project for one year met to share their experiences, advance their own training, and begin the training of a new group of teachers. . . . Much of our time was spent in observing ourselves in complex problem-solving situations — observing the ways in which we, as learners, generate and reconstitute problems through the use of the social, symbolic, technical, and material resources at our disposal, and then

go on to invent new procedures and arrive at instrumental solutions. Some teachers and administrators participated in the collaborative problem-solving situations, while others observed and took notes which were later shared and analyzed by all those who participated in the institute. In this way, we advanced our own understanding of the social construction of cognitive tasks, while at the same time the teachers new to the project had the opportunity to think about the possibilities of establishing classroom environments in which they could observe children engaged in *solving the problem of problem-solving literacy.* (p. 10)

Cross-institutional communities of teachers pose distinctive problems for themselves, and hence build knowledge in different domains. Often this is a reflection of their origins and their affiliations with various programs, universities, and institutes, or with particular ideologies. In each case, the community of teachers constructs knowledge for its own consideration and use. By investigating the function of talk in classrooms across the grades and curriculum, for example, participants in the Brookline (Massachusetts) Teacher Researcher Seminar, affiliated with the Literacies Institute in Boston, build their own distinctive knowledge base about classroom discourse.

Teacher-researcher groups at the Breadloaf School of English (Goswami & Stillman, 1987) and other graduate programs in writing and language (Bissex & Bullock, 1987; Calkins, 1991), as well as groups associated with sites of the National Writing Project — in the San Francisco Bay Area, Philadelphia, Detroit, Northern Virginia, Baltimore — focus on the interrelationships of language, literacy, and learning. Finally, inquiry-centered pre-service programs, such as Project START (Cochran-Smith, 1991) and the University of Wisconsin elementary education program (Zeichner & Liston, 1987), and in-service teacher communities (Evans, 1989; Lytle & Fecho, 1991; Yonemura, 1982) explore the processes of learning to teach across the developmental continuum and thus build knowledge for the local community about teacher knowledge, teacher thinking, and professional socialization. When teachers build knowledge in these domains, they begin to develop local criteria for evaluating questions, evidence, and interpretive frameworks.

TEACHER RESEARCH AND PUBLIC KNOWLEDGE

In addition to its function as a way of knowing for teacher researchers in their local communities, teacher research has the potential to be a significant way of knowing for the larger communities of both school-based teachers and university-based researchers and teacher educators, as well as policymakers and school administrators. There have been relatively few forums for the presentation and publication of teacher research and an even smaller subset of these where school- and university-based teachers and researchers join together. Further, there have been limited opportunities to explore empirically the ways teachers' texts are being read and interpreted by university-based researchers and teacher educators, or whether and how teacher research is beginning to alter understandings of classroom practice.

Increasingly, communities of teacher researchers from different parts of the country are disseminating their work to one another and developing a classroom-grounded knowledge base from the collective inquiries of teachers across contexts. Growing networks of teacher researchers have thus begun to provide access to their teaching colleagues through conferences and publications. When teachers are the audience for teacher research, the task, as Fecho (1990) has suggested, is to read like a teacher; that is, to bring teachers' analytic frameworks to bear on the questions, issues, and interpretations presented by other teachers. As teacher research becomes public knowledge, teachers — and not university-based researchers or teacher educators — will determine its value for the broader community of school-based teachers.

From our perspectives as researchers, however, we would argue that teacher research has particular potential for transforming the university-generated knowledge base. In a recent address to the American Educational Research Association, Jackson (1990) discussed the changing venue of educational research and its current emphasis on particular contexts. He points out:

> In recent years we have witnessed a growing interest within our research community in the use of techniques and scholarly traditions that provide a close look at the everyday affairs of educational practitioners and those they serve. . . .[There has also been] a decline of interest on the part of many of us in what used to be looked upon as our main business, which was the discovery of rules and principles of teaching and of running schools that would prove to be universal or nearly so in application and invariant or nearly so over time. That dream of finding out once and for all how teaching works or how schools ought to be administered no longer animates nearly as many of us as it once did. In its place we have substituted the much more modest goal of trying to figure out what's happening *here and now* or what went on *there and then*. This does not mean that we have given up trying to say things that are true from situation to situation or that we are no longer interested in making generalizations. But the kind of truth in which more and more of us seem interested these days takes a very different form than it once did. (p. 7)

Jackson's discussion suggests to us that there are several ways teacher research might be a way of knowing for the larger community of both school-based and university-based teachers and researchers. Just as critical scholarship has challenged many of the norms of interpretive social science (Lather, 1991), teacher research may make problematic in a different way the relationships of researcher and researched, theory and practice, knower and knowledge, process and product. When teachers do research, the gap between researcher and researched is narrowed. Notions of research subjectivity and objectivity are redefined: subjective and local knowing, rather than objectified and distanced "truth," is the goal. The teacher researcher is a native inhabitant of the research site — not a participant observer over a bounded period of time, but a permanent and "observant participant" (Florio-Ruane & Walsh, 1980) who knows the research context in its richest sense of what Geertz (1973) calls shared webs of significance.

Because it often investigates from an emic perspective topics that are already widely researched by university-based researchers, teacher research is a source of new knowledge in many of the domains of teaching and learning, and also has the potential to open up new areas of study. Further, because teaching requires simultaneous attention to many agendas and because it provides the opportunity for constant observation of particular phenomena, such as children's drawing or writing, teacher researchers' analytic frameworks are extraordinarily rich and complex. What we mean here is that when teacher researchers turn their attention to children's drawing, for example, they bring a historical framework based on a thousand other drawings and what these drawings meant for particular children at particular times and places. Hence, they ask questions that other researchers may not ask, and they see patterns that others may not be able to see.

Teacher research is concerned with the questions that arise from the lived experiences of teachers and the everyday life of teaching expressed in a language that emanates from practice. Teachers are concerned about the consequences of their actions, and teacher research is often prompted by teachers' desires to know more about the dynamic interplay of classroom events. Hence, teacher research is well positioned to produce precisely the kind of knowledge currently needed in the field.

Almost by definition, teacher research is case study — the unit of analysis is typically the individual child, the classroom, or the school. Whether and how case studies function in knowledge generation is part of a larger set of questions about the relationships between qualitative research and practice, which have long been topics of considerable debate. As Eisner (1991) points out, this debate hinges on what is meant by the accumulation of knowledge in a field — on whether we mean that knowledge accumulates in the sense that dollars and garbage do, a view that presumes that knowledge is an "inert material" that can be collected, stored, and stockpiled. Eisner argues, to the contrary, that knowledge growth in the social sciences is "more horizontal than vertical," not at all like building with blocks, but, rather, yielding multiple conceptual frameworks that others use to understand their own situations:

> My point . . . is not to claim that the products of research have no bearing on each other, or that they do not connect in any way. It is, rather, to challenge the notion that all researchers must use a common intellectual currency whose profits are additive in the same way in which money accumulates in the bank. Research studies, even in related areas in the same

field, create their own interpretive universe. Connections have to be built by readers, who must also make generalizations by analogy and extrapolation, not by a water-tight logic applied to a common language. Problems in the social sciences are more complex than putting the pieces of the puzzle together to create a single, unified picture. (p. 210)

We think that with teacher research, knowledge will accumulate as communities of school-based and university-based teachers and researchers read and critique each other's work, document and perhaps disseminate their responses, create a network of citations and allusions, and, hence, begin to build a different kind of "interpretive universe."

One domain in which K-12 teacher researchers have been especially active is the area of language and literacy, where teachers have studied their own and their students' experiences reconstructing the traditional language/literacy curriculum. For example, Wiggington (1985) explores writing and oral history, while Stumbo (1989) relates oral history and cultural identity. Atwell (1987) focuses on self-initiated writing; Five (1986) on dialogue writing; Ashton-Warner (1963) on a culturally responsive reading curriculum; Lumley (1987) on social interaction and peer group dialogue journals; Holmstein (1987) on students' interpretations of writing with word processing; Branscombe (1987) on students as language researchers; Buchanan (1989) on the language of whole language; Johnston (1989) on social scenes of reading; Ray (1986) on talk and writing conferences; Starr (in press) on deaf children's composing processes; Headman (in press) on parents' and teachers' perspectives on literacy; Morizawa (1990) on writing, dramatization, and children's social worlds; Wilson (1990) on students' and teachers' talk and writing; Buchanan (1989) on learning from one child's writing; and Farmbry (1993) on dialect and standardization. In addition, a number of National Writing Projects publish collections on various aspects of teaching and learning writing. What we know from each domain of teacher research is not simply a series of discrete findings, but a sense of the multiple perspectives teachers bring to their work, which together generate unique interpretive universes.*

None of the examples of teacher research we have mentioned is what Calkins (1985) has referred to as "field-testing" research, in which practitioners test out new ideas that they are already convinced are exemplary. The goal of teacher research is not product testing, but "the development, assess-

---

* Other domains of active teacher research include: progressive education (Howard, 1989; Kanevsky, 1993; Kanevsky & Traugh, 1986; Philadelphia Teachers Learning Cooperative, 1984; Streib, 1985); critical pedagogy (Brown, 1992; Ellsworth, 1989; Lather, 1991; Lewis, 1989; Miller, 1987); teaching and learning to teach (Brody et al., 1993; Cochran-Smith, Garfield, & Greenberger, 1992; Colgan-Davis, 1993; Dicker, 1990; Dunstan, A., Kirscht, J., Reiffer, J., Roemer, M., & Tingle, N., 1989; Fecho, 1989; Guerin, 1985; Harris, 1993; Kean, 1989; Pincus, 1991, Reither, 1990; Rotchford, 1989; Wunner, 1993; Yagelsky, 1990); and theories of teacher research itself (Burton, 1991; Hahn, 1991; Queenan, 1988; Schwartz, 1990).

ment, and revision of theories that inform practice" (p. 143). As Calkins reminds us, teacher researchers, like Freud, Erikson, and Bettelheim, are practitioners as well as theory-builders:

> Through working with patients and through related study they developed theories that informed their practices. They also acted as researchers, observing their own work and the results of it and letting these observations guide them as they studied. This constant interaction between practice, reflection, and study led them to flesh out and refine their theories. . . . Each case report provides a forum for integrating theory and practice. (p. 143)

Teacher research, then, is a way of knowing for the larger communities of teachers and researchers because it contributes both conceptual frameworks and important information about some of the central domains of the knowledge base.

Finally, the texts of teacher research provide data about teacher knowledge itself — a burgeoning area of study since 1975, when university-based researchers began to study teaching as a cognitive activity. Research conducted by pre-service and in-service teachers provides a window into the nature of their perspectives on teaching, learning, and schooling. Using teacher research itself as data contrasts with some of the more common methods for exploring teachers' thinking and knowledge, including stimulated recall, policy capturing, and repertory grid techniques, which are often supplemented by interviewing, observation, and narrative descriptions (see Clark & Peterson, 1986). Of necessity, these methods typically focus on simplified and researcher-created tasks, constructs, or *a priori* categories. Consequently, these techniques do not account for the ways in which teacher inquiry is mediated by, and essentially embedded in, the cultures of classrooms, schools, school districts, and teacher-research communities. Because teacher research emerges from praxis and because it preserves teachers' own words and analyses, it has the potential to be a particularly robust method for understanding whether and how pre-service and in-service teachers construct their knowledge and theories of practice, how these may change and develop over time, and the impact of these on teaching and learning.

For example, there is considerable discussion in the field about the content and form of teacher knowledge (Shulman, 1986b, 1987; Sockett, 1987), especially about the nature of teachers' practical knowledge (Fenstermacher, 1986; Saunders & McCutcheon, 1986). Teacher research often reveals teachers' explorations of the discrepancies they perceive between their theories of practice and their actual practices. If university-based researchers use as data the texts written by teachers themselves, it is likely that the domain of teacher knowledge will be refined and eventually redefined as a field of study.

Although we see clear advantages to understanding teachers' knowledge through teachers' own representations, we also have reservations about what might happen if teacher research were the object of others' interpretations without serious attention to the ethical and epistemological issues entailed in this form of inquiry. Although university-based researchers routinely locate their own work in relation to others in the field, with rare exception they do not use their colleagues' research as data for their own analyses. Hence, when university-based researchers use teacher research as data, this raises sensitive and provocative issues of power, status, and representation. When university-based and school-based researchers collaboratively use teacher research as data, however, they may more closely attend to these ethical and epistemological concerns. In these instances, the tension between collaboration and critique is often heightened considerably, while the potential for breaking new ground is also dramatically increased. What seems to us most important is that each case be regarded on its own terms, with members of both school- and university-based communities participating in identifying the issues, making arguments, and deciding how teachers' texts are to be used for different purposes.

REDEFINING THE KNOWLEDGE BASE

In conclusion, we want to come full circle by returning to the traditional notion of knowledge for teaching with which we began this article. As we have argued, in the epistemology implied in the AACTE volume and in other similar compilations of university-based research, knowledge is something received by teachers, who are expected to adapt it to their particular situations. Underlying this perspective is the assumption that knowledge for teaching is predominantly "outside-in" — generated at the university and then used in schools, a position that focuses on the linear transmission of knowledge from a source to a destination. Those who hold this view often regard the central problem in improving teaching as one of translation from theory to practice, of making university-based research findings more accessible, more relevant, and more utilized by school-based teachers. In this epistemology, school-based teachers themselves are not a primary source of knowledge generation for the field.

In this article, we have sketched a different theory of knowledge for teaching — one in which teachers play a critical role as knowers. As we have shown, inquiry conducted by teachers is one way to build knowledge both locally and publicly — for the individual teacher, for communities of teachers, and for the larger field of university-based researchers and teacher educators, policymakers, and school administrators. Through examining cases of individual teachers in a variety of contexts, we have shown how inquiry provides teachers with a way to know their own knowledge — how they and their students negotiate what counts as knowledge in the classroom and how interpretations of classroom events are shaped. Along these same lines, we have explored how teacher-research communities conjoin their under-standings to construct curriculum, to compare interpretive frameworks, and to analyze data gathered in settings across classrooms, schools, and commu-nities. And, finally, we have argued that teacher research also contributes to more public knowledge, primarily through qualitative case studies that build new bodies of information about language and literacy, critical pedagogy, and teacher inquiry itself. Together these reveal the multiple perspectives teachers bring to their work and generate unique interpretive universes.

The notion of knowledge for teaching that we propose is "inside/outside" rather than "outside-in" (Cochran-Smith & Lytle, 1993), a juxtaposition that calls attention to teachers as knowers and to the complex and distinctly non-linear relationships of knowledge and teaching, as they are embedded in the contexts and the relations of power that structure the daily work of teachers and learners in both schools and universities. As teacher research of various kinds accumulates and is more widely disseminated, we believe it will present a radical challenge to current assumptions about the relation-ships of theory and practice, schools and universities, and inquiry and re-form. Research by teachers represents a distinctive way of knowing about teaching and learning that will alter, not just add to, what we know in the field. Because we see teacher research as both interpretive and critical, how-ever, its contribution will not be in the form of generalizations about teach-ing (this time from the "inside" perspective), nor will teacher research be benign and evolutionary, a process of accumulating new knowledge and gradually admitting new knowers to the fold. Rather, this different theory of knowledge fundamentally redefines the notion of knowledge for teaching, alters the locus of the knowledge base, and realigns the practitioner's stance in relationship to knowledge generation in the field.

Legitimating the knowledge that comes from practitioners' research on their own practice is a critical dimension of change in both school and university cultures. In challenging the university's hegemony in the genera-tion of expert knowledge for the field, teacher research also challenges the dominant views of staff development and pre-service training as transmission and implementation of knowledge from outside to inside schools. Thus it has the potential to reconstruct conceptions of the ways teachers learn across the professional lifespan, so that inquiry is regarded as an integral part of the activity of teaching and a critical basis for decisions about practice. Class-rooms and schools are treated as research sites and sources of knowledge that are most effectively accessed when teachers collaboratively interrogate and enrich their theories of practice.

When teacher development is reconfigured as inquiry and teacher re-search as challenge and critique, they become forms of social change wherein individuals and groups labor to understand and alter classrooms, schools, and school communities. These transformations will inevitably cause conflict as those traditionally disenfranchised begin to play increasingly important roles in generating knowledge and in deciding how it ought to be interpreted and used. Teacher research, furthermore, makes visible the ways teachers and students negotiate power, authority, and knowledge in classrooms and schools. As a way of knowing, then, teacher research has the potential to alter profoundly the cultures of teaching — how teachers work with their students toward a more critical and democratic pedagogy, how they build intellectual communities of colleagues who are both educators and activists, and how they position themselves in relationship to school administrators, policymakers, and university-based experts as agents of systemic change.

REFERENCES

Ashton-Warner, S. (1963). *Teacher.* New York: Simon & Schuster.

Atwell, N. (1987). *In the middle: Writing, reading and learning with adolescents.* Portsmouth, NH: Boynton/Cook.

Baum-Brunner, S. (1993). Stepping and stepping out: The making of hindsight, revision, and teacher research. In M. Cochran-Smith & S. L. Lytle, *Inside/outside: Teacher research and knowledge.* New York: Teachers College Press.

Berthoff, A. E. (1987). The teacher as researcher. In D. Goswami & P. R. Stillman (Eds.), *Reclaiming the classroom: Teacher research as an agency for change.* Upper Montclair, NJ: Boynton/Cook.

Bissex, G., & Bullock, R. (1987). *Seeing for ourselves: Case study research by teachers of writing.* Portsmouth, NH: Heinemann.

Bloome, D., & Green, J. (1984). Directions in the sociolinguistic study of reading. In P. D. Pearson (Ed.), *Handbook of reading research.* New York: Longman.

Boomer, G. (1987). Addressing the problem of elsewhereness: A case for action research in schools. In D. Goswami & P. Stillman (Eds.), *Reclaiming the classroom: Teacher research as an agency for change.* Upper Montclair, NJ: Boynton/Cook.

Branscombe, A. (1987). I gave my classroom away. In D. Goswami & P. Stillman (Eds.), *Reclaiming the classroom: Teacher research as an agency for change.* Upper Montclair, NJ: Boynton/Cook.

Branscombe, A., Goswami, D., & Schwartz, J. (1992) *Students teaching: Teachers learning.* Portsmouth, NH: Heinemann.

Britton, J. (1987). A quiet form of research. In D. Goswami & P. Stillman (Eds.), *Reclaiming the classroom: Teacher research as agency for change* (pp. 13–19). Upper Montclair, NJ: Boynton-Cook.

Brody, D., Cornman, E., Crouse, M. R., Greenspun, L., Klavens, J., Miller, T. D., Patton, K., Powers, E., Ritchie, M. C., Rogers, P., & Schefer, D. (1993). Faith, love, and polka music: Writing essays, building theories. In M. Cochran-Smith & S. L. Lytle, *Inside/outside: Teacher research and knowledge.* New York: Teachers College Press.

Brown, S. (1993). Lighting fires: One teacher's intellectual journey and its effect on the classroom. In M. Cochran-Smith & S. L. Lytle, *Inside/outside: Teacher research and knowledge.* New York: Teachers College Press.

Buchanan, J. (1989). The language of whole language. *The Voice of the Philadelphia Writing Project, 1*(1), 1–2.

Burton, F. (1991). Teacher-researcher projects: An elementary school teacher's perspective. In J. Flood, J. M. Jensen, D. Lapp, & J. R. Squire (Eds.), *Handbook of research on teaching the English language arts.* New York: Macmillan.

Calkins, L. M. (1985). Forming research communities among naturalistic researchers. In B. McClelland & T. Donovan (Eds.), *Perspectives on research and scholarship in composition.* New York: Modern Language Association.

Calkins, L. M. (1991). *Living between the lines.* Portsmouth, NH: Heinemann.

Carini, P. (1986). *Prospect's documentary processes.* Bennington, VT: Prospect Center and School.

Clark, C. C., & Peterson, P. L. (1986). Teachers' thought processes. In M. C. Wittrock (Ed.), *Handbook of research on teaching* (3rd ed.). New York: Macmillan.

Cochran-Smith, M. (1991). Reinventing student teaching. *Journal of Teacher Education, 42,* 104–118.

Cochran-Smith, M., Garfield, E., & Greenberger, R. (1992). Student teachers and their teacher: Talking our way into new understandings. In A. Branscombe, D. Goswami, & J. Schwartz (Eds.), *Students teaching, teachers learning.* Portsmouth, NH: Heinemann.

Cochran-Smith, M., & Lytle, S. L. (1990). Research on teaching and teacher research: The issues that divide. *Educational Researcher, 19*(2), 2–11.

Cochran-Smith, M., & Lytle, S. L. (1993). *Inside/outside: Teacher research and knowledge.* New York: Teachers College Press.

Colgan-Davis, P. (1993). Learning from and about diversity. In M. Cochran-Smith & S. L. Lytle, *Inside/outside: Teacher research and knowledge.* New York: Teachers College Press.

Cone, J. (1990). Untracking advanced placement English: Creating opportunity is not enough. In *Research in writing: Working papers of teacher researchers.* Berkeley, CA: Bay Area Writing Project.

Crawford, M., & Marecek, J. (1989). Feminist theory, feminist psychology: A bibliography of epistemology, critical analysis, and applications. *Psychology of Women Quarterly, 13,* 477–491.

Crouse, M. R. (1990). Fantastic Mr. Fox: *What about the farmers?* Unpublished manuscript, University of Pennsylvania, Philadelphia.

Dewey, J. (1904). The relation of theory to practice in education. In C. A. McMurry (Ed.), *The third NSSE yearbook* (Part 1). Chicago: University of Chicago Press.

Dicker, M. (1990). Using action research to navigate an unfamiliar teaching assignment. *Theory Into Practice, 29,* 203–208.

Dunstan, A., Kirscht, J., Reiffer, J., Roemer, M., & Tingle, N. (1989). Working in the classroom: Teachers talk about what they do. *English Education, 21*(1), 39–52.

Edelsky, C. (1988). Living in the author's world: Analyzing the author's craft. *The California Reader, 21*(3), 14–17.

Eisner, E. (1991). *The enlightened eye.* New York: Macmillan.

Elbow, P. (1973). *Writing without teachers.* New York: Oxford University Press.

Ellsworth, E. (1989). Why doesn't this feel empowering? Working through the repressive myths of critical pedagogy. *Harvard Educational Review, 59,* 297–324.

Erickson, F. (1986). Qualitative methods in research on teaching. In M. C. Wittrock (Ed.), *Handbook of research on teaching* (3rd ed.). New York: Macmillan.

Evans, C. (1989, April). *The educators' forum: Teacher-initiated research in progress.* Paper presented at annual meeting of the American Educational Research Association, San Francisco.

Farmbry, D. (1993). The warriors, the worrier and the word: Language at odds in the classroom. In M. Cochran-Smith & S. L. Lytle, *Inside/outside: Teacher research and knowledge.* New York: Teachers College Press.

Fecho, R. (1989). *On becoming mean and sensitive: Teacher to student writing conferences in the secondary classroom.* Champaign-Urbana, IL: NCTE Research Foundation.

Fecho, R. (1990). Reading like a teacher. *The Voice of the Philadelphia Writing Project, 1*(2), 14–16.

Fecho, R., Pincus, M., & Hiller, N. (1990). *"Crossroads" proposal to Philadelphia Schools Collaborative.* Philadelphia: Philadelphia Schools Collaborative.

Feiman-Nemser, S., & Featherstone, J. (1992). *Adventures in teaching.* New York: Teachers College Press.

Fenstermacher, G. (1986). Philosophy of research on teaching: Three aspects. In M. C. Wittrock (Ed.), *Handbook of research on teaching* (3rd ed.). New York: Macmillan.

Five, C. L. (1986). Fifth graders respond to a changed reading program. *Harvard Educational Review, 56,* 395–405.

Florio-Ruane, S. (1986, April). *Taking a closer look at writing conferences.* Paper presented at the American Educational Research Association, San Francisco.

Florio-Ruane, S., & Walsh, M. (1980). The teacher as colleague in classroom research. In H. Trueba, G. Guthrie, & K. Au (Eds.), *Culture in the bilingual classroom: Studies in classroom ethnography.* Rowly, MA: Newbury House.

Freire, P. (1971). *Pedagogy of the oppressed.* New York: Herder & Herder.

Geertz, C. (1973). *The interpretation of cultures.* New York: Basic Books.

Geertz, C. (1983). *Local knowledge: Further essays in interpretive anthropology.* New York: Basic Books.

Giroux, H. (1984). Rethinking the language of schooling. *Language Arts, 61,* 33–40.

Greene, M. (1973). *Teacher as stranger.* Belmont, CA: Wadsworth.

Goswami, D., & Stillman, P. (1987). *Reclaiming the classroom: Teacher research as an agency for change.* Upper Montclair, NJ: Boynton/Cook.

Guerin, K. (1985). "Bounced around": Teachers and leftover children. *Education and Urban Society, 17,* 284–291.

Griffin, G. (1989). Coda: The knowledge-driven school. In M. C. Reynolds (Ed.), *Knowledge base for the beginning teacher.* Oxford: Pergamon Press.

Hahn, J. (1991, February). *Teacher research as a catalyst for teacher change.* Paper presented at the Ethnography and Education Forum, Philadelphia.

Harris, M. (1993). Looking back: Twenty years of a teacher's journal. In M. Cochran-Smith & S. L. Lytle, *Inside/outside: Teacher research and knowledge.* New York: Teachers College Press.

Headman, R. (1993). Parents and teacher as co-investigators: Uncovering parents' perspectives on their children's literacy. In M. Cochran-Smith & S. L. Lytle, *Inside/outside: Teacher research and knowledge.* New York: Teachers College Press.

Hiller, N. (1991). *A year in transition.* Unpublished manuscript.

Holmes Group. (1990). *Tomorrow's schools: A report of the Holmes Group.* East Lansing, MI: Author.

Holmstein, V. (1987). We watched ourselves write: Report on a classroom research project. In D. Goswami & P. Stillman (Eds.), *Reclaiming the classroom: Teacher research as an agency for change.* Upper Montclair, NJ: Boynton/Cook.

Howard, J. (1989). On teaching, knowledge, and "middle ground." *Harvard Educational Review, 59,* 226–239.

Jackson, P. (1990). The functions of educational research. *Educational Researcher, 19*(7), 3–9.

Johnston, P. (1989). A scenic view of reading. *Language Arts, 66,* 160–170.

Kanevsky, R. (1993). Descriptive review as oral inquiry. In M. Cochran-Smith & S. L. Lytle, *Inside/outside: Teacher research and knowledge.* New York: Teachers College Press

Kanevsky, R., & Traugh, C. (1986). Classroom life: Some interpretations. In C. Traugh, R. Kanevsky, A. Martin, A. Seletsky, K. Woolf, & L. Strieb (Eds.), *Speaking out: Teachers on teaching.* Grand Forks: University of North Dakota.

Kean, E. (1989). Teachers and administrators eyeing each other (No one stops to clap). *The Teachers' Journal, 2,* 1–7.

Knoblauch, C. H., & Brannon, L. (1988). Knowing our knowledge: A phenomenological basis for teacher research. In L. Z. Smith (Ed.), *Audits of meaning: A festschrift in honor of Ann E. Berthoff.* Portsmouth, NH: Boynton/Cook.

Lather, P. (1986). Research as praxis. *Harvard Educational Review, 56,* 257–277.

Lather, P. (1991). *Getting smart: Feminist research and pedagogy with/in the postmodern.* London: Routledge, Chapman, & Hall.

Lewis, M. (1989, April). *Politics, resistance, and transformation: The psycho/social/sexual dynamics in the feminist classroom.* Paper presented at the Annual Meeting of the American Education Research Association, San Francisco.

Lortie, D. (1975). *School teacher: A sociological study.* Chicago: University of Chicago Press.

Lumley, D. (1987). An analysis of peer group dialogue journals for classroom use. In D. Goswami & P. Stillman (Eds.), *Reclaiming the classroom: Teacher research as an agency for change.* Upper Montclair, NJ: Boynton/Cook.

Lyons, N. (1990). Dilemmas of knowing: Ethical and epistemological dimensions of teachers' work and development. *Harvard Educational Review, 60,* 159–180.

Lytle, S. L., & Cochran-Smith, M. (1990). Learning from teacher research: A working typology. *Teachers College Record, 92*(1), 83–103.

Lytle, S. L., & Fecho, R. (1991). Meeting strangers in familiar places: Teacher collaboration by cross-visitation. *English Education, 23*(1), 5–28.

Michaels, S., Ulichney, P., & Watson-Gegeo, K. (1986). *Writing conferences: Innovation or familiar routine?* Unpublished manuscript, Harvard University, Cambridge, MA.

Miller, J. L. (1987, October-November). *Points of dissonance in teacher/researchers: Openings into emancipatory ways of knowing.* Paper presented at the Conference on Curriculum Theory and Classroom Practice, Bergamo, OH.

Morizawa, G. (1990). Acting out. In *Research in writing: Working papers of teacher researchers.* Berkeley, CA: Bay Area Writing Project.

Myers, M. (1985). Institutionalizing inquiry. *National Writing Project Quarterly, 9*(3), 1–4.

Noffke, S. (1990, April). *Knower, knowing, and known in action research.* Paper presented at the Annual Meeting of the American Educational Research Association, Boston.

Paris, C. (1993). *Teacher agency and curriculum making in classrooms.* New York: Teachers College Press.

Phelps, L.W. (1991). Practical wisdom and the geography of knowledge in composition. *College English, 53,* 863–885.

Philadelphia Teachers Learning Cooperative. (1984). On becoming teacher experts: Buying time. *Language Arts, 61,* 731–736.

Pincus, M. (1991). Following the paper trail. *The Voice of the Philadelphia Writing Project, 2*(1), 1, 14–16.

Polanyi, M. (1967). *The tacit dimension.* Garden City, NY: Anchor Books.

Queenan, M. (1988). Impertinent questions about teacher research: A review. *English Journal, 77*(2), 41–46.

Ray, L. (1986). Reflections on classroom research. In D. Goswami & P. Stillman (Eds.), *Reclaiming the classroom: Teacher research as an agency for change.* Upper Montclair, NJ: Boynton/Cook.

Reither, J. A. (1990). The writing student as researcher: Learning from our students. In D. Daiker & M. Morenberg (Eds.), *The writing teacher as researcher.* Portsmouth, NH: Boynton/Cook.

Reynolds, M. C. (Ed.). (1989). *Knowledge base for the beginning teacher.* Oxford: Pergamon Press.

Rotchford, M. (1989). Student teachers focus on their students. *The Teachers' Journal, 2,* 42–52.

Saunders, D., & McCutcheon, G. (1986). The development of practical theories of teaching. *Journal of Curriculum and Supervision, 2*(1), 50–67.

Schaefer, R. J. (1967). *The school as a center of inquiry.* New York: Harper & Row.

Schön, D. A. (1983). *The reflective practitioner: How professionals think in action.* San Francisco: Jossey-Bass.

Schwartz, J. (1990). On the move in Pittsburgh: When students and teacher share research. In D. Daiker & M. Morenberg (Eds.), *The writing teacher as researcher: Essays in the theory and practice of class-based research.* Portsmouth, NH: Boynton/Cook.

Shulman, L. (1986a). Paradigms and research programs in the study of teaching: A contemporary perspective. In M. C. Wittrock (Ed.), *Handbook of research on teaching* (3rd ed.). New York: Macmillan.

Shulman, L. (1986b). Those who understand: Knowledge growth in teaching. *Educational Researcher, 15*(2), 14.

Shulman, L. (1987). Knowledge and teaching: Foundations of the new reform. *Harvard Educational Review, 57,* 1–22.

Sockett, H. T. (1987). Has Shulman got the strategy right? *Harvard Educational Review, 57,* 208–219.

Starr, P. (1993). Finding our way: A deaf writer's journey. In M. Cochran-Smith & S. L. Lytle, *Inside/outside: Teacher research and knowledge.* New York: Teachers College Press.

Stenhouse, L. (1985). *Research as a basis for teaching.* London: Heinemann.

Strieb, L. (1985). *A Philadelphia teacher's journal.* Grand Forks, ND: Center for Teaching and Learning.

Stumbo, C. (1989). Beyond the classroom. *Harvard Educational Review, 59,* 87–97.

Taylor, D. (1990). Teaching without testing [Special issue]. *English Education, 22,* 4–74.

Westerhoff, J. H. (1987). The teacher as pilgrim. In F. S. Bolin & J. M. Falk (Eds.), *Teacher renewal.* New York: Teachers College Press.

Wiggington, E. (1985). *Sometimes a shining moment: The Foxfire experience.* Garden City, NY: Archer Press/Doubleday.

Wilson, S. (1990). Spinning talk into writing: Behind the scenes of a research project. In *Research in writing: Working papers of teacher researchers.* Berkeley, CA: Bay Area Writing Project.

Wunner, K. (1993). Great expectations. In M. Cochran-Smith & S. L. Lytle, *Inside/outside: Teacher research and knowledge.* New York: Teachers College Press.

Yagelsky, R. P. (1990). Searching for "sloppy trees": How research shapes teaching. In D. Daiker & M. Morenberg (Eds.), *The writing teacher as researcher: Essays in the theory and practice of class-based research.* Portsmouth, NH: Boynton/Cook.

Yonemura, M. (1982). Teacher conversations: A potential source of their own professional growth. *Curriculum Inquiry, 12,* 239–256.

Zeichner, K., & Liston, D. (1987). Teaching student teachers to reflect. *Harvard Educational Review, 57,* 1–22.

Teachers Reflect
on Their Own
Classroom Practice

Because You Like Us: The Language of Control

CYNTHIA BALLENGER

This article is the result of a year spent in conversations about teaching — difficult conversations in which I, a seasoned teacher and fledgling sociolinguist, was only rarely the informed party.[1] Mike Rose, in *Lives on the Boundary* (1989), uses the metaphor of "entering the conversation" to describe the process of learning to participate in academic discourse. In my case, there was a multitude of different conversations I was trying to enter, and in each I had a different role to play.

During that same time I was teaching preschool, as I have done for most of the past fifteen years. The school was in the Haitian community in Dorchester, Massachusetts, and primarily served the children of Haitian immigrants. I went there because in my previous work as an early childhood special education teacher I had noticed that more and more Haitian children were being referred to my class. These children were arriving attended by all kinds of concerns from the educational professionals: they were "wild," they had "no language," their mothers were "depressed." There were certainly some children I saw who had genuine problems, and yet time and time again I found that, after a period of adjustment, they were responsive, intelligent children; their mothers were perhaps homesick and unhappy in a strange, cold country, but generally not clinically depressed. During that period, however, we did make many mistakes, and I became interested in learning the Haitian culture and language in order to see the children more

[1] Earlier versions of this work have been presented at the Penn Ethnography in Educational Research Forum in February 1991 and the Brookline Teacher-Researcher Seminar in June 1990. My research was carried out as a member of that seminar with teachers and children at my school. In this article, all teachers' and children's names have been changed.

Harvard Educational Review Vol. 62 No. 2 Summer 1992, 199–208

clearly. After a period of graduate school studying sociolinguistics, I took a position as a preschool teacher in a bilingual school where both Haitian Creole and English were spoken and where, as I came to understand, Haitian culture was quite central. I was the only teacher at this school who was not Haitian and, although by this time I spoke Creole, I was still getting to know the culture.

During that time I was one of two instructors of a course in child development that a local college offered for Haitian people who wished to work in day-care centers. My Haitian co-instructor and I designed this course based on the model of a conversation about child rearing — a dialogue between Haitians and North Americans about their attitudes on the subject. I was also a new member of the Brookline Teacher-Researcher Seminar (BTRS), a group of public school teachers and academic researchers who are attempting to develop a common language and a shared set of values with which to approach classroom issues (Michaels & O'Connor, in press; Phillips, 1991). As a graduate student in sociolinguistics, I had done research; as a teacher, I had thought about teaching; I was now involved in trying to approach issues in ways that incorporated both of these perspectives. The work that I will report on here was part of these conversations. I will try to let the reader hear some of the different voices that I heard.

In this article, I will discuss the process I went through in learning to control a class of four-year-old Haitian children. Researchers who regard language as the principal vehicle by which children are socialized into their particular family and culture have consistently regarded control and discipline as central events — events where language patterns and cultural values intersect in visible ways (Boggs, 1985; Cook-Gumperz, 1973; Watson-Gegeo & Gegeo, 1990). When, as in my case, the adult does not share the same cultural background and the same experience of socialization as the children, one becomes very aware of learning how to enter and manage the relevant conversation. Although it can be argued that my participation in the events I relate here was in some ways informed by sociolinguistic theory, I present this more as a story than as a research report. This is my attempt to discuss this experience in a way that will not deny access to the conversation to those who helped form my understanding of it. I must stress, however, that all of these conversations would not have been possible if there hadn't been room in the preschool day for talk — the school was run jointly by the teachers and we spent considerable time each day together — and if there had not been some financial support for the Brookline Teacher-Researcher Seminar (Phillips, 1991). This support, in the form of small stipends, photocopying, money for an occasional day off to reflect, and a sense of being valued, combined with the nature of the school where I was teaching, made my situation luxurious compared with that of many teachers faced with problems similar to mine.

THE PROBLEM

Having had many years of experience teaching in early childhood programs, I did not expect to have problems when I came to this Haitian preschool three years ago. However, I did. The children ran me ragged. In the friendliest, most cheerful, and affectionate manner imaginable, my class of four-year-olds followed their own inclinations rather than my directions in almost everything. Though I claim to be a person who does not need to have a great deal of control, in this case I had very little — and I did not like it.

My frustration increased when I looked at the other classrooms at my school. I had to notice that the other teachers, all Haitian women, had orderly classrooms of children who, in an equally affectionate and cheerful manner, *did* follow directions and kept the confusion to a level that I could have tolerated. The problem, evidently, did not reside in the children, since the Haitian teachers managed them well enough. Where then did it reside? What was it that the Haitian teachers did that I did not do?

The group of Haitian preschool teachers whom I was teaching in the child-development course recognized the problem in their own terms. As part of the course, they were all interning in various day-care centers, some with me at the Haitian school, the majority in other centers. Many of the teachers in the other centers were extremely concerned about behavior problems. What they told me and each other was that many of the children in their centers were behaving very poorly; many felt that this was particularly true of the Haitian children. They felt that the way in which they were being instructed as teachers to deal with the children's behavior was not effective. One woman explained to me that when she was hit by a four-year-old, she was instructed to acknowledge the anger he must be feeling, then to explain to him that he could not hit her. She told me that, from her point of view, this was the same as suggesting politely, "Why don't you hit me again?"

When I talked with Haitian parents at my school, I again heard similar complaints. From the point of view of many of the people I talked with, the behavior tolerated in their neighborhood schools was disrespectful; the children were allowed to misbehave. A common refrain in these conversations was, "We're losing a generation of children"; that is, the young children here now, who were not brought up first in Haiti, were not being brought up with the same values. However, when I asked for specific advice about things I might do to manage the children better, the teachers and I could never identify any behaviors of mine that I could try to change.

I took my problem to the Brookline Teacher-Researcher Seminar. The members of BTRS have come to share a focus on language — the language of instruction; children's language in a wide variety of situations; the language of science talk, of book talk, of conflict; and so on. Thus, in our conversations, the BTRS group encouraged me to approach my problem by discovering what it was that the Haitian teachers *said* to the children in situations where directions were being given. The Seminar members have also come to believe that an important part of a research project is examining where a particular research question comes from in one's own life — why it seems important, what its value is to the teacher-researcher. In many cases, this is a matter of investigating one's own socialization, a kind of self-reflection that became an important part of my investigation.

SITUATIONS AS TEXTS

I began to write down what the Haitian teachers said to the children in situations where the children's behavior was at issue. I then carried these texts to the various conversations of which I was a part: the Haitian teachers in the child development course, the North American teachers in the Brookline Seminar, and the parents and teachers at the school where I was teaching. I will present here some texts that I consider typical in their form and content, and then share some of the responses and the thinking engendered by these texts among the people with whom I had been conversing.

I present first Clothilde's account of an event at her day-care center. Clothilde is a middle-aged Haitian woman and a student in the child-development course. She has a great deal of experience with children — both from raising her own and from caring for other people's — and many of her classmates turn to her for advice. The text below is from a conversation in which she had been complaining to me about the behavior of the Haitian children in the day-care center where she was student teaching. She felt that the North American teachers were not controlling the children adequately.

One day, as Clothilde arrived at her school, she watched a teacher telling a little Haitian child that the child needed to go into her classroom, that she could not stay alone in the hall. The child refused and eventually kicked the teacher. Clothilde had had enough. She asked the director to bring her all the Haitian kids right away. The director and Clothilde gathered the children into the large common room. The following is the text of what she told me she said to the children:

Clothilde: Does your mother let you bite?

Children: No.

Clothilde: Does your father let you punch kids?

Children: No.

Clothilde: Do you kick at home?

Children: No.

Clothilde: You don't respect anyone, not the teachers who play with you or the adults who work upstairs. You need to respect adults — even people you see on the streets. You are taking good ways you learn at home and not bringing them to school. You're taking the bad things you learn at school and taking them home. You're not going to do this anymore. Do you want your parents to be ashamed of you?

36

According to Clothilde, the Haitian children have been well-behaved ever since. Other Haitian teachers with whom I have shared this text have confirmed that that was what the children needed to hear. However, they also said that Clothilde will have to repeat her speech because the children won't remain well-behaved indefinitely without a reminder.

The next text involves an incident at my school. Josiane, who has taught for many years both here and in Haiti, was reprimanding a group of children who had been making a lot of noise while their teacher was trying to give them directions:

Josiane: When your mother talks to you, don't you listen?

Children: Yes.

Josiane: When your mother says, go get something, don't you go get it?

Children: Yes.

Josiane: When your mother says, go to the bathroom, don't you go?

Children: Yes.

Josiane: You know why I'm telling you this. Because I want you to be good children. When an adult talks to you, you're supposed to listen so you will become a good person. The adults here like you, they want you to become good children.

Finally, we have Jérémie's father speaking to him. Jérémie is a very active four-year-old, and the staff had asked his father for help in controlling his behavior:

Father: Are you going to be good? (Jérémie nods at each pause)

Are you going to listen to Miss Cindy?

Are you going to listen to Miss Josiane?

Because they like you.

They love you.

Do it for me.

Do it for God.

Do you like God?

God loves you.

REFLECTING

The content and the form of these texts are different from what I, and many other North American teachers, would probably have said in the same circumstances. I shared these and other texts and observations with many parents and teachers, both Haitian and North American. I asked them to reflect with me on how these conversations were different and what underlay them.

What follows is a blend of many people's observations and self-reflections, including my own. Here I want to note that I am assuming that the North American teachers, including myself, shared similar training and enculturation. Although we differed in many ways, I would characterize our culture — as Heath does in *Ways with Words* (1983) — as "mainstream culture." The Haitian teachers also shared some, although not all, values and assumptions. Although I am trying to distill these conversations in order to identify "typical" practices of Haitian or North American teachers, I do not mean to imply that all North American or all Haitian teachers are the same.

The Haitian preschool teachers had clear insights into behavior characteristic of North American teachers. Clothilde commented that the North American teachers she knows frequently refer to the children's internal states and interpret their feelings for them; for example, "you must be angry," "it's hard for you when your friend does that," and so on. Clothilde pointed out to me that in her speech she makes no reference to the children's emotions; other Haitian teachers I have observed also do not do this as a rule.

Rose, another Haitian teacher, also commented that North American teachers often make reference to particular factors in the child's situation that, in the teacher's opinion, may have influenced his or her behavior. For example, Michel, whose mother had left him, was often told that the teachers understood that he missed his mother, but that he nevertheless needed to share his toys. When a child pushes or pinches another child sitting next to him or her, many North American teachers will suggest that, if the child does not like people to sit so close, he or she should say so rather than pinch. Rose felt, and from my observation I concurred, that Haitian teachers rarely do this. Josiane suggested further that if she were concerned about an individual child and his or her particular problems, instead of articulating them for him or her, her goal would be "to make him or her feel comfortable with the group." If the child were misbehaving, she felt she would say, "You know I'm your friend," and then remind him or her that "we don't do that." In fact, I have seen her do exactly that many times, with excellent results.

These examples suggest to me a difference in focus between the North American and Haitian teachers. It seems that North American teachers characteristically are concerned with making a connection with the individual child, with articulating his or her feelings and problems. On the other hand, Clothilde, Josiane, and the many other Haitian people I spoke with and observed, emphasize the group in their control talk, articulating the values and responsibilities of group membership. For example, we have seen that both North American and Haitian teachers make reference to the family, but in different ways. North American teachers are likely to mention particular characteristics of a child's family, characteristics that are specific to that family and are seen as perhaps responsible for the child's individual actions.

The Haitian teachers emphasize instead what the families have in common. The families do not differ in their desire that the children respect adults, that the children behave properly, and that their behavior not shame them. The children's answers, when they are given in unison as in Josiane's text above, present a vivid enactment of the sort of unity the Haitian teachers' approach may engender.

Another difference the Haitian teachers noted is the use of consequences. North American teachers typically present the particular consequences of an act of misbehavior. For example, I often say something like, "He's crying because you hit him," or, "If you don't listen to me, you won't know what to do." Haitian teachers are less likely to differentiate among particular kinds of misbehavior; they condemn them all, less in terms of their results than as examples of "bad" behavior. Clothilde is typical of the Haitian teachers in that the immediate consequences are not made explicit; she does not explain why she is against biting or punching. She instead refers to such behavior as "bad," and then explains to the children the consequences of bad behavior in general, such as shame for the family. Jérémie's father simply tells Jérémie to be good, to be good for those who love him. Josiane, too, tells the children to be good because the people who like them want them to be good. I have heard other Haitian teachers refer to the impression that bad behavior would create in a passer-by, or to the necessity of modeling good behavior for younger children. But Haitian teachers rarely mention the specific consequences of particular acts, a clear difference from North American teachers.

In the Haitian texts, one has the impression that the children share the adult's understanding of what bad behavior is. Clothilde's series of rhetorical questions, like "Do your parents let you kick?", is an example of the form that many Haitian teachers adopt when addressing children about their behavior. The children understand their role without difficulty; they repeat the expected answers in choral unison. The choice of this form — that is, questions to which the answer is assumed — emphasizes the fact that the children already know that their behavior is wrong.

In the North American control situation, on the other hand, the child often appears to be receiving new information. If there is a consensus about behavior — certain behavior is bad, certain other behavior is good — we don't present it this way. North Americans frequently explain the consequences of particular actions as if they were trying to convince the child that there was a problem with his or her behavior. As presented in school, misbehavior is considered wrong not because of anything inherent in it, but because of its particular consequences, or perhaps because the behavior stems from feelings that the child has failed to identify and control.

These differences, as I came to recognize them, seemed significant enough to account for some of the difficulties I had been experiencing in my classroom. But what to do about them?

PRACTICE

With the overwhelming evidence that these children were used to a kind of control talk other than what I had been providing, I have since begun to adopt some of the style of the Haitian teachers. I assume that I am not very good at it, that I have no idea of the nuances, and I continue to include many of the ways I have typically managed behavior in my teaching. Nevertheless, I have developed a more or less stable melange of styles, and my control in the classroom has improved significantly. In addition, I find that I love trying out this Haitian way. I was struck by an experience I had the other day, when I was reprimanding one boy for pinching another. I was focusing, in the Haitian manner, on his prior, indisputable knowledge that pinching was simply no good. I also used my best approximation of the facial expression and tone of voice that I see the Haitian teachers use in these encounters. I can tell when I have it more or less right, because of the way that the children pay attention. As I finished this particular time, the other children, who had been rapt, all solemnly thanked me. They were perhaps feeling in danger of being pinched and felt that I had at last been effective. This solemn sort of response, which has occurred a few other times, gives me the sense that these situations are very important to them.

The following anecdote may suggest more about the way in which these interactions are important to the children. Recently I was angrily reprimanding the children about their failure to wait for me while crossing the parking lot:

Cindy: Did I tell you to go?

Children: No.

Cindy: Can you cross this parking lot by yourselves?

Children: No.

Cindy: That's right. There are cars here. They're dangerous. I don't want you to go alone. Why do I want you to wait for me, do you know?

"Yes," says Claudette, "because you like us."

Although I was following the usual Haitian form — rhetorical questions with "no" answers — I had been expecting a final response based on the North American system of cause and effect, something like, "Because the cars are dangerous." Claudette, however, although she understands perfectly well the dangers of cars to small children, does not expect to use that information in this kind of an interaction. What, then, *is* she telling me? One thing that she is saying, which is perhaps what the solemn children also meant, is that, from her point of view, there is intimacy in this kind of talk. This is certainly the feeling I get from these experiences. I feel especially connected to the children in those instances in which I seem to have gotten it right.

THE LARGER CONTEXT

North American teachers generally think of reprimands — particularly of young children who are just learning to control their behavior — as put-downs, and are reluctant to give them. North American preschool teachers, in particular, will take great pains to avoid saying "no" or "don't." In contrast, I have learned from working with Haitian children and teachers that there are situations in which reprimands can be confirming, can strengthen relationships, and can, in a sense, define relationships for the child, as seems to have been the case for Claudette in the example given above.

Such an opportunity may be lost when we go to great lengths to avoid actually telling a child that he is wrong, that we disagree or disapprove. When we look at the difference between the ways in which things are done at home and at school, and the negative consequences that may result from these mismatches for children coming from minority cultural backgrounds, the area of misbehavior and the way it is responded to seem particularly important because it affects so directly the nature of the relationship between child and teacher.

I was not unaware when I began that this subject was a hotbed of disagreement: North Americans perceive Haitians as too severe, both verbally and in their use of physical punishment, while Haitians often perceive North American children as being extraordinarily fresh and out of control.[2] Haitian immigrant parents here are at once ashamed and defiantly supportive of their community's disciplinary standards and methods. In order to represent the views of Haitians I spoke with independent of my process of understanding, I asked them to reflect again on our two cultures after they had heard my interpretations.

People, of course, offered many varied points of view, yet everybody emphasized a sense of having grown up very "protected" in Haiti, of having been safe there both from getting into serious trouble and from harm. This sense of being protected was largely based on their understanding that their entire extended family, as well as many people in the community, were involved in their upbringing. Haitian families in the United States, some pointed out, are smaller and less extended. The community here, while tight in many

---

[2] It must be stated that the consequences of this disagreement are, of course, vastly more painful for the powerless. Contact with schools, with social service institutions, with the police, is in many cases highly problematic for Haitian families. The Haitian family, in these situations, is frequently met with a lack of understanding that leads easily to a lack of respect. Mainstream assumptions about "proper" ways of talking and dealing with children's behavior often stand in the way of distinguishing a functioning family, for example, from a dysfunctional one, in distinguishing a child whose parents are strict in order to help him or her succeed from one whose family simply does not want to deal with the child's problems. Such assumptions often stand in the path of appropriate help as well. The school where I taught was often called upon to discuss cultural differences with social service groups, hospitals, and other schools. Occasionally, we were asked to provide some assistance for particular cases. But, of course, there were countless instances in which Haitian families were involved with these various powerful institutions and the families were without such aid.

ways, is more loosely connected than in Haiti. This change in social structure was bemoaned by the people I spoke with, especially with reference to bringing up children. They attributed to this change their sense that this generation of children, particularly those born here, is increasingly at risk. They are at risk not only of falling away from their parents' culture, but also, and consequently, of falling prey to the drugs, crime, and other problems of urban life that they see around them.

And yet everyone I spoke with also recalled some pain in their growing up, pain they relate to the respect and obedience they were required to exhibit to all adults, which at times conflicted with their own developing desire to state their opinions or make their own choices. This pain was nevertheless not to be discarded lightly. For many of the Haitian people with whom I spoke, religious values underlie these twin issues of respect and obedience; respect for parents and other adults is an analogue for respect and obedience to God and God's law.

Many people seemed to agree with the ambivalence expressed by one Haitian lawyer and mother who told me that, while she had suffered as a child because of the uncompromising obedience and respect demanded of her in her family, she continued to see respect as a value she needed to impart to her children. She said to me, "There must be many other ways to teach respect." She was one of many Haitians who told me of instances where a child from a poor family, a child with neither the clothes nor the supplies for school, had succeeded eventually in becoming a doctor or a lawyer. In these accounts, as in her own case, it is in large measure the strictness of the family that is regarded as the source of the child's accomplishment, rather than the talent or the power of the individual.

Presumably, there is some tension in all societies between individual and community. In these accounts is some suggestion of the form this tension sometimes takes within Haitian culture. For my part, I am struck and troubled by the powerful individualism underlying the approach I characterize as typical of me and many North American teachers. It appears that North Americans do speak as if something like the child's "enlightened self-interest" were the ultimate moral guidepost. In comparison to the language used by the Haitian teachers, North American teachers' language seems to place very little emphasis on shared values, on a moral community.

The process of gaining multicultural understanding in education must, in my opinion, be a dual one. On the one hand, cultural behavior that at first seems strange and inexplicable should become familiar; on the other hand, one's own familiar values and practices should become at least temporarily strange, subject to examination. In addition to the information I have gained that helps me to manage and form relationships with Haitian children in my classroom, I also value greatly the extent to which these conversations, by forcing me to attempt to empathize with and understand a view of the world that is in many ways very different from my customary one, have put me in a position to reexamine values and principles that had become inaccessible under layers of assumptions.

I am not teaching Haitian children this year, although I continue to visit them. Next year I expect to have a classroom with children from a wide range of backgrounds. It is difficult to say how my last experience will illuminate the next — or, analogously, how my experience can be of use to teachers in different kinds of classrooms. I do believe that teachers need to try to open up and to understand both our own assumptions and the cultural meaning that children from all backgrounds bring to school. It seems to me that accommodation must be made on all sides so that no group has to abandon the ways in which it is accustomed to passing on its values. I have been fortunate that the knowledge and collaboration of so many people, Haitian and North American, were available to help me begin to understand my own experience. All of these conversations have been their own rewards — I have made new friends and, I believe, become a better teacher.

REFERENCES

Boggs, S. (1985). *Speaking, talking and relating: A study of Hawaiian children at home and at school.* Norwood, NJ: Ablex.

Cook-Gumperz, J. (1973). *Social control and socialization.* London: Routledge & Kegan Paul.

Heath, S. B. (1983). *Ways with words.* Cambridge, Eng.: Cambridge University Press.

Michaels, S., & O'Connor, M. C. (in press). *Literacy as reasoning within multiple discourses: Implications for policy and educational reform.* Newton, MA: Education Development Center.

Phillips, A. (February, 1991). *Hearing children's stories: A report on the Brookline Teacher-Researcher Seminar.* Paper presented at the Penn Ethnography in Educational Research Forum, Philadelphia, PA.

Rose, M. (1989). *Lives on the boundary.* New York: Penguin.

Watson-Gegeo, K., & Gegeo, D. (1990). *Disentangling: The discourse of conflict and therapy in the Pacific Islands.* Norwood, NJ: Ablex.

A Curious Plan:
Managing on the Twelfth

PATRICIA CLIFFORD

SHARON L. FRIESEN

The Mock Turtle went on:
   "We had the best of educations — in fact, we went to school every day."
   "And how many hours a day did you do lessons?" said Alice, in a hurry to change the subject.
   "Ten hours the first day," said the Mock Turtle, "nine the next, and so on."
   "What a curious plan!" exclaimed Alice.
   "That's the reason they're called lessons," the Gryphon remarked; "because they lessen from day to day."
   This was quite a new idea to Alice, and she thought it over a little before she made her next remark. "Then the eleventh day must have been a holiday?"
   "Of course it was," said the Mock Turtle.
   "And how did you manage on the twelfth?"
(Carroll, 1865/1966, pp. 95–96)

INTRODUCTION: PLANNING A LIVED CURRICULUM

Every September, teachers and students gather together in our classroom to learn. Each of us, teacher and child alike, walks through the door bringing experiences and understandings that are ours alone. Yet, each person is also embarking on a journey that he or she will come to share with others. This journey is made anew every year with every class.

   Travelers prepare more or less carefully for the adventures they hope to have, but the itineraries, maps, and plans do not in themselves create the

Harvard Educational Review Vol. 63 No. 3 Fall 1993, 339–358

voyage. The journey is an experience, lived as just the thing it turns out to be: moment-by-moment, day-by-day, month-by-month. As teachers, we prepare for each year's journey in big ways and in small ways. We make decisions, design plans, and outline key strategies to help us set directions for the coming year. In this article, we hope to share some of our decisions, plans, and strategies, therein describing the factors we consider as we prepare for an authentically engaging journey with each new class of children.

Some travelers keep diaries, which we, too, have done, recording actual situations that took place in our classroom from September 1991 to June 1992. In terms of its multi-aged, open-area configuration, our class was like others in the primary division of our school. The number of children varied throughout the year, as families moved in and out of the community. At any time, the two of us team-taught between fifty-five and fifty-eight children in grades one and two. In many ways, our classroom would be familiar to anyone used to teaching in middle-class neighborhoods. In other ways, however, there are important differences. First of all, the children in our class vary more widely in their abilities, backgrounds, emotional and physical needs than one might expect. In this class, ten students were second-language learners. One child was in a wheelchair. Several had behavioral problems severe enough that social workers, psychologists, and psychiatrists had been involved before the children entered grade one. Some had been identified as gifted, others as learning disabled.

For twenty-five years, our school has maintained a tradition of multi-aged, open-area classrooms as part of its demonstration function for the local university. Because innovative structures and teaching practices are expected and encouraged, we were supported in our request both to teach together and to conduct action research. From the earliest days of our work as a team, everyone knew what we were setting out to do. Never content simply to replicate existing best practices, our school wanted to find out what would happen if we did what teachers at our school, University Elementary School, have always done: question, challenge, and change fundamental assumptions about the education of young children.

Using excerpts from the diaries we kept last year, we hope in this article to illustrate some of the struggles and successes in our way of thinking about teaching, learning, curriculum, and planning. We feel such examples suggest a quality of children's thought and work that some may find astounding, given the fact that our students are only six and seven years old. We feel strongly, however, that this is an example of the kind of work and thinking in which *all* children could engage and that all teachers could endeavor to bring forth. We would like to pose serious questions about how teachers can prepare themselves to create situations in which the voices of children genuinely inform the construction of each year's curriculum. For some teachers, administrators, and staff developers, these questions may be uncomfortable to hear because they call into question much of what is currently recognized as sound professional practice, practice that stands squarely in the way of the kinds of educational reform our profession needs most urgently to begin.

When schools open each year, one of the first things many teachers do is begin making long-range and unit plans that outline what they hope to accomplish by Christmas or, perhaps, for the whole year. If you are an administrator, we would like to give you some things to think about as you request such plans. If you are a classroom teacher, we would like to give you things to consider before you actually sit down to plan. If you are a teacher of teachers, we would like to give you pause as you prepare student teachers for their work with children. We would like, in short, to add our voices to the conversations aimed at ensuring that lessons do *not* lessen from day to day, from year to year, for children who have no choice but to come to school. We are committed to developing a classroom where teachers and children are passionate, robust learners. This commitment requires something more than new programs or new methods. It calls forth what we can only characterize as a philosophy of education, an attitude toward teaching and learning, and a fundamental disposition that permits teachers to live differently with the children in their care.

We are searching for a school curriculum that acknowledges the importance of the lived experience of children and teachers; that understands growth as more than an interior, private, individual matter of unfolding development; that situates teaching and learning within the context of an educative community; and that asks hard questions about the fuzzy, feel-good legacy of much of what teachers now do in the name of "progressive" practice. Creating such a curriculum is a life's work. Perhaps it is significant, however, that neither of us came to early childhood education as our first career. One of us worked for five years as a systems analyst, and the other taught senior high school for fifteen years. For different reasons, and on different paths, we had both developed similar concerns about public education long before we actually met each other. We were worried about the boredom, drop-out rates, and general lackluster performance of many students. In that we were not alone; we were part of a growing public concern that young people in North America were not learning as much as they might. Two things were different for us, however. First, we resisted the return to traditional images and practices that seem almost inevitably to accompany criticism of schools. And second, each of us knew (again, long before we met) that attempts to reform schools by concentrating mainly on the attitudes and achievements of secondary students, the young people we had been hiring and teaching, was unlikely to succeed. Each of us had already decided that the most promising place to create genuinely new practices was with the very young.

We endeavored initially to find out something about what a classroom would look like if we called into question some of our profession's most ordinary assumptions about teaching and learning. We have now studied, taught, and written together for four years. In that time, we have learned a great deal, and we fight constantly with the temptation to try to say everything at once. In this article, we hope to make a small start by posing three important questions:

- How can curriculum remain open to children's unique experiences and connect with the world they know outside the school?
- Why is imaginative experience the best starting place for planning?
- What happens when teachers break down the barriers between school knowledge and real knowledge?

DAVID'S STORY: ON KEEPING THINGS CONNECTED

"I would ask you to remember only this one thing," said Badger. "The stories people tell have a way of taking care of them. If stories come to you, care for them. And learn to give them away where they are needed. Sometimes a person needs a story more than food to stay alive; that is why we put these stories in each other's memory. This is how people care for themselves." (Lopez, 1990, p. 48)

We met David and his parents on the first day of school.[1] They had just returned to Canada after spending seven years in Africa, where they had lived and worked among the Masai. Although he was of European descent, David had been born in Africa. He went to a village kindergarten, and played and tended cattle with the Masai children. No one in our class, including us, knew much about Africa. Though we had listened carefully to what David's parents told us at the beginning of the school year, we remembered embarrassingly little of it because we had been trying to learn about our fifty-four other children at the same time. So, as we watched David take his first tentative steps in school, we often forgot that the life David had been living until the end of August was radically different from the one he now had to negotiate in our large, complicated, noisy Canadian classroom.

Throughout September and into October, David spoke very little. He would answer direct questions briefly, but never offered to share much of himself. Once, in response to an assignment to tell a personal story, he told a small group of children how he and his family had gone camping — and had woken up to find lions crouching under their truck. The other children acted the story out, growling and shrieking with frightened delight. But aside from this story, we knew little about David. As time went on, David made a friend in class, hooking up with Jason out of mutual need. David was lonely, and he wanted to establish himself in a new country. Jason needed a companion to coerce, command, and bully. This friendship worried David's par-

---

[1] The names of the students we use in this article are pseudonyms for the children in our class.

ents. David had spent all of his life nurtured within a trusting, gentle community, and he approached his friendship with Jason with the same quality of trust. David got into trouble almost daily because of Jason, and David's parents found themselves having to talk to him about the inappropriateness of some people's intentions. They were heartsick — both about what was happening to David and about the ugly lessons about "the real world" that their gentle, naive son was beginning to absorb.

One day in early October, David arrived at school with a huge book about the Masai and asked if he could show his book to the other children. This was the first time David had ever offered to share part of his life experiences with the whole class, to teach us all what he knew best — life among the Masai. David stood in front of the class with his book. He flipped to a few pictures and spoke softly — so softly that only the children near the front could hear him. We tried to offer a few details about the Masai, but we knew so little. In spite of these difficulties and limitations, the children were entranced. They had so many questions to ask David, so much they wanted to know. This was the second time we had seen the children respond with enthusiasm to David's life in Africa. This time we recognized the power of the invitation that he had offered us. Here was the perfect chance to bring David into the full life of the classroom.

That afternoon, David's mother came to volunteer in the classroom. We asked her if she would speak to us about the Masai. She agreed, took her place in a small chair at the front of the group, and opened David's book. As she spoke, David stood quietly at her shoulder, gently stroking her long hair. He seemed to relax into the memories of that safe, familiar place, trusting the intimacy of his mother's voice and body to secure the connection between here and there.

As our eyes met above the heads of the children, we knew we had been waiting for this all along, without knowing it: waiting for David's life in Africa to come alive for us. Up to now, David had blended in too readily with all the other children. We had had no images to help us understand that this new country, this new classroom, held few connections with the world he had known in Africa.

Our effort to see all children as contributing members of our classroom community is a kind of standing invitation, but we never know who will take it up, or how they will do it. It appeared that David had decided that *now* was his time, and he made the first essential move. David and his mother shared their life among the Masai with us, and in that sharing helped forge new links between David, his classmates, and us. The class was filled with curiosity, and questions overflowed the hour we spent together. Because of the intensity of the children's interest in David's experiences in Africa and the potential to find, in their pleasure, a new place for David in the classroom, we felt committed to act beyond the delights of that afternoon. We accepted eagerly when David's mother asked if we were interested in using a children's book about the Masai that they had at home.

The next day David brought us *Bringing the Rain to Kapiti Plain*. As we read the story to the class, David sat at the back mouthing every word to himself. Once again we saw David relaxed, smiling, basking in the genuine delight of hearing that well-loved story again, this time in the world of his classroom in Calgary. This book was just the beginning of the stories about Africa, for we found others: *The Orphan Boy; Rhinos for Lunch, Elephants for Supper;* and *A Promise to the Sun*. David brought in other things to share with us, such as elaborate beaded collars and knives used to bleed cattle.

Months later, when the children drew maps of their known worlds, David's map showed his house in Africa, the cheetah park, the camping place where the lions crouched under the truck, a Masai warrior. We sensed then how much of his heart was still there and were honored that he felt safe enough among us to share himself in this way, for as David now tells us, he is "a very private person." We are also keenly aware that we would have known nothing about these places had David not come into our lives. Recently, when we were reading about Mongolian nomads' living on animal blood and milk, many children remembered what David had taught them about the Masai. They speculated about why the animals didn't die when they were bled, and looked to David for confirmation that such a thing was, indeed, possible.

We continually ask ourselves: How much of the life that is lived completely outside of school is welcomed into the classroom as knowledge and experience that can enrich us all? How much of each child gets to come to school? When a child says, "This is me, and I am ready for you to know it," we feel we must try to honor this offering, not shut it out, control it, or hurry to get on with the curriculum. An invitation is more than words. Offered sincerely, invitations create obligations to welcome and to provide. Having extended an invitation to David, we felt compelled to act. David's knowledge and experiences needed to become part of the curriculum, part of the life of the group.

Bringing David into the class in this way opened up new possibilities for him, but it did something just as important for the whole class. All of the children lived the experience of a standing invitation. By observing how we attended to David and to others who also offered *their* stories, the children came to understand the importance of what each of them might bring to the journey our class had embarked on together.

Our curriculum work demands mindful, deliberate improvisation at such moments. It goes far beyond "Show and Share," which can be a perniciously inauthentic practice: "You show me yours and I'll show you mine." Children's sharing is often limited to a slot in the daily agenda. While such activity is designed to bring home into the school, the activity of sharing can, unfortunately, become an end in itself, requiring no further commitment from the teacher than to provide the opportunity for each child to bring in a favorite object or news event. That is not at all what we mean when we speak of invitations. We mean, rather, that each child's voice can be heard, and that their speaking can make a difference to our curriculum decisionmaking.

Improvising on children's responses to our standing invitation demands a commitment to recognizing human relationships as a fundamental source of knowledge. At the beginning of the year we could not plan for these moments, but we were prepared for them because we knew that they would inevitably arise. We knew that the children would give us what we needed to know, as long as we remained open to the possibilities.

Determined to foster continuity between personal and school knowledge, we work in a constant state of watchfulness. Children's authentic offerings are often made tentatively. Unlike David's, they can be subtle and easy to miss, but they are nevertheless vital components of a lived curriculum. We know that when curriculum includes only the plans teachers make to deliver instruction, the child who emerges is usually what we might call a "school child," one who is either compliant with or defiant of the exercise of institutional power. It is our belief that when curriculum is divorced from real life, children often lose connections with their own memories and histories. They lose touch with who they are. They may exist in our eyes more as students than as emerging selves, and we wonder if they continue to learn in any passionate sense of that word.

LEARNING: FROM THE KNOWN TO THE UNKNOWN

Children develop most fully as passionate learners when they — like all of us — are allowed to claim fully their own experience of the world. We are not, however, talking about the type of experience that is made relevant to children through its commercial appeal or immediate access: Ninja Turtles and Barbies, video games, superheros, or cartoons. Nor are we talking about the immersion in local experience that some call "the belly button curriculum": me and my house, me and my family, me and my neighborhood. Much traditional thought in early childhood education is grounded in a view of learning as predictable development through ages and stages, from familiar to strange, from concrete to abstract, from (supposedly) simple to complex.

In one sense, we accept these assumptions. After all, David *did* want to share his daily experiences in Africa with his classmates in Canada, and we watched David blossom as he accepted the invitation to connect his life in Africa with life in Canada. In another sense, however, what happened to David is best understood as a starting point for even richer engagement. What intrigued the children was not the sharing of "me and my family." They did not want to talk about *their* daily lives in Calgary in response to David's stories. They wanted, rather, to talk about knives and arrows, about drinking blood and milk, about women who shaved their heads, and about children who tended cattle all day long, far from the gaze of watchful adults. What was familiar and well-known to David called out to the imagination in each of us. Enriched by David's knowledge, we began to experience new worlds together, creating within our classrooms the kinds of imaginative experiences that Egan (1986, 1992) describes: those imaginative experiences that

51

engage, intrigue, interest, puzzle, and enchant; those imaginative experiences that call forth sustained and key conversations about freedom, loyalty, responsibility, strength, and human relationships. When we speak of imaginative engagement, we mean the kind of engagement that invites children most fully, most generously, into the club of knowers; not at some unspecified time in the future when they are all grown up and able to use their knowledge, but today — and each and every day they spend with us.

Egan (1992) invites us to consider that "even the briefest look at children's thinking from this perspective opens profound conflicts with some of the ideas that dominate educational thinking and practice today" (p. 653). When we learn to look at children with new eyes, we can see clearly that, by the time they come to school at age five, they have already learned about some of the most complex, abstract, and powerful ideas they will ever encounter. Simply by virtue of their humanity, they have experienced joy and fear, love and hate, trust and betrayal, power and oppression, expectation and satisfaction — all, as Egan notes, before they have even learned how to ride a bicycle (1986, pp. 28–29).

Our study of a fairy tale familiar to many of us shows how this view of imaginative experience can challenge dominant educational thinking. Early last year, the children in our class listened to *Rumpelstiltskin*, an ordinary experience in a primary classroom. In choosing that story, we were depending on the children's knowledge in important ways. We did *not* assume that they had had direct experience with princes and princesses, much less with malevolent dwarves and alchemic transformations. Indeed, if learning is understood to proceed from concrete to abstract, from familiar to strange, from daily experience to the world of wonders, then *Rumpelstiltskin* should make little sense to children. But they loved the story, debating fiercely about issues such as whether parents, like the miller, have the right to put their children in danger; whether people have the right to ask for help without pledging something in return; whether adults should be allowed to give their children away, and the grief that may follow if they participate in such bad bargains. In order for children to understand this story, they needed to know about deception, the politics of rescue, false pride, boasting, and the indomitable human spirit.

As Egan (1992) notes, "to teach concrete content untied to powerful abstractions is to starve the imagination" (p. 653). David's story is important to us because of what it tells us about hearing each child's voice and bringing each child into the life of the classroom. However, it is also important to us because of what it says about children's interest in places and times long ago and far away. The great stories of history and literature are as fascinating to the children in our class as David's accounts of Africa. Stories about Leonardo da Vinci, Columbus, Ghengis Khan, Radames and Aida, Pythagoras, and King Arthur and his court prompted the same kind of lively debate and discussion of big questions about the human condition that we saw in their response to *Rumpelstiltskin*. Retellings of *Romeo and Juliet, Beowulf,* and parts of Chaucer were as enchanting as readings of *The Lady of Shalott, The Highwayman,* and *The Rime of the Ancient Mariner.* All of these stories have engaged the imagination of generations of adults because of the engagement they demand. We have discovered that these stories touch young children with as much power. They connect each of us with the past, ground us firmly in the present moment of listening to their rich language and images, and cause us to contemplate together what life holds in store.

Thus, for us, a second important planning issue centers on the "big questions" we offer to — and accept from — our children. Without those big questions, tied to great literature that engages the imagination, the spirit, the feelings, and the intellect, curriculum is likely to be thin and unsubstantial, fully satisfying to neither teacher nor child. Arising from questions about the human condition that engage each of us because we share the planet together, the curriculum we have created with our children permits them access to intellectual and aesthetic traditions that are thousands of years old. Children often ask some of the same questions the ancients asked, and discover anew, for themselves, the power of learning both to create and to solve important, engaging questions.

We have many, many typed pages of notes we took while the children were discussing stories and films about Columbus, Leonardo da Vinci, Ghengis Khan, the Arthurian saga, outer space, Greek myths, and Chinese legends. These subjects may not be considered the usual fare offered to six- and seven-year-olds. Indeed, we had no idea in September, when we were writing our plans, the various directions our studies would take. How could we have imagined, for example, that Jason would bring us back again and again to the idea that human knowledge is really a model of how we think things work? He asked us over and over how people know when their models are wrong. And over and over, we thought about that question as a way of understanding what adults have come to call "history," "mathematics," "science," "literature," "ethics" — and "education." How do any of us find out if our models are wrong?

How could we have anticipated the amazement of Diana, a child in grade one who could not yet read, when she learned that the ancient Greeks had known the earth was spherical, but that people had subsequently *lost* that knowledge for thousands of years. They had lost precious knowledge about space, Diana's passion. She was offended by the carelessness of her ancestors, and endlessly intrigued by how we had gotten that knowledge back again. Had there been one person, she wondered, who had just stood up and said, "Look, you guys, this is how it is"? Or had there been many people at the same time who figured it out together?

Could we ever have guessed that Edward would lean over to Sharon during a reading of *The Rime of the Ancient Mariner* and whisper, "It feels like the ghost of the ancient mariner is in this room right now. Do you think he's here? Do you?" Until Christmas, Edward had hardly spoken to us. He was so withdrawn from others that he often buried his face in the hood of his kangaroo shirt and rocked back and forth during lessons and class meetings. He seldom wrote, preferring to sit by himself and draw minutely detailed mazes of miniature battle scenes, seemingly obsessed with blood dripping from gaping wounds and vicious swords. On a blustery January day, Coleridge's words had reached across time and space to touch a little boy who wanted, for the very first time, to talk to his teachers about the world inside his head. The next day, he picked up the conversation again. "Do you know," he told us, "that an imagination is a terrible thing? The pictures in my mind really, really scare me." For Edward, the thing that had frightened him most — his ability to conjure detailed, vivid images — became the vehicle through which he was able, for the first time that we could see, to connect with others in the classroom.

Would we ever have expected that, after several weeks of reading, discussion, and project work about human discoveries, dreams, hard work, courage, tenacity, and integrity, the children would have pulled together the following questions about knowledge and work, questions to which they — and we — returned again and again in the months that followed:

– Where do you go looking for knowledge?
– How do you learn the secrets of the world?
– The more you learn, the more you get to know what you have to do. Why?
– Why do things come alive when you put yourself into your work?
– What do you need to give so you can get knowledge?

The children drove us deeper and further than we could possibly have gone on our own, demanding more stories, more history, more problems, more answers. The children stretched our knowledge and our capacity to hear, in their demands, the next best step to take. We haunted stores and libraries, searching for books to bring back to them and for books to help *us* learn more physics, mathematics, mythology, history, literature. When, for example, we read the children *I, Columbus* — excerpts from the log Columbus reputedly kept on his journey to learn what he called the secrets of the world — they asked many questions. Was Columbus the only person who believed that the earth was a sphere? What must it have been like to be Columbus, certain of your own knowledge but wrong in the eyes of many of your peers? Where did Columbus get his maps from, anyway? How did he navigate once he had passed the boundaries of the known world? Where was the Sargasso Sea, and was that where the Ancient Mariner had been becalmed? Why do people say Columbus discovered America when there were people living here already?

As teachers, we saw opportunities in these questions to bring in more and more material about maps and map-making, astronomy, geography, and history. One child brought in an article from the Manchester *Guardian* about Renaissance maps. We found stories such as Yolen's *Encounter*, which raised important issues about the effect of European contact on aboriginal peoples, and we introduced the children to the fact that the First Nations of Canada struggle to this very day with the consequences of voyages of so-called discovery that ended up on shores we now think of as our own.

During each story, lesson, and discussion, we would sit side by side at an easel at the front of the group. One of us would facilitate the children's conversation, and the other would scribe as quickly as possible, catching wherever we could the actual words of the children, and paraphrasing when the talk moved too quickly. Earlier in the year we had tried to tape-record these conversations, but the microphones let us down. First, the conversation was too complex for a machine to capture properly. Second, capturing key elements of the discussion required a teacher's judgment. Which were the comments and questions we wanted to formulate for the whole group? Which were the threads that seemed, even in the moment, to hold real promise of future exploration? Where were the moments that allowed us to make powerful connections between the mandated program of studies and the children's own questions?

At the end of days on which the children had been engaged in such discussions, we would sit at the easel re-reading and organizing what they had said and asked. We would highlight for ourselves what the next step ought to be. What had the children said that we could most profitably mine? Sometimes we knew exactly what resources we could use. We would go to our class library, the school collection, or to the public library for books and films we already knew about and bring them in for future classes. At other times, we would just go looking. If a question seemed sufficiently promising or intriguing, we would look for material we were certain must exist.

Curriculum planning that takes the voices of children seriously represents a kind of openness. As we tell stories about our classroom, we feel that teachers need to remain open to children's experience in the world and construct curricula that are deeply resonant with what each child knows, who each child is. We feel that teachers also need to understand that it is only the big, authentically engaging questions that create openings wide and deep enough to admit all adventurers who wish to enter. Three things are important in this regard. First, when children raise the kinds of questions that capture their attention in our studies of literature, history, and mathematics, it becomes possible for each of them to find compelling ways into the discussion and work that follows. Individuals cannot tell in advance when moments of connection will occur — for themselves or for others. Our experience has shown us time and again that questions about fairness, justice, knowledge, learning, courage, and oppression, sparked by stories of substance and worth, seem to free children to engage deeply with complex aspects of the world and of their own experience. There is little in traditional curricula that calls forth children's capacity for profound philosophical engagement made possible through the power of such stories.

Second, these kinds of questions are ones that intrigue adults as much as they enchant children. The conversations, the debates, and all of the work that flow out of these questions are deeply engaging for us, as teachers. The children experience our own genuine sense of excitement and commitment to the world of the mind and the spirit as they struggle with us to relive, in the present moment, dilemmas that were equally real to our ancestors. Moreover, when the children see their own questions returned to them as the basis for subsequent work and study, they come to know curriculum as a living, deeply connected experience. Curriculum is not delivered to them through activities made up by others; it is created with them, inspired by the work of the community of which each of them is a valued member.

Third, the worlds made available to children through stories and philosophizing of this sort form strong links with the complicated, everyday world in which they live. When the dean of the local law school, the mother of one of our students, came into the classroom during our study of *Rumpelstiltskin* and saw a child's comment written on chart paper, she hastened to copy it down: "When parents give their child away for gold, they will regret it later on, when they've had time to think about it." She was about to make a presentation about surrogacy contracts to the legal community, and she was delighted that young children, inspired by this classic tale, had articulated so clearly the dilemma that many legal scholars were now exploring. Thus, we *must* remain open to the power of real literature, real science, real mathematics, real art to touch all of us profoundly — not only the children.

REAL KNOWLEDGE AND SCHOOL KNOWLEDGE: EXAMPLES FROM MATHEMATICS

Our understanding of what *counts* as knowledge goes beyond the view that currently dominates school curricula — a view that carries with it the assumption that school knowledge, bound up in curriculum guides and school texts, is the same as "real" knowledge. Coming to know the world as mathematicians or scientists — like becoming a reader and writer — involves authentic engagement in mathematical and scientific experiences, not the busy work that often comes to count in school as math and science or reading and writing. Many school textbooks and workbooks are organized to encourage mindless recitation. Most math curricula are organized to support the notion that accuracy in computation equals excellence in understanding. Even our province's new math curriculum, which states that problem-solving is at the heart of mathematics, relegates problems to a separate unit. Many curriculum designers seem to think that problem-solving means doing word problems. It is also clear that many teachers think that they are teaching math when they are merely covering the textbook or the workbook. Unfortunately, the result often is a student who is schooled in "school math" — a form of math that bears little resemblance to the "real math" that mathematicians, physicists, and engineers experience, or to the math that sparks the imagination and ignites a passion for understanding the world mathematically and scientifically.

We want children to experience mathematics as a powerful language of the imagination that allows them to explore big mathematical ideas like balance, space, time, patterns, and relationships. We have come to see that they enjoy thinking about these matters, exploring, debating, solving problems, and learning together. Too many school children learn only "school math," a dull, lifeless, scary, and irrelevant round of pluses and minuses that usurps the real, much more engaging, thing.

How might it look in a classroom if teachers set about to make math real? The Alberta science and math curricula both state that children in the primary grades must know certain things about time: they must know how to read both analog and digital clocks, know the days of the week, the months of the year, and something about the seasons and the phases of the moon. When we sat down to talk about how to teach this part of the curriculum, we saw that among our options were activities that would encourage children to think that time resided in a clock or a calendar. Such activities would have satisfied the curriculum objectives, but we wanted more. We wanted children to learn that time is a mysterious and puzzling phenomenon.

We felt that if we restricted an understanding of time to the narrow view of "telling time" contained within most curriculum guides, we would transmit a useful skill, but not much more. Instead, we thought that if we paid attention to what physicists ask about time, we might give children access to what is undeniably one of the secrets of the world.

Here is what Bruce Gregory (1990), the Associate Director of the Harvard-Smithsonian Center for Astrophysics, tells us about the human understanding of time:

> Galileo's accomplishment was made possible by his decision to talk about the world in terms of motion through space and time. These concepts seem so obvious to us that it is difficult to remember that they *are* concepts. Time is normally measured in terms of motion, from the swing of the pendulum of a grandfather's clock to the oscillations of a quartz crystal in a modern watch. Apart from such periodic behavior, how could we even talk about the uniformity of time? In the words of the contemporary American physicist John Wheeler, "Time is defined so that motion looks simple." Wheeler also said, "Time? The concept did not descend from heaven, but from the mouth of man, an early thinker, his name long lost." Einstein demonstrated the power of talking about space and time as though they were a unity, and in the process he showed that both space and time are human inventions — ways of talking about the world. (p. 70)

In order to let children in on some of the secrets of this way of talking about the world, we need to let them in on two other big secrets. First of all, they *must* come to understand that human knowledge is humanly constructed. As a culture, a society, a community — and as a classroom — we make decisions about what will and will not count as knowledge, and those decisions make some understandings of the world possible, as much as they render other perspectives impossible.

If we really want our children to face the challenges of the twenty-first century with confidence and skill, we must teach them not only that they can acquire current knowledge, but also that they have voices that can shape what *their* society comes to accept as knowledge. This philosophy of teaching is exemplified in the following illustrations drawn from a series of lessons and activities about time.

We began one morning by asking the children to talk to us and each other about what they knew about time. Seated on the floor in front of the easel, they began to talk. As they offered examples of how time works, we recorded the following comments:

- It's something you have to use.
- You need to wear a watch to know what time it is.
- You need it — you can be late if you don't know the time.
- You can run out of time when you are playing or when people bother you.
- Sometimes grown-ups say, "You have two minutes to do something!" They really mean get it done quickly.
- You need to know time to know how fast you run in a race. You win when you have the least time.
- You can waste time.
- It is important to tell time.
- People get worried if they think they are running out of time.
- A day and a night equals twenty-four hours.
- Time can be fast and slow.
- Time lets you know when you should be doing things.
- Time goes fast when you're playing. It goes slowly when you're not having fun.
- Everyone in the world needs to know what time is the right time. You need to synchronize time with world events, like the Olympics on TV.
- Adults are expected to tell time. Children don't have to.
- If your house is flooded, it takes a long time to get it out.
- When we're doing projects, people always ask, "How much time until lunch?"
- You can tell time by counting by fives.
- People need to be home on time.

Clearly, this long list shows that the children had many experiences with time. For example, they knew about clocks and strategies about how to read clocks, they knew time was related to astronomical and geographical phenomena, and they knew time experientially. One of the children asked, "How can you tell time without a watch?" This question was to lead to intriguing explorations into the history of time and time-keeping devices and opened the possibility to explore time and its astronomical relationships. When one child recalled that a member of Columbus's crew was charged with the responsibility of turning the hour glass over when it emptied and keeping track of how often this occurred, another remarked that at one time people used sundials. This idea of the sundial caught the children's imagination, and they wanted to know exactly how a sundial told time. Fortunately, the sun cooperated with us and we went outside to begin some preliminary investigations.

In order to understand what happened next, it is important to know something about how our day is structured. We reserve a two-hour block of time between morning recess and lunch for the integrated study of literature, social studies, science, and mathematics. This time might be devoted on one day to conversations such as the one described above, and on another it might be used for a lesson and supporting activities. Sometimes we read stories and explore the children's responses; sometimes the children conduct investigations and experiments; sometimes we all listen to a guest speaker who can shed light on a question that has emerged on previous days. Often, the children paint or perform plays.

The flexibility of this long block of time permits us to follow up promising questions and comments like the ones about sundials. On this particular day, we had enough time left before lunch to go outside to explore the daytime astronomy of the sun's light and motion. Before leaving the classroom, we asked the children to observe where their shadows were and to try to make them fall in a different direction. Once outside, they turned and twisted themselves about in the sun, succeeding only in making their shadows change shape, not direction. A group of five children called us over to where they were standing. They proudly announced that they had found a way to tell time using the sun and their bodies. The children had positioned themselves in a circle and explained that one of them was at twelve, one at three, one at six, and one at nine, with the fifth child in the center. They had formed a clock and the direction of the shadow that was cast by the center person indicated the time.

Inside again, the children made further observations and asked more questions:

- If you stood in the same place for a whole day you would see your shadow change places because the earth changes position.
- Clouds can block the sun's rays so sundials won't work on rainy days.

- Can you tell time with one "hand"?
- Why is my shadow longer than I am in the evening but shorter than me at noon?
- People can't make time go faster because they're not the boss of the world. Even if you change the hands of the clock, you aren't changing time, itself.
- How do we know what the real time is?
- How did people start to tell time?

By now, two hours had passed. What had seemed like a simple beginning had flowered into exciting possibilities for future investigations. From the children's work and conversation, we saw themes on which we could now begin to improvise.

On another day, we asked the children to name all the ways they knew to record time. We learned that they knew about months, hours, and minutes; that sixty minutes equalled an hour; that 120 minutes made up two hours; and that thirty minutes was half an hour. Time, some said, could be measured in years, seconds, days, weeks, decades (which we told them meant ten years), and centuries (which they knew meant one hundred years). There were birth years, seasons, milliseconds, generations, and lifetimes (which we all decided together usually lasted from about seventy to about ninety years.)

The next question was easy for us to ask:

"Which of these measures of time is the longest?"

We even expected an easy answer: centuries. But we didn't account for children like Michael, whose hand shot up at once.

"I know, I know," he said, "it's seasons!"

"Why, Michael? Tell us what you are thinking about."

"Well, you see, seasons keep going on and on. You can have summer and fall and winter and spring. Then you keep having them all over again, and they make a pattern. See?"

And all of a sudden, we did see: not only that we had both locked into a narrow focus when we thought centuries was the best (even the only) answer, but also that Michael understood something important about the concept of relativity: that is, that "right" answers had everything to do with the framework you adopted. We looked at other measurements on the list. We asked if some of *those* could be candidates for "longest" as well. Joseph responded that generations were even better than seasons because generations went on and on with parents and children, and then their children and their children and *their* children. It all ended up in Heaven, he added, where time went on forever and ever. This idea of generations set another conversation in motion. To how many generations could each of us belong in a lifetime? Could they ever be in the same generation as their parents? As the children they would come to have? Would they *want* to be?

And so it went — from topic to topic, question to question, insight to insight. By the end of yet another discussion, we reached a conclusion to which everyone agreed: When you talk about days, seasons, or whatever in a general way, many units of measurement could be considered "longest" because they repeat themselves in a patterned way. As Michael's and Joseph's comments indicate, duration can also be understood as cycles — a fundamentally different framework from a linear one. Moreover, the children spoke of freezing time. They gave the example of designating a time — say, Friday, June 5, 1992, 11:48 a.m. — which is the precise time we had this part of the conversation. That moment will never repeat itself, they reminded us. The instant it passes, it becomes part of history. You can never, ever go back and do *that* time again the way you can repeat summers, year after year.

As the discussion continued, thoughtful and excited murmurs passed through the group like a wave.

"You mean, if we just waste that time we can't ever get it back?"

"Like, if we just were fooling around right now, we wouldn't get to come back to 11:48 because it was gone forever?"

"No, not gone forever, because tomorrow there will be another 11:48. But *this 11:48 can't come back."*

We pushed them by asking: "How precisely do you have to indicate a time before you know that that particular moment would never repeat itself?" Clearly, every day had 11:48's in it (and Maria reminded us that there was an 11:48 for the morning and one for the night time because there were always two 12:00's in every day). Fridays would repeat themselves, and so would Junes. But the Friday that occurred on the fifth day of June in 1992 — not 1993 or some other year — was the one that wouldn't come back. The 11:48 that belonged to only that Friday was the moment that was now part of our collective history.

This discussion was in June; we had worked hard since September to create an intellectual community. We were witnessing the work and dispositions that we had nurtured throughout the year bearing fruit. The next time the children gathered to talk about time, their observations bore the mark not only of their individual experiences of time outside the classroom, but also of the hours we had spent in exploration together. We decided to ask them what we thought was a harder question: "What is time?" This is what the children told us:

- Time is something that keeps on going.
- It helps you keep track of the events in a day and also of the day.
- It's not in a clock — it's everywhere.
- It's something we use.
- It's invisible — like air.
- It's part of our lives.
- We can't hear it, we can't see it, but we can use it and waste it.
- We live time, we make it.

- You can't speed it up or slow it down.
- Planets use time to travel around the sun.
- It's a different time in every country. When we have morning other countries have night.
- If everything stopped, we would float quickly off to the sun — like a very fast airplane ride.
- The clocks we use can be wrong — but time itself can't be wrong.
- The sun uses time — it takes Mercury less time than any other planet to go around the sun. Pluto takes much more time to orbit the sun.
- If we didn't have any time we would be dead. We wouldn't have any time to be born or to live.
- Time was in the past and it is still part of the world.

They were also left with questions:

- How do we know if our clock is wrong?
- When was math invented?
- Was there time before there was a universe? Did time exist before the Big Bang?
- Where would stars and planets "go" if time stopped?
- How did time get started?

As we went over the list, we noticed that much of what they discussed referred to the solar system. We recalled that, for a number of weeks, a group of children had worked together to create an elaborate, scaled model of the sun and the planets with all sixty of their respective moons. All of us had been involved in lively discussions about outer space, gravity, density, and light. The children brought forward into this current conversation on time some of the questions and issues they had visited before. We hadn't planned to integrate or summarize their experiences, but then Scott looked pensively at the ceiling and said, "Time is the whole universe. If there was not time everywhere, there would be no time. The only way time could stop is if the universe stopped." He formulated for all of us an understanding made possible by the history we shared together.

We were excited and honored to have been part of this conversation. These children were pursuing knowledge, making conjectures, reasoning with each other. They were asking the kinds of questions that Einstein, Feynman, Sagan, and Hawkings ask. They were coming to understand that mathematics is a way of speaking. It is a language that permits us to experience the world in particular ways. It is a tool that allows us to explore other, larger ideas. The ability to think mathematically is not simply the ability to produce number facts. It is not even the ability to solve word problems. If we want to nurture children who are passionate about science and mathematics, we have to start right (in both senses of the word) from the beginning:

> Because the discourse of the math class reflects messages about what it means to know math, what makes something true or reasonable, and what doing math entails, it is central to both what students learn about math as well as how they learn it. Therefore the discourse of the math class should be founded on math ways of knowing and ways of communicating. (*Professional Standards*, 1991, p. 54)

Did the children ever learn to tell time? Absolutely. It took only one hour for fifty of them and an additional thirty minutes for the other five to learn *that* kind of math language, too. Many of the grade one's and all of the grade two's could tell time to the quarter hour, and a substantial number mastered the grade-three objective: they could tell time to the minute. As for problem-solving, a group of children created, and then set about solving, their own problems. Nathan, for example, wanted to know how many seconds were in an hour. A group of five children who had already completed the required exercises on telling time and who were interested in solving Nathan's problem gathered around him. While the rest of the class worked in small groups with clocks and question sheets, Nathan and his friends figured out what they thought they would need to know in order to solve the problem and then set about doing the computation. This was no mean feat, considering that none of them knew how to multiply. But they *did* know that mathematics is about patterns and relationships, so they were able to draw upon what they knew about addition, set organization, and place value to solve this real and interesting problem.

There is more to our story of time. The children's questions about the beginnings of clocks led us to ancient Egypt and Stonehenge, to early calendars and struggles to align solar and lunar years, to the mythological sources naming months and weekdays.

Unfortunately, like the sands in an hour-glass, we ran out of time. But we were left with a wonderful and exciting starting place for the following September, when we teach these same children again.

CONCLUSION

These are not easy times for public education. Beset on all sides by calls to do better work on behalf of children, it is difficult not to feel defensive or defeated when others far from the daily life of a classroom call for school reform. For a long time, teachers have been charged with implementing theories developed by others. Those of us who have been teaching for a long time have seen many theories come and go, and we have worked hard to keep up with what was expected of us. Increasing numbers of us have, however, begun to sense that the educational conversation is changing in important ways. Often excluded in the past, the voices of teachers and children are being welcomed as ones that can inform both theory and practice in unique ways. For it is teachers who spend their daily lives in the presence of children; teachers who are better placed than anyone to see what can happen when they begin to think differently about their work with children; teachers who can make change happen.

In our daily work, our reflection, and our writing, the two of us have taken seriously the challenge of thinking about education from deep inside its most fundamental structures. We began our work together knowing *that* we wanted to challenge basic assumptions about primary practice. As our research proceeded, we began also to be able to talk about *how* we thought changes in teaching practice might come about. First, we came to see, in the relationships that we established with each child in our care, the importance of offering invitations to connect the life each child lived fully and completely outside the school with the life we were offering inside its doors. For us, David's story was perhaps the most dramatic and obvious of fifty-four other stories we could have told. As we sat together at the end of the school year thinking about the children and the journey on which each had embarked with us, we understood for ourselves that the successes — and the failures — of our attempts to connect with each child marked the successes — and the failures — of our work with each.

We do not think that observation will come as any great surprise to good teachers. Nor will it come as a surprise to anyone when we say that living out the implications of this understanding is an awesome responsibility. What *did* come as more of a surprise to us was to see, in our relationships with the children, the power of imagination to build connections that were not only personally gratifying, but also educationally profound. Imaginative engagement in questions and issues that were big enough to enchant each person in class, child and adult alike, created the space within which each child could move with strength and freedom. Each found his or her own ways into the conversations and the work throughout the year, and the conversation and work were glorious because each voice contributed uniquely.

Perhaps what is most unexpected about what we found as we began to explore the world with children in the ways we have described here is the extent to which they learned more than we had ever imagined possible. We heard some of them recite parts of Tennyson by heart on the playground, loving *The Lady of Shalott* as much as David had loved *Bringing the Rain to Kapiti Plain*. We did physics experiments with some, and investigated ancient number systems with others. Together, we and the children built models of the solar system, medieval castles, and the Great Wall of China. We thrilled in their retellings of ancient Chinese legends and plots of Italian operas. With each and every study, the children kept pushing: tell us more. Given access to real science, real mathematics, real literature, and art of substance and merit, they seemed insatiable.

We began this article with a quotation from *Alice in Wonderland*. Like many teachers, we are fond of Alice. Indeed, there are days when we find ourselves, like her, wandering around asking foolish questions about matters that seem quite settled to others. The Mock Turtle and the Gryphon listen patiently to Alice's bewildered inability to understand what schools are for, and we wonder what — if anything — they made of her question, "And how did you manage on the twelfth?" We wonder if they clucked their beaks, rolled their eyes, and wished she'd just go away.

Having begun to create for ourselves a completely different framework from the one presented by the Turtle and the Gryphon, however, we are no longer left to resolve the beastly paradox that so bedeviled Alice. Lessons need *not* lessen from day to day, month to month, year to year. Children and teachers *can* find new and powerful ways to come to know each other through real work that engages their minds, hearts, and spirits.

We can all, in fact, manage quite nicely on the twelfth.

REFERENCES

Aardema, V. (1981). *Bringing the rain to Kapiti Plain*. New York: Dial.

Beowulf. (1982). Oxford: Oxford University Press.

Coop, P., & Coop, C. (Eds.). (1990). *I, Columbus: My journal*. New York: Avon Books.

Carroll, L. (1966). *Alice's adventures in wonderland, and Through the looking glass*. New York: Macmillan. (Original works published 1865)

Coleridge, S. T. (1992). *The rime of the ancient mariner*. New York: Atheneum.

Egan, K. (1986). *Primary understandings*. London: Routledge.

Egan, K. (1992). The roles of schools: The place of education. *Teacher's College Record, 93*, 641–655.

Gregory, B. (1990). *Inventing reality: Physics as language*. New York: John Wiley.

Harris, D. J. (1991). *Rumpelstiltskin*. Toronto: Oxford University Press.

Lopez, B. (1990). *Crow and weasel*. Toronto: Random House.

Mollel, T. M. (1990). *The orphan boy*. Toronto: Oxford University Press.

Mollel, T. M. (1991). *Rhinos for lunch, elephants for supper*. Toronto: Oxford University Press.

Mollel, T. M. (1992). *A promise to the sun*. Boston: Little, Brown.

Noyes, A. (1981). *The highwayman*. Oxford: Oxford University Press.

Price, L. (1990). *Aida*. San Diego: Gulliver Books.

Professional standards for teaching mathematics. (1991). National Council of Teachers of Mathematics.

Tennyson, A. (1986). *The lady of Shalott*. Oxford: Oxford University Press.

Yolen, J. (1992). *Encounter*. New York: Harcourt Brace.

White, E. B. (1952). *Charlotte's web*. New York: Harper & Row.

Appearing Acts:
Creating Readers in a
High School English Class

JOAN KERNAN CONE

"They're never going to read Dickens. . . ."
One Saturday evening in mid-November, during a conversation about teaching, a friend of mine — a computer genius and Tom Clancy fan — said to me, "You're having your kids read the wrong books. They're never going to read Dickens when they get out of school. You need to introduce them to authors they *will* read."

At first I was irritated by his words. What did he know of the books I was teaching? What did he know of my commitment to expand the canon, to bring new writers into my classroom who represented the cultural and racial backgrounds of my students? Yet, as much as I wanted to dismiss his suggestion as another example of everyone-knows-how-to-teach-better-than-teachers, I could not. He had touched a nerve.

For all of the attention I pay to literature in my classes, I am not producing readers: that is, students who choose to read on their own for pleasure and for knowledge. That saddens me. A friend of mine tells her students a truth I've known since I was five: "If you don't read, you can only live one tiny life" (a paraphrase of an S. I. Hayakawa idea). I want my students to share my experience of living many lives through reading. I, a wife, a mother, and a veteran teacher, have become Antonia Shimerda, Franny Glass, and Jing-Mei Woo; have traveled to Mahfouz's Cairo, Gordimer's Johannesburg, and Vargas Llosa's Milaflores; and have discovered the identity of Mr. Rochester's first wife, the intricacies of Willie Stark's politics, and the political intrigues of Deep Throat.

Harvard Educational Review Vol. 64 No. 4 Winter 1994, 450–473

The habit of reading not only opens a world of vicarious adventure to students; it also encourages them to weigh ideas, take informed stands, and think deeply. Reading offers them insights into themselves and their worlds — private, national, global — insights that allow them to speak intelligently, vote wisely, rear kind children, counsel, lead. What happens to students who graduate from high school barely literate, reading only books assigned in class and having neither the skill nor the confidence to read a book on their own? Just as important, what happens to students who *can* read but do not; who go to college, perhaps to professional schools, and yet read only the daily newspaper, an occasional weekly news magazine, or the *New Yorker* in the dentist's office? My friend's words challenged me to examine the way I was teaching literature, challenged me to find a way to lead students to become readers.

CREATING READERS: WAS CHOICE THE ANSWER?

The next Monday I went to class, told my first- and second-period seniors what my friend had said about my teaching "the wrong books," and then gave them a reading assignment. If they wanted to earn an A for the semester, they had to read a novel of at least five hundred pages (or two of 250 pages) written since 1985, that had no Cliff notes and had not been made into a film. I gave them two opportunities to take a test on the books. The first, two days before winter vacation; the second, one week before the end of the semester. The students immediately posed questions: Was a "novel" a fiction or nonfiction book? Did they have to buy the book, or could they check it out of the library? What if they chose a book with 480 pages? Would I be assigning other homework at the same time?

After answering their questions, I posted the deadline for finishing the book in large letters on my front chalk board and moved on to *Othello*. A week before the independent reading book was due, I asked students to write a letter telling me how they were doing in each of their classes and how they thought they would do on their upcoming progress report, a written evaluation of their grade up to that point in the semester. In terms of English class, I asked them to discuss their independent reading book.

As I read over their papers, I grew uneasy. Some students, like Tassie, were excited about the assignment: "The outside reading is a wonderful idea. I love it! It gives me options. I can read eighty pages in two days or three pages in one day. It's up to me." Some, like Wilson, were moving along with the assignment: "I'm determined to finish my outside book since it tells a lot of things about China and I want to see how the student movement began." A few students had already finished their books. But the majority of the responses were not promising. Many students gave me what I felt were teacher-pleasing responses. Danielle wrote, "My independent reading book is *Misery* by Stephen King [no apology for reading a book made into a film]. Everything about this book is a mystery. I find myself really committed to this book." Others were even less specific — they had praise for the book, or they were doing fine with the reading, but they did not include the name of the book nor discuss its plot or characters. As Jeff commented, "My outside book is easier than I thought it would be because I barely have time to take a leak. I found something I could relate to and in turn it caught my attention."

My uneasiness about students' progress with their independent reading was confirmed the day I gave the first test. When asked to retell the ending of the book from the main character's point of view and to discuss why the ending was satisfying or unsatisfying, only nine students of thirty-four in first period and eleven of thirty-five in second period could do so in a way that demonstrated that they had read their book thoroughly and thoughtfully. A few tried to fake their answers. Craig wrote of *Remains of the Day,* "Well, in the end, Mr. Stevens drove off and was excited to show his employer all that he had learned on this interesting journey of his." What had happened to Jeff and Danielle, who had written only a few days before of being "really into" their books? "The book got boring and I didn't have time to start a new one." "I'll read a 500-page book next time." Others made no excuses or promises.

What had gone wrong? I had given students a choice of books, homework time to read, and, in the last few days before the test, class time for reading. Yet the majority of the students had not finished a book.

Despite the disappointing results, I was not willing to give up on the independent reading idea. Over the December vacation, I thought about what I could do. Clearly, I needed to check that students were reading books that fit the previously established criteria (such as no Cliff notes, no books made into movies). My leniency with the first book had led to students "fudging": they had reported about novels that had been turned into films ("But I didn't see the movie"), books that were used in other classes, and autobiographies of current star athletes that bore a close resemblance to articles I had read in recent sports pages. In addition, I realized that waiting until close to the assignment deadline to give students in-class reading time was not a good idea. I needed to allocate time early in the term so that students had read enough of their books to complete the assignment.

When school reconvened in January, I was determined to make the next independent reading assignment a success. After handing back the December tests, I talked about the results and asked students to write about, and then discuss as a class, why they had read or not read the first book. I hoped that by forcing them to reflect first in writing and then aloud, I would help them take responsibility for reading and thereby inspire more of them to finish the next book. Several students said they had trouble finding a book. "I went to [a chain book store]," Kema announced, "and asked the lady to recommend a book written by an African American after 1985 and she said there weren't any." Students who were taking an elective class in African American literature were horrified — at the saleswoman's ignorance as well as at Kema's believing her. "What are you talking about?" they asked her.

"What about Toni Morrison and Alice Walker? You need to go to another bookstore." Those comments created an opportunity for me to mention the names of bookstores easily accessible in nearby Berkeley — bookstores with readers as salesclerks and tables laden with books by African Americans, Asian Americans, Latinos, Native Americans, women, gays, new writers. Students who knew of other sources for books offered suggestions to those who didn't want to buy books. Next we talked about the criteria for choosing the books. The page limit this time was determined by what they had done on the previous independent reading assignment. If they had read a five hundred page book, they had no further independent reading requirement; if they had read a 250-page book, they had to read another book of at least 250 pages; and if they had not read a book, they needed to choose a book of five hundred pages. The students stated that the 1985 publication date was too limiting and asked that it be changed to at least 1980 — I agreed. I restated my insistence on novels, not biographies or books from which movies had been made. The students asked if I had any suggestions, which I did. I had lots of books to lend and encouraged them to come in to talk with me so I could help them find books that were right for them.

I set aside the first three days of the following week for in-class silent reading. On Monday, several students came without books: they had forgotten their book at home, they hadn't had time to buy one or go to the library, or they couldn't find anything interesting. I handed out anthologies of short stories to these students and we all settled down for silent reading. The next day, every student had a book. During this time, I did not allow students to do other homework — despite their promises to read at home if they could just do their biology in class or protests about not being able to read without listening to music. If a student dropped her head in her arms for a nap, I sent her out to get a drink of water; the second time it happened I threatened to mark her absent.

At the end of the third day of reading, I asked students to write about their books: What is the title? What has happened so far in it? Do you like or dislike it? Why? What is it going to take for you to finish it by the due date?

In late January I tested students on their second independent reading book. Students who had read a five hundred page book the first time and students who had not finished the second book used the test period as a study hall. Again, because I had not read all of the books my students had chosen, I wrote a generic prompt:

PART 1: Due at the end of the period.
— Give the title and author of your book. Summarize what happened in it in such a way that I will understand the plot.
— Choose the most unforgettable scene, describe it fully, and tell why that scene affected you as it did.

PART 2: Due at the beginning of class tomorrow.
— Tell me in detail why you chose the book.
— Thoroughly describe your process of reading this book: When did you read, for how long? When did you finish? How did you feel as you were reading it?

The results were better this time. In first period, seventeen out of thirty-four students had read books; in second period, twenty out of thirty-five had. For the second test, some students chose new books and some finished books they had started for the previous assignment. More significant than the results on the Part 1 recall and analysis sections were the comments on Part 2 about choices and processes:

Craig: I grabbed this book because I knew I could finish it fast. What can I say? I was in the mood for some cheese-ball action.

Jeannine: I chose *The Temple of My Familiar* because I like Alice Walker.

Kandi: My aunt told me about this book — she read it two times.

Whatever the reason for choosing a book, once students were into it, most of them finished. Students, like Tachia, who had not read the first book, finished the second one:

I loved *The Street* because it related to the streets around where I live. It's interesting to learn about the struggle of some Black poor people trying to go somewhere in life. . . . I read the book daily when possible, usually after I had done my other homework. I finished early.

As I read these comments and listened to the discussion in my classroom, I was filled with excitement. Changes were taking place in students' knowledge about and enthusiasm for reading. Students were recommending books to each other and were asking each other for recommendations:

Tassie: If you don't read any other book this year, read *Disappearing Acts*!

Kema: Jalaine, do you know a good book for me — not one you'd like, one I'd like.

They were also asking me for books to read. "Now don't get me wrong," Kandi said one day after class, "but are there *any* Black books that aren't about slavery?" I discovered they were even asking other teachers for books: "I hope it's okay with you that I told Rebecca to read an Anne Rice," a science teacher told me one morning. "I'm a total science fiction freak and Anne Rice is my favorite."
Along with my excitement came questions: What had brought about the change in Kema? In December she had written, "I have not read my inde-

pendent book like I'm supposed to. I think to have an independent book was a burden on me and it makes me feel guilty." In January she was writing, "*Mama* is so good. I got it yesterday and I can't believe I'm on page 53. This book has 260 pages so I'll be able to finish it by Wednesday because of the long weekend." Why was Nikki, a University of California-bound student, not reading? In December she had selected *Beloved* because "schools should teach more works by African American writers" and in January she chose *Mama* "because I've heard a lot about it being a quality novel and it is written by an African American woman," and yet she had finished neither book. Why was it that some students had read several independent books and some, like Nikki, had trouble finishing any?

LOOKING FOR ANSWERS

Assuming that what happens to children early in their school careers affects them as learners, I found some insights into my students' reading habits in university research on young children. Work by Rosenholtz and Simpson (1984) suggests that a determining factor in my students' success or failure on the independent reading assignments was their self-perception. In their seminal study on the formation of ability constructions, Rosenholtz and Simpson found that children's conceptions of their intellectual ability were "socially constructed during their early school experiences" (p. 55) and that schools "typically 'reproduce' institutionalized ability conceptions because their 'deep structure' produces patterns of performance and performance evaluation that make it logical for children to interpret their academic abilities unidimensionally" (p. 55). Research on self-fulfilling prophecy by Weinstein (1986) stressed the cumulative effect of differential teacher treatment of students. "What begins as small differences in student skills, grows due to coverage differences and to accompanying changes in children's behavior, self-esteem, and motivation" (p. 30). In their work with upper grade elementary school students labeled "poor readers," Brown, Palinscar, and Purcell (1986) found that students who have formulated a negative diagnosis of their ability to succeed in school display "a typical pattern of learned helplessness" and "often develop compensatory coping strategies for preserving their self-worth" — strategies that include "devaluation of academic tasks, goals, and desired outcomes, and the justification of a lack of effort" (pp. 123–124).

My own work as a classroom teacher supports the connection between students' self-perceptions about ability and their school performance. For years I have watched students assigned to remedial classes wither, while students in "gifted" classes blossom. I have observed students in low-track classes act out, drop out, misbehave, and "give up and withhold effort . . . because failure given high effort inevitably will imply low ability and generate subsequent feelings of shame" (Rosenholtz & Simpson, 1984, p. 54). Students become non-learners as a result of teachers' and their own low expectations. Was my students' success or failure with independent reading a result of their perceptions of themselves as readers? I needed to find out, and so I asked them to write an extended definition of a *reader*, and how they defined themselves in terms of that definition.

— HOW "READERS" SAW THEMSELVES:

Students who identified themselves as readers saw reading as an opportunity to learn, to escape, to experience an adventure. Andrew wrote, "A reader is someone who can pick up a book and be transported to a new place, a place where the writer is in control but the reader is free to fill in the blanks, to view the scene as he wishes to." Students who identified as readers wrote about reading constantly and widely. "A reader," reflected Sarah, in e.e. cummings's style to capture the need for eclecticism, "is someone who reads — books novels plays newspapers magazines poetry prose, fiction and non-." "Readers," students said, read everywhere — waiting in lines, on the BART (Bay Area Rapid Transit) train, in classes when they finished assigned work, late at night. Students wrote of finishing a book and starting another immediately, of reading two books at the same time, of getting lost in reading. These "readers" finished books — even books they did not like. They knew where to get books: they wrote of libraries and bookstores and people they could rely on for suggestions. They had lists of books they wanted to read. They read some books more than once. They knew when they had become readers. "When I was in fourth grade," Keesha said, "I started reading Judy Blume books. That's how I became a reader. I read one of her books and decided it was good and she had to have more books that were just as good. One book from an author is all it takes."

— HOW "NON-READERS" SAW THEMSELVES:

Not surprisingly, students who identified themselves as non-readers also saw that being a reader was a matter of action. "They read when they have to and when they don't," commented Freddie. Karen noted that "Readers don't read by chapters — they just read." According to these students, readers read fast, readers read long books, readers understand what they read, readers don't quit books. Many students who labeled themselves as non-readers wrote of a change in their lives as readers:

August: When I was in the fourth grade, I was in a class for the gifted or whatever. Our teacher read us a book called *Never Cry Wolf* which she thought was so good. This was my first taste of literature and I hated it. I didn't want to hear about some man in the freezing cold, studying some wolves. That turned me off from books.

Lan: In my freshman year, I loved all the books [my English teacher] introduced us to, especially *Jane Eyre*. But now, it seems that every time we read a book, we have to analyze it. No matter how easy or hard the book is, we have to analyze what the author is saying.

What did these students do when assigned books for school? "If the book starts out boring, then I'll just pass and hopefully they'll have a movie out on it so I can watch it," wrote Freddie. "I always put off reading it until the last minute," Sean said. "It's funny how I work it out. If I start today, I have to read 80 pages a day and if I start next week, I'll have to read 150 pages a day. I procrastinate until my pages per day ratio is at my personal maximum. Time pressure gets me motivated."

Self-designated non-readers were adamant about being *able* to read. They saw a real difference between reading habits and reading ability. As Laura commented, "Just because you don't read book after book, doesn't mean you can't read." In fact, these students' sixth- and eighth-grade scores on the California Achievement Test supported that distinction in most cases. That is, their scores indicated that in junior high, they were reading close to, at, or above grade level. The scores of ten self-designated non-readers, however, did reflect reading problems. One, a special education student, scored in the eighteenth percentile, two scored in the high twenties, one in the thirty-first, and the rest in the fortieth percentiles in total reading. These students defined the act of reading quite differently from their "reader" and other "non-reader" classmates. For them, reading was not a comprehension activity, but a decoding skill or a performance opportunity. Nate wrote, "My life as a reader has been hell!! Don't get me wrong I can read, but it's just I hate doing it. I seem to have a little studdering [sic] problem and there's nothing more embarrassing when you're reading is to studder [sic]."

From my reading of students' reflections on themselves as readers and on the work they did in class, I drew the following general conclusions:

1. High grades did not necessarily correspond with the students' self-designation as a reader. Among those who saw themselves as readers were students who had earned straight A's or close to straight A's and students whose grade point averages were as low as 2.0 and 1.97. Low grades and self-designation as a non-reader, however, did correlate.

2. High SAT scores did not necessarily correspond with a student's self-designation as reader. Some students with combined SAT scores as low as 470 saw themselves as readers and others with scores as high as 1400 labeled themselves non-readers.

3. Among high-achieving students, both readers and non-readers, no relationship existed between self-perception and performance on the independent reading assignments. Whatever label they gave themselves, high-achievers completed the independent reading. Among low-achieving students, however, a relationship did exist. That is, low-achievers who labeled themselves as non-readers did not do the reading. The only exception to this self-perception/ performance association was a group of five low-achievers who said they were readers but did not finish one independent book. These students, all young women, typically wrote

statements about the place of reading in their lives using language that suggested that sounding like a reader and knowing the names of writers and works were as important as actually doing the reading. Alice, for example, declared, "I go through stages where I live, breathe, eat, and sleep with a book in my hand." Jalaine, a high-achiever, was the only example of a deflation rather than an inflation of self-perception: she identified herself as a non-reader, when a good deal of evidence pointed to the contrary. Jalaine wrote that although she reads, she does not see herself as a reader because "I can't really get into books until I read a really good one. Once I do, I hunt for as many books by that author as I can. If I can't find any, I listen to what other people (mostly college students) are saying about books they're reading and then I go read those. . . . If I like a book, I read until I'm done with the entire book." The fact that she had so many books that she liked highlighted a seeming contradiction in her refusal to identify herself as a reader. Among her favorites: *I Know Why the Caged Bird Sings, The Color Purple, The Joy Luck Club, Wuthering Heights, Crime and Punishment.* When interviewed about her seeming self-mislabeling, Jalaine grew adamant. "No, I am not a reader. I read but I am not a reader. You want me to change what I wrote and I don't want to. I AM NOT A READER!" Her insistence on differentiating between reading a lot and being a reader intrigued me. What was she telling me that I couldn't hear?

4. School labels related to reading ability — "remedial," "average," and "fast" — did not necessarily affect the labels students used for themselves. While some students attributed their being non-readers to school, the majority of the self- designated non-readers did not blame school. Clifton stated, "There are two things that make me the reader I am: procrastination and laziness. . . . Reading is a bit like having a foreign accent. If you don't use it, you lose it."

In fact, several students saw themselves as readers despite a school label to the contrary. Frank identified himself as a reader, even though "in elementary and junior high I always, I mean *always,* scored below average in reading" and was "*always* assigned to below average reading groups and English classes." Rahima adamantly declared herself a reader despite being labeled a remedial student in seventh grade. "When I was in fourth grade, I read a lot and they wanted to skip me up to fifth grade but my mom didn't want me to do that. In seventh grade they put me in a dumb class, a reading class, with kids who couldn't read. I kept telling them I was in the wrong class, but they didn't believe me. So I just sat and read by myself. Then one day I got into a fight and when the principal called me in to suspend me, she checked my records. She asked me why was I in that reading class and I *told* her I had told them it was a mistake. The next day they moved me to the right class."

— ANOTHER CATEGORY — A "SOMEWHAT" READER:

While most students designated themselves as readers or non-readers, several students were not comfortable with either label. "I think I am almost a reader," wrote Rebecca. "It wasn't until this year that I realized I liked reading and that reading doesn't have to be a task — it can be fun." Antoinette noted, "I believe I am becoming a reader. I am a beginning reader. I am beginning to read books on my own with pleasure." "I am somewhat of a reader," said Rob.

As I studied what these students had to say about readers and reading, I saw that they were indeed in between the two categories of reader and non-reader. This group of students had a hard time finding books, they procrastinated about starting books, and they often chose to watch TV rather than read, but once they got into a book, they read it. They also read newspapers and periodicals regularly and saw reading as valuable. "I know that if I was encouraged to read," Patty said, "I would read more."

CREATING READERS:
WAS THE ANSWER A NEW CURRICULUM?

As helpful as the research and student reflections were, they did not answer my question about how to transform students into readers. I needed to look further. I decided to focus on my second-period English class, a broad mix of students who had not elected to take Advanced Placement (AP) English Literature or AP English Language and Composition, or who had not completed the required summer work for those classes. Of the thirty-five enrolled in my second-period class, eight were labeled "certified gifted" and three were labeled "special ed." Students' academic interests and achievement levels varied widely: there were students who were taking calculus and those who had never taken algebra; students who were in French V and students assigned to social studies classes for English as a Second Language learners; students who were headed to UC Berkeley and students taking night classes to make up for lost credits so they could graduate with their class in June. Grade point averages ranged from 3.84 to 1.06. Two of the students cut class almost daily, and two others were absent at least once or twice a week. The twenty-three females and twelve males in the class represented almost all of the major racial and ethnic groups at our school, and students were from both the most affluent and poorest parts of our school district.

I chose this class for a variety of reasons. First, it included six "somewhat" readers, a group that intrigued me. What was it that held them back, made them tentative? What would it take for them to become real readers, students who would choose to read on their own for pleasure and knowledge? Second, of my four classes of seniors, second period had the widest range of students in terms of academic achievement. What I learned from studying them might help me in other classes and in my advocacy to end tracking schoolwide. And finally, unlike my AP English Language and Composition class, where the curriculum almost demanded I spend the third quarter preparing students for the national AP examination, the curriculum in English 4 was open. We had completed our school district's required readings and had practiced writing the required discourse modes. I was free to experiment, free to try out my belief about the role written reflection might play as a tool to affect students' perceptions of themselves as learners.

I decided to make independent reading the focus of the second semester and then to arrange all other reading and writing activities around it. Since many "readers" had expressed pleasure in reading books by and about people who shared their race or ethnicity, I thought that "somewhat" readers and "non-readers" might enjoy these writers too. The first day of the third quarter, I gave out a new independent reading assignment: read a book written by or about someone in an ethnic or racial group with which you identify. I gave students three days to find a book and then allowed them two days for in-class silent reading.

My new curriculum plan called for alternating whole-class activities with independent reading activities. When students were working on an independent book, homework assignments were mostly limited to that book; I did not ask them to read two novels at the same time or ask them to write at home the essay forms we studied in class. In addition to studying plays and short stories, we spent a good deal of time working on argumentation through discussing current political events — the Rodney King verdict, the national election, the family values issue — and reading and writing argumentative essays on a wide range of topics. We also watched and discussed films, practiced a variety of writing activities — scholarship essays, letters to next year's seniors, and personal credos — and prepared a piece for the end of the year literary magazine. Along with these activities, I regularly asked students to tell me in writing about their independent reading book. This practice kept me informed of their progress and encouraged them to continue reading at a steady pace. When I felt that students were falling behind, I talked with them about the importance of keeping up with the assignment, helped them get connected to the book, or found them a different book. Occasionally I called parents to enlist their support.

For the second independent reading assignment of the quarter, I asked students to choose a book written by or about someone from a racial or ethnic group of which they were not a member. Again, I allowed a few days of in-class silent reading for them to get into the book, and I gave homework assignments related to the independent reading.

At the end of the third quarter, I had mixed feelings about the results of the independent reading assignments. I was heartened by all the book talk I was hearing in the room and delighted with the quality of the books students were reading: *Mama, Animal Dreams, Tracks, Praisesong for the Widow, The Joy Luck Club, Family, Migrant Souls, Tar Baby, Winter in the Blood, Spring Moon, Vampire Lestat, Macho, Gather Together in My Name, Jasmine, Lucy, Cere-*

mony, Yellow Raft in Blue Water, How the Garcia Girls Lost Their Accents, Slave Girl, You Can't Keep a Good Woman Down, Cider House Rules, Iron and Silk, Manchild in the Promised Land, Black Elk Speaks. Students' eclectic tastes moved me to ease my rule about novels written in the last ten years. I made exceptions easily, allowing students to read older books, books of short stories, biographies, and non-fiction works. Reading was what mattered, not genre or publication date. Dimming my excitement, however, was the worry that for all of my encouragement and allowances, not all students were reading. Nineteen students finished the first book, eighteen the second. I was particularly concerned about the six students who had read neither book. What would motivate them?

CREATING READERS:
THE EMERGENCE OF TALK AS AN ANSWER

The first day of the fourth quarter was unusual. About one-third of the students in second period were absent, out of class to set up for a school carnival. Rather than begin a new lesson, I told students they could use the period as a study hall. But as I looked around at who was present, it occurred to me that there were several students who had done all of the independent reading assignments. Why not use the period to interview them? I escorted them into a small workroom adjacent to my classroom and said I wanted them to talk about themselves as readers — their history as readers, their process of reading, and whatever else that came up about reading. Because I did not want to lead or impede their discussion, once I got them started talking, I left them alone — with the tape recorder on. When I returned forty minutes later, they were involved in a lively sharing of most loved and most hated books. In the last few minutes of their discussion, I asked them for ideas about where we needed to go during the rest of the year with independent reading. They wanted to read books that they hadn't read in high school, "missed classics" that they thought would be expected of them as college freshmen. *And* they wanted to discuss the books. I laughed when I heard this — why hadn't I thought of adding "talk" to the independent reading project? Talk had been the main focus of the books we had studied as a class, and I had forgotten its importance when I moved to independent reading.

That night, as I listened to the tape, I was moved by my students' passion and the breadth of their reading:

Jalaine: When I was in tenth grade, I read this book called *Wuthering Heights.* And at first I would've never . . . just, just, picked that book up. But it was — I don't know — it was weird. Because the teacher was like "Well, read it and you'll understand it." And I did. And I thought that was kind of neat because, you know, I wouldn't never just read it myself . . . because it was . . . like a fifteenth century book.

Phillipa: I always wanted to read that book.

Jalaine: It was, it was hecka good, it was . . .

Phillipa: It's a love story, isn't it?

Jalaine: Yeah, yeah, and when you pick it up and stuff you wouldn't think it was good. And there's scandal in there and . . .

Phillipa: It's not filled with that Shakespeare stuff?

Jalaine: No, it's not really a lot of Shakespearean language. It's just — at times it will be . . . but it's hecka good.

Phillipa: I'm about to read it then. What's it called?

Jalaine: Wuthering Heights. I forgot who wrote it, though, but she has a sister.

David: Bronte.

Jalaine: Bronte! Bronte! And she has a sister who writes books, too, and . . . uh . . . I think my tenth-grade English teacher . . . Mr. Martin . . .

Antoinette: I remember him.

Jalaine: The one who used to ride a bike all the time . . .

Phillipa: Yeah, with a backpack.

Jalaine: Yeah, introduced us to them. The Bronte sisters — and that was when I started really reading a whole lot of stuff. Now I even read science fiction books.

They talked about becoming readers:

Antoinette: It was last year when I got into Black literature and started reading books that I enjoyed. Because at first I didn't think I was a reader because the books we read, I couldn't . . . relate to things and it was . . . I don't know . . . but after I started reading books that I liked . . . I could . . . I went back to read those same books and I could read them with an open mind. I didn't think I was [a reader] because I didn't think I was getting the point that everyone else was and because I felt I was reading books just for the class — which I was — but now I read things on my own, instead of just for the class.

Rob: I haven't been a reader all that long. A couple of years ago — even last year — I wasn't. I wasn't really. I couldn't be called a reader. I didn't read the books really. I just scammed through.

Antoinette: Aren't you afraid to take the test though?

Jennifer: What happened when the teacher picked the wrong place — the part you scammed through?

Rob: Well, you know, see, you've just got to play it off. See, well, I'd just read a little bit of it. I'd always be . . . the night before the test, I'd always be somewhere around page 50 of the book so I'd know some of the characters, you know. You know, I could wing it through because a lot of the time the books were old books that I already knew something about. I just didn't read 'em. I was on the wrong side of the tracks. But, but . . .

Jalaine: What changed you over then?

Rob: I really, I really can't say. I came into this class and I think I just had a different mentality, a mentality of . . .

Antoinette: Because we're *seniors.* [Laughter]

Rob: Something — I wanted, you know, I wanted to work hard and uh, uh, I guess, uh, I just wanted to . . . I knew I could do it. I just didn't 'cause I was being lazy. So I said, "this is, like, the time to just go all out" and I s'pose . . . I mean, I've read all the books in the class and took all the tests and, uh, so I'm just now becoming a reader, really. I 'spose. But see, it's still different, because I might watch — if given the choice, you know, I might still watch the news instead of reading the newspaper or something.

They talked of books — their favorites, *Catcher in the Rye, Beloved, Cider House Rules, The Bluest Eye;* books they wanted to read or reread, *1984, Animal Farm, Crime and Punishment, Hamlet* ("Is that the 'to be or not to be' one?"); books they had not understood, *Woman Warrior, Crime and Punishment, The Joy Luck Club.*

Jennifer: Another hard book is *Beloved.*

Jalaine: That's weird. Because I picked that up and read it straight through. I don't know. It was good — to me. I had read other Toni Morrison books and I kind of understood her style. I had read *The Bluest Eye* and then I read something else, I can't remember . . .

Phillipa: Sula?

Jalaine: Yeah, *Sula.* And then I said, "Well, I'm going to read *Beloved* now." It was different, but it was the same. She, like, used her style — the normal style that she did in the other two books — but she added stuff, like with the baby character, the ghost spirit — whatever you want to call it. That was different. You could understand why. I liked the book myself. And then I was listening to an interview she did on TV with that guy on Channel 9 [Bill Moyers on PBS] and she was kind of explaining it and I was, like, "Yeah, that's true, that's true." You know, it was, to me, it was, *Beloved* was easy to read. And I read it in like in a weekend. I read it while I was eatin' dinner and in the tub. All weekend.

They asked each other questions: Can you read anywhere? Can you read a book in one night? What do you do when a book starts out boring? They talked about the "gaps" they saw in their reading education:

Phillipa: When I was in ninth grade we had this crazy teacher and we didn't get to read much. The lady was crazy! Miss _____. Remember her? Remember her? She was crazy. The only book I remember reading was *Animal Farm.* And I feel like I've missed out on a lot of ninth-grade reading — that everyone else, that ninth-grade classes read, that I still didn't get to read. I still haven't read *Mice and Men.* There was another book I wanted to read and I haven't read it.

[Here I returned to the room and, because I couldn't resist, entered the discussion.]

Cone: So, sometimes teachers don't hit on books you think you should read because . . . they're a part of the "conversation?" Like everyone has read *Of Mice and Men* so you should read it? But sometimes students don't want to read those books — the books that you're "supposed" to read.

Jennifer: But even though you don't want to read them, you need to be exposed to them, or you feel left out. . . . I mean, like she [Phillipa] says — she might not like *Mice and Men* but now she's regretting not having read it because she can't be part of the conversation. And she feels neglected. Even if you don't like a book at least it helps to be exposed to it and make the choice from there, you know, instead of not knowing whether you would have liked it or not.

As I listened, I also discovered the reason Jalaine had labeled herself a non-reader. "I signed up for AP," Jalaine began. "I read the first book. I read it to the best of my ability. So my [required summer] paper on this book was like fifteen pages. I sent it to Ms. Cone's house and about a week later I got this postcard saying, 'You did not read this book thoroughly. Pleeeeassee rewrite the summary.' I said, 'Oh, no. I spent fifteen dollars for this book and she's telling me to read it and write again — oh, no, I'm not.' I said, 'I'm not reading it over again. And, um, I just got really discouraged when she said I didn't read it. I read it and she said I didn't read it." Reflecting on Jalaine's comments, it's little wonder that when I asked her to label herself, she wrote "non-reader": my rejection of her paper was a rejection of her as a reader.

The next day in class I suggested the "missed classic" idea for their next book. I said it was fine with me if they didn't all want to read the same book, but that whichever book they chose, they needed to read it well enough to discuss it in a group. The assignment that night was to think of a book they had always wanted to read, bring their suggestion to class the next day, and convince a group of classmates to read it with them and discuss it. The titles they came back with were revealing. No one proposed *Jane Eyre, Animal Farm,* or *Brave New World* — not even the students who had suggested on the tape that they wanted to "fill in the gaps" in their reading history. They did not suggest books on the basis of what might impress a college. They wanted to read more current literature: *Disappearing Acts, Slaughterhouse 5, Her, The Color Purple, Speaker for the Dead, The Autobiography of Malcolm X.* Students made their choice and agreed to get a copy of the book they had selected. Four days later they met with their group leader (the student who had suggested the book) to decide how they wanted to begin the reading. The next two days in class, students met in their groups — in the classroom or in an adjacent empty classroom — either to read aloud or silently.

I joined the science fiction group, mainly to show the leader of that group that I wasn't as narrow-minded about science fiction as he had accused me of being. As I read the book, I found myself procrastinating, falling asleep, resisting rereading parts I was confused about, hating what I judged as silly pseudo-scientific language, disliking the characters, not caring about the action. I was irritated with myself for choosing the book and wished that I could find an audio tape of the book to listen to on my drive to school so that I didn't have to waste reading time on it. When I realized what was happening to me, I laughed out loud: my resistance to a book I did not want to read had turned me into a Freddie, a Karen, an August. I had taken on the characteristics of a non-reader.

The date for the book discussion arrived, and I was filled with apprehension, not for the students, but for me. Not because I hadn't finished my book — the achiever in me had pushed me through it — but because two visitors were coming. Carol Tateishi, Director of the Bay Area Writing Project, University of California at Berkeley, and Richard Sterling, Director of the Institute for Literacy Studies, Lehman College, City University of New York, wanted to observe the class as part of their study of the work of teacher researchers. The source of my apprehension was the largest independent reading group, the students reading *Disappearing Acts*. The day before, the leader of the group, Keesha, had told me that she and two other strong discussants in the group were going to miss the next day because of a field trip.

"What about the discussion?" I asked them. "Who's going to lead it?"

"Clifton says he'll do it," they told me.

My heart sank. Clifton has not finished one book all year.

"Clifton," I moaned. "Isn't there anybody else?"

"Don't worry," they reassured me, "he's reading the book."

When class began the next day, we moved into our discussion groups. Tateishi joined the *Malcolm X* group, Sterling went to Clifton's group, I went to my group. Occasionally, I looked around: all was going well. Every group was involved in animated talk. Clifton's group seemed the most excited. I relaxed.

At lunch I met with the visitors who were full of praise for the students' choice of books and the quality of their talk. When I shared my fears about Clifton's leading the group, Sterling assured me that Clifton had met the challenge. He knew the book, he was engaged with the characters, and he insisted that everyone participate in the discussion. When one girl tried to get out of answering by saying she felt the same as the last student who had spoken, Clifton said, "You know you can't get away with that in here — what do *you* think?"

For their last book, I asked students to read *Walkabout*, by James V. Marshall. The book, a story of racial and cultural misunderstanding and tragedy, seemed a fitting final project after our reading of books from the many cultural, ethnic, and racial groups in our class. This time I allowed no in-class reading and gave students a deadline of one week to finish the book. I wanted to give them practice in reading a book on their own in a short amount of time and I wanted to see what they would do with a book of my choosing. Twenty-nine out of thirty-five read the book.

Instead of a final examination, I asked second-period students to do a series of writings based on the reading they had done over the course of the year. I was particularly interested in their views about the place of independent reading in a high school curriculum and what suggestions they had for me that would improve my teaching. Students who had not done the independent reading — any or all of it — did not want the independent assignments. The great majority of students, however, found real value in it. Amaka wrote, "Independent reading should be a requirement for each grade level in high school." "If I were a teacher, I would make it mandatory to read at least three independent books a semester to pass my class," commented Phillipa. And Jalaine observed, "Independent reading should be a class in itself. It gets you motivated to read."

Among their suggestions for the next year:

Keesha: Let the class have more of their own picks on books they want to read and less of the requirements. Every student cannot get into Shakespeare's thou's and art's and thee's. Why should we have to be required to know them? Less requirements will make a lot of difference.

Angel: I think that independent reading should divide equally with chosen reading — meaning, we should read independently as much as we read in school. The reading we did this year in and out of class let me know that I am a diverse reader, that I can read many different styles of literature and like them.

Jenna: Add Stephen King.

Wilson: Let students read non-fiction.

David: I hereby suggest to English teachers that they drop the hatred they have for science fiction. The prejudice I see of the medium of science fiction is annoying.

CREATING READERS BY CREATING COMMUNITY: "C'MON, GIRL, YOU GOT TO READ IT."

By the end of the year, most students in second period wrote about positive changes in their perceptions of themselves as readers. Kema's written reflections illustrate the kind of change that took place:

September 16th: The only book I have read on my own was *Daddy Cool* by Donald Gaines and *Heart of a Woman* by M. Angelou. . . . When and if I have an assignment to read a book, I do all my other homework first because I know if I pick that book up I would get restless especially if I don't want to do it. I know it's sad, but that how I feel.

January 27th: No! I do not see myself as a reader because I'm very picky about what I read. . . . I don't consider myself a reader especially in this class where I'm compared against students who have been on honor roll all of their lives. I would never take the chance to read or do any other things they do. Why? because that's how it is. [I chose the last book] because it is written by a female which happens to be black. She's telling my story. How I feel inside. What I see in life. What I'm going to get out of life. Terry McMillan is a powerful writer.

February 24th: Most of the books I have read in the past were fairy tales. I wanted to read something that I can apply to my life that might help me in the future — especially if it is by an African American writer. I stated [at the beginning of the year] that there is not a lot of them out there but boy was I wrong. At first I hated this book assignment. Now I'm getting used to it. I'm finding me in each one of the books I read. I don't like how things end sometimes but that's part of life. I read when I have time. Like when I'm not working or not at school. With these last two books I've read, I hate to put them down because they didn't bore me. I just had other things to do.

April 9th: I don't consider myself a reader yet. I'm getting there though. It's probably because I couldn't find something to read written by a true black woman until I read books by Terry McMillan. That's when I found myself trying to read more and more. . . . Until this year I hated reading with a passion until I learned how to pick out books that interested me.

May 24th: I didn't think I'd make it with *Walkabout*. I couldn't get into that book. Keesha kept telling me, "C'mon, girl, you got to read it — it's good." But I kept asking, "Why I can't see how good it is?" But then I got to the part where the boy died and it was good — just like Keesha said. . . . I still feel intimidated with some kids in here — kids like Keesha and Jalaine and David, especially David. He is never without a book. But I read all my books this year, every one of them. The other day Keesha and me were at the mall and we saw this bookstore and we thought we saw you in there. Keesha said, "There's Joan, let's go in." But it wasn't you. We saw Toni's new book and Keesha want to buy it but it's too expensive so she'll wait 'til it comes out in paperback.

What had brought about the change so clearly in Kema and in other students' perception of themselves as readers? As I made sense of what had happened over the year, I saw that it was not the freedom to choose books, not the independent reading assignments themselves, not the students' reflections on themselves as readers that had brought about the change. It was the combination of all those things — choice, assignments, reflections — in a community of readers that had brought about the change. The secret was creating the community in which students could chose books, read them, talk about them, and encourage each other to read.

I realize now that creating that community had started early in the year with my belief in talk as a way to create an environment where students of all ability levels could succeed, something I had worked on with AP students but had experienced only limited success with in other classes (Cone, 1992). From the first book we read in second period, I stressed the need for students to assist each other in making meaning together. We started with *Sula*. The first day, Melissa asked, "What's up with Shaddrack — are his fingers really growing or is he freaking out?" She asked what other students were afraid to ask and thereby set an example for them. As we made our way through books, students asked questions of each other, cleared up confusions, defended their analysis, reinterpreted the text with each other — and in doing so, taught each other how to read and analyze literature. "Did Sula plan to kill Chicken Little?" "That's not right — Sula doing that with Jude — didn't she know it would hurt Nel? Why'd she come back in the first place?" "What did it mean when it said at the end that it was Sula Nel missed and not Jude?" And so it went — with novels like *Woman Warrior* and *One Flew Over the Cuckoo's Nest* and short stories like "The Tree" and "The Handsomest Drowned Man in the World." The emphasis was always on asking questions, looking back at the text for substantiation, trying out interpretations, coming to agreement or living with disagreement. Students were creating meaning together and teaching each other. And always, it was writing begetting talk and talk begetting understanding.

On the second day of our study of *Othello,* for example, I asked students to write down everything they knew about the characters from Act I. Phillipa said she knew nothing. "Then write about what you don't know," I told her, "and then we'll talk."

She wrote:

> I know I hate Shakespeare. I know I don't understand this play. I know nothing about this stupid play. And I hate it.
> Okay, so I know there's this guy named Othello who is a famous soldier and he fell in love with this young girl. Another guy's in love with her, too. I forgot his name. Her name is Desdemona and she eloped with Othello. And there's this other guy who is jealous of Othello and mad at him. He works for Othello, I think. I can't remember why he's mad. Anyway this guy is setting out to destroy Othello. Who is black but Desdemona's dad, who is white, doesn't like him because he's black.

In fact, Phillipa knew a good deal about the play, which she discovered in the course of writing. When she shared that writing with her classmates, they learned from her and she learned from them. They explained the conflict between Iago and Othello, and they filled in the gaps of her understanding just as she had filled in gaps for them. Once they had gotten the first act straight, they could move to the second act. With each piece of literature, students wrote about what they knew and didn't know and then talked about it in a way that cleared up confusion and deepened understanding. With each piece students learned that saying they were confused wasn't going to get them off the hook. "What is confusing?" I'd ask. "What don't you understand?" "If you could ask a question of your classmates, what would you ask?" Gradually they came to see that asking questions was not a sign of stupidity, that getting lost in a book did not mean they had to reread or discard it or cut class until the book was finished, and that when students taught each other, they often explained material in a more accessible way than when teachers explained it. When the time came for the independent reading project, a sense of community had been established along with a sophisticated model for how to read a book.

The extent of our sense of community as readers is reflected in our connection to writer Terry McMillan. Early in the year, Tassie lent me *Disappearing Acts.* "You have *got* to read this. My sister-in-law gave it to me last Friday and I finished it this weekend. Now I'm reading her first book. Don't be shocked by the language." When I finished the book and gave it back to Tassie, she lent me *Mama.* Other girls in first and second period heard of the books, and began reading and recommending them. I bought copies to lend. Gradually a McMillan fan club developed. Kandi wrote, "*Disappearing Acts.* Everywhere I go I hear people talking about that book. I'll read it again right after my aunt is finished with it. It was so good I just gave it to her and told her to read it and that she'll love it. Sure enough she's in the middle of it and can't put it down. Just last week in my church a woman was reading the book (not in church, at choir practice). She told me that they are going to make a movie out of it. I can't wait to see it." After so much talk about McMillan's work, little wonder that *Disappearing Acts* was one of the books chosen as a group discussion book.

A few days after Clifton had led the discussion on the book, a notice came out in the newspaper advertising McMillan's new book, *Waiting to Exhale,* and a reading by her at a San Francisco bookstore. I told my students I planned to go to the event and said I was going to write a note inviting McMillan to visit our class. "You shouldn't write," Clifton said, "we should." And so they did; they wrote notes and letters to tell her of their admiration. Clifton did not have enough time in class to finish his letter, so he brought it to me at the end of the day, two pages long: "Truthfully I planned to dog-out your book just as I've done everyone else's. I just don't know what happened. As I started to read your book (I do start all the books I'm supposed to read) I found myself unable to leave it alone or put it down. It was almost as if I was addicted to this book. *Disappearing Acts* not only moved me but it became a part of me. Me, a person who doesn't by a long shot consider himself a reader knocked out your masterpiece of writing in less than seven days. I have now started on the book prior to *Disappearing Acts, Mama.*" His postscript: "Thank you for changing my life. It was a change well needed."

I went to the reading with one of my second-period students and gave McMillan the packet of letters and my classroom phone number. The next morning, at 9 o'clock, she called. "I'd love to visit your class. I've got to meet Clifton." As it worked out, McMillan could not come — she was leaving the next day on her book tour and would not arrive back in the Bay Area until the day before graduation, too late to visit the class. The fact that she had wanted to visit, however, impressed my students. An author was interested in them.

A postscript to the independent reading assignment came with a visit from Kema in October of 1992. She came to visit on Back-to-School Night to tell me of the books she is reading in community college. "I'm waiting for *Waiting to Exhale* to come out in paperback." I told her I'd lend her my copy of it — she could send her younger sister by the next day to pick it up. A month later I got the book back with the following note:

Mrs. Cone,

Thank you for sharing yet another piece of important literature with Kema, Keesha, and I.
 Terry McMillan is really a gifted author and we all shared the book with our mothers. We even had a discussion group. I can't thank you enough.

Love,

Your former students,

Jalaine
Kema
Keesha

CREATING STUDENTS AS READERS: PRINCIPLES FOR CHANGE

By the end of a year of asking students to write and reflect, I had gotten to know my students as readers — their reading tastes, habits, problems — in a way I had never known them before, and I had come to know high school reading instruction in a way that would dramatically change the way I teach. I reached the following conclusions:

1. High schools can create readers.

In their study, "Poor Readers: Teach, Don't Label," Brown, Palinscar, and Purcell (1986) argue that the "effects of inadequate early experiences with the types of knowledge that clarify, elaborate, and extend knowledge can be overcome by providing the missing experience with explicit intervention" (p. 138). My study of senior English students corroborates those findings. Once students learned how to summarize, formulate questions about what they were reading, and discuss text in an environment that encouraged collaborative meaning-making, they gained confidence as readers.

Beyond classroom instruction, other things also encouraged students as readers. Primary among these was the personal connection teachers made with individual students — finding a "match" between writers and students or subject matter and students. Jalaine wrote, "When I was in Black lit, I started reading a whole bunch of different stuff because that's the kind of teacher Mr. Greene is. He was like, 'Read Malcolm X,' *The Autobiography of Malcolm X*, and then 'Read somebody else's opinion of the book' and stuff like that. That happened in the tenth grade and then during that year I had Ms. Gocker and I started reading poetry."

The use of literature related to students' lives is also an important element in encouraging students to become readers. Teachers can make these connections by helping students see themselves in books, by choosing books that mirror their experience, and by helping them see the relevance of other people's stories to their own:

Jennifer: As a child, I never found reading difficult, it just wasn't enjoyable. We were always forced to go the library, pick out our favorite book, take it home, and that's all I'd do. Pick out a book, take it home, and return it when it was due. I never found reading could be an enjoyable experience because it was never taught to be fun or interesting, just a lot of words on several pieces of paper. Then as I grew older and entered junior high school, we were assigned books and given more pages to read. This was also not enjoyable because to me it was hard, painful work. Each day we would be assigned a certain number of pages to read, then the following day we would be tested. In my opinion this was not an encouraging or accurate way to get students, like me, to read because there were always other ways of getting the answer to the test. Then finally as I entered high school, reading slowly became more enjoyable. Not because we were forced to read thousands of pages but just because we were being taught how to read and how to make meaning out of what we were reading. I no longer felt inferior to the texts. One of my most favorite books is *Black Boy*. It was my understanding of his triumphs and struggles through life that made the book enjoyable. Finally I was reading something that I felt like I could relate to and most of all understand.

2. High school literature programs need to include independent reading as an integral part of the curriculum.

With very few exceptions, the students in my second-period class who labeled themselves "non-readers" had not been expected to read independently or encouraged by teachers to develop the habit of independent reading. The literature they had previously studied was read in class — mostly aloud — with short reading assignments for homework. When lengthy independent reading was assigned, it was usually for extra credit, an inducement that had little attraction for most of them.

Just as students who were taught in early elementary grades that reading was comprehension had an advantage over students taught that reading was decoding (Brown, Palinscar, & Purcell, 1986), students who were expected to read independently in high school had an advantage over those who were not expected to read on their own. Students who were assigned independent reading matured as readers. Again, Jennifer comments: "I've learned to speed read and I know for a fact it will help me in college. When I used to read, I would examine every book, word for word for meaning. Now I know how to scan paragraphs and make meaning out of them — although I must admit that sometimes I reread parts to make sense. Now that I have learned to read faster, reading has become more enjoyable for me because it doesn't take me so loooonnnnngggg."

Asking students to read independently was not new to me. For years I had assigned "outside books." I took my students to the library, helped them find books, set a deadline for the book to be finished, and tested them with some kind of writing task. But independent reading was not an important part of my curriculum, mainly because readers read the books, and non-readers did not — students who needed no motivation to read got A's, the rest got F's. Since independent reading was not a successful activity, I had (except for AP students) nearly discarded it in favor of having all students read the same book together according to a set schedule. That was not such a bad option: I chose books carefully, making sure I mixed complex works and not-so-complex ones to address the reading levels of my students, selected books that reflected the racial and ethnic background of my students, and brought in complementary films, essays, and short stories.

My study of the reading habits of students pointed out what was wrong with my avoidance of independent reading for all students: the longer I chose the books and assigned the pages, the more I reinforced my students' reading dependence on me, the teacher. More importantly, in not setting aside time for independent reading, I was not encouraging students to practice the comprehension skills they were learning in class, skills that I was carefully scaffolding with discussions and writing assignments. When I did not ask students to use those skills on their own, I was, in effect, implying that they either could not apply the skills on their own or they did not need to read independently — both messages that potentially reinforced their negative self-perceptions as learners.

3. High school literature programs need to provide an opportunity for students to choose texts.

For five students in second period, choice made no difference: with or without the right to choose a book on their own, they did not read. As Nina explained, "I didn't really choose not to read a book. I just never got around to reading one. I really don't know what your [sic] looking for in a book for us to read. I would like to read one by a Hispanic author, but I have no idea how to really find one. I know if I tried I could but I really didn't." For a few others — readers, non-readers, somewhat-readers — choice was of little consequence. "Actually I preferred having no choice at all. I read what I'm assigned. I'd much rather read books that were already chosen. For the next year, less choice," wrote Sam. But most students saw choice as essential in getting students to read. Rebecca was enthusiastic: "Reading in class and out of class this year has let me explore a part of my world I never knew. It has given me a great sense of pride and accomplishment. I never really read until this year and I like it. I've read all the books except the last independent one. I've read more books this year than in my whole life put together. I've read from mysteries to vampire books to romances — a wide variety. I know now I can develop a good habit, reading. I can do it!"

For some students, choice provided the opportunity to pursue an interest in a specific genre, author, or issue. Jennifer was one of these students: "I hate to limit myself right now, but I'm going through a phase. An Alice Walker phase. All the books that I have read have been from Black writers because I find those interesting and I like to see how each writer is different." And Angel explained her preference: "I am really into reading books that involve a struggle of some type. Sometimes it makes me sad to read these kinds of books, but at the same time I can't keep my hands away from them."

For others, choice built confidence. "After I finish a book," wrote Kandi, "I feel as if I'm a whole different person. I don't know how to explain it, but I feel powerful, like I'm getting smarter or something." "When I didn't have to read the same thing as the person in front of me, I didn't have to worry about whether or not I got behind in the assigned reading. I took a chance with reading *House of Spirits* because it was really long and political which intimidated me a little. But I read it and I enjoyed it," Tassie wrote.

Advocating that students be given a choice of literature does not imply that books traditionally taught as part of the canon should be eliminated. Readers, somewhat-readers, and non-readers alike often chose traditionally taught books as well as other, more contemporary, stories as their favorites. Common favorites included the following: *Grapes of Wrath, The Great Gatsby, One Flew over the Cuckoo's Nest, Where the Red Fern Grows, Their Eyes Were Watching God, Lord of the Flies, Cider House Rules, The Autobiography of Malcolm X, 1984, Catcher in the Rye, Sula, Black Boy, Disappearing Acts, The Color Purple.* Most students saw a need to balance teacher-selected books and student-selected books. Angel summed up her feelings: "I think it was a good idea [to have a choice] because we got to read books that the teacher liked and felt we should read, plus what we liked. In class we read books like *Sula, Woman Warrior, Othello, Pygmalion* and *A Doll's House,* all of which were pretty good reading but honestly speaking, I wouldn't have picked those books up at the library. But I'm glad we read them."

4. Literature teachers need to make talk an essential part of reading.

Besides assisting students with understanding sophisticated text, talk inspired by writing can create a classroom atmosphere in which the most and least able reader can collaborate in making meaning and can learn from each other by sharing their insights, experiences, questions, and interpretations:

> *Phillipa:* I don't think I could read [*Romeo and Juliet*] by myself because I don't like Shakespeare and . . . and it's easier when you do in class because you can talk about it and . . . Like a person like Shakespeare — you can understand it better if, you know, if you talk about it.
>
> *Jennifer:* And make it interesting like when we read *Othello*.
>
> *Jalaine:* You know how she'd [the teacher] say like, "Othello, what's up with you?" And, "Cassio, what's up with you?"
>
> *Phillipa:* Really, really. I wouldn't have understood at all if we didn't review.
>
> *Jennifer:* She'd say, "Desdemona, what happened" and I'd go like "Uh, uh," and Jalaine'd say, "Remember — " then something would trigger in my mind and I'd say, "Oh, okay," and I could go on and expand from there. But just off the bat if she'd say, "Here's a test," everyone would be going, "What's number one?"

CREATING READERS:
INVITING EVERYONE INTO THE CONVERSATION

Rob wrote at the end of the year about his transformation into a reader, "I now consider myself a reader. Before I didn't read books. I did not consider myself a reader. But I've read every book assigned this year, class book and independent reading book. After I finished my last book I saw a book lying on my shelf. *A Summer Life* by Gary Soto. I don't know how it got there or who put it there but I picked it up and I began reading it. I began reading a book for no ulterior motive. I can't remember the last time I did that. I wanted to read for no one but myself, my own quest for further knowledge, my own enjoyment. I am a reader and I owe it all to this class. I've unlocked a chest full of hidden desire and emotion toward reading that I didn't know was there. Who knew?"

As successful as Rob's final reflection made me feel, I knew that for every Rob and Kema there were also Cliftons and Amakas graduating from high school, just beginning to see themselves as readers, as well as Nikkis and Nates who were leaving high school not having read a single book on their own. And that continues to sadden and concern me.

The issue of reading instruction, like most pedagogical issues, is a political one. Who are the students taught early on that reading is meaning-making, and who are the students taught that reading is decoding? Which students are asked to read on their own and which are not given independent reading assignments? What are the consequences when an education system invites one group of students to see themselves as independent thinkers and another to remain dependent on teacher instruction and teacher motivation?

If teachers intend for students to leave school as readers — to say nothing of leaving with positive perceptions of themselves as learners — then teachers must make dramatic changes in reading and literature instruction in ways that assist students in reading thoroughly and thoughtfully, encourage them to read on their own, and help them to develop the habit of reading.

At the end of the school year, Jennifer asked, "Ms. Cone, do you teach ninth graders the same as us?"

I replied, "After this year, yes."

REFERENCES

Brown, A. L., Palinscar, A. S., & Purcell, L. (1986). Poor readers: Teach, don't label. In U. Neisser (Ed.), *School achievement of minority children: New perspectives* (pp. 105–143). Hillsdale, NJ: Lawrence Erlbaum.

Cone, J. K. (1992). Untracking AP English: Creating opportunity isn't enough. *Phi Delta Kappan, 73,* 712–717.

Rosenholtz, S., & Simpson, C. (1984). The formation of ability conceptions: Developmental trend or social construction? *Review of Educational Research, 54,* 31–63.

Weinstein, R. (1986) The teaching of reading and children's awareness of teacher expectations. In T. E. Raphael (Ed.), *Contexts of school-based literacy* (pp. 232–252). New York: Random House.

Arts as Epistemology: Enabling Children to Know What They Know

KAREN GALLAS

One afternoon in early June, six children and I crowd around a butterfly box watching a painted lady chrysalis twitch and turn as the butterfly inside struggles to break free. Juan, who is seated on a chair next to the box, holds a clipboard on his lap and is carefully sketching the scene. This is his third sketch of the day chronicling the final stage in the life cycle of the butterfly. It will complete a collection he began in early May, when mealworms arrived in our first-grade classroom. As he draws, the children agonize over the butterfly's plight. They have been watching since early that morning, and they all wonder if the butterfly will ever get out. Sophia smiles to herself and then begins to hum a tune.

"I'll sing it out," she says.

"Yeah, let's sing it out!" agrees Matthew, and all of the children begin to improvise a song. Juan looks up, smiles, and continues to sketch.

Events such as these have become almost commonplace in my classroom. Over the course of the school year, this class of children questioned, researched, wondered, and discussed their way through a wide variety of subject matter and concepts. What distinguished their learning process from that of many other children, however, was the presence of the arts as an integral part of their curriculum: as a methodology for acquiring knowledge, as subject matter, and as an array of expressive opportunities. Drawing and painting, music, movement, dramatic enactment, poetry, and storytelling: each domain, separately and together, became part of their total repertoire as learners.

Harvard Educational Review Vol. 61 No. 1 February 1991, 19–31

By describing the development of a unit on insects, this article will show how the arts can play an essential role in forming and extending all aspects of a curriculum. The concept of life cycles, which informed our study throughout, was the focus of several months of work for my first-grade class. Eighteen children, from a range of socioeconomic, racial, and cultural backgrounds, and including four different language groups, participated in this study from late winter through the month of June. What happened in this class could happen in any class of children. Each group brings a wide range of life experience to school, and, though we are often initially separated by language, culture, and racial barriers, I have learned that the creative arts, rather than labeling our differences, enable us to celebrate them.

Juan arrived in September from Venezuela, speaking no English but filled with joy at being in school. As I struggled during our first few weeks together to find out what he could and could not do (and found out that, according to my teacher's agenda, he could not do many things), Juan very graciously attempted to help me understand what he could do. He would tolerate a few minutes of my informal assessment activities and then use his one word of English: "Paint?" he would suggest cheerfully, and by that time I would agree. "Paint," for Juan, meant drawing, painting, modeling, or constructing, and it was his passion. As the weeks passed, I continued to be amazed by his talent and frustrated by his inability to learn the alphabet and basic readiness skills. However, Juan's own nonchalance about the process of learning to read and write was somewhat contagious, and I began to see that his art was presenting both what he had already learned at home and in school, and what he desired to learn. It soon became clear that our forays into the world of number and letter recognition would be fruitless without Juan's skill as an artist. His visual representations became a catalogue of science information and science questions, and that information began to provide material for his involvement in reading and writing — and learning a new language. As Juan drew, we built a reading and speaking vocabulary from his pictures, and that vocabulary, together with his interest in representing science, also became the subject matter of his writing.

Juan was teaching me once again a lesson that I seem to have to relearn each year: when given the opportunity, listen to the children. They will show you what they know and how they learn best, and often that way is not the teacher's way. Because I am a teacher, my unspoken agenda is shaped by academic expectations: I am supposed to present concepts and skills, and the children are supposed to "master" those skills and concepts. Unfortunately, the journey towards mastery of a subject is often inextricably tied to instruments of assessment, presentation, and communication that are designed by and for teachers. Tests, workbook pages, teacher-led discussions, textbooks, charts — each of these assumes a commonality of experience that the children in a classroom may not share. Each artificially separates the process of mastery from that of individual expression. Each of these excludes the full participation of some portion of the population I teach.

Illustration by Juan

How do young children convey their understanding of the world around them? Before they begin school, and even in the primary grades, most children depend on play, movement, song, dramatic play, and artistic activity as their means of making sense of the world. That these pastimes gradually give way to predominantly "adult" styles of communication is more a tribute to the power of traditional schooling and parental pressure than a statement of the natural process of expressive maturation. What unfolds each year in a classroom that places the arts as a centerpiece of the curriculum is simply a continuation of the early preoccupations of childhood. Children, unlike most of their teachers and parents, are comfortable using virtually all of the expressive modalities. Because one does not need to teach the "how" of the artistic process to them, their ability to use the arts for their own educational process is expansive.

Developing a multi-arts curriculum allows me to follow the children's own expressive interests while also using the artistic process as an integral part of the identification and expansion of their knowledge in different areas. This method goes beyond the use of art as an enhancement or enrichment of an already established curriculum and places the arts as central to the

95

completion of the curricular process. For both teacher and child, the arts offer an expanded notion of classroom discourse that is not solely grounded in linear, objective language and thinking, but rather recognizes the full range of human potential for expression and understanding.

From the first days of our study of the life cycle of insects, we used basic creative and critical thinking skills to identify our existing knowledge base. What did these children know about insects, and what did they want to know? As a group, we brainstormed, sharing our common knowledge, and in the process generated questions we wanted to answer. Later we drew a semantic map to extend and relate our ideas.

What We Know About Insects	*Questions About Insects*
Birds eat them.	Are caterpillars insects?
They have six legs.	How many legs do beetles have?
Some are furry or slimy.	Do all insects have legs?
Some help trees.	Do all insects fly?
Some fly.	How do fireflies light up?
Some eat fruit.	Why do fireflies light up?
Some people eat them.	How do insects grow?
They could destroy the earth.	How do insects swallow?
Some eat wood.	Do they have teeth?
Some live underground.	How old can an insect get?
Some are dangerous.	How do they smell?
Some insects eat other insects.	How many kinds are there?
Most have antennae.	Do insects have lips?
Some have wings and don't fly.	Do they all hop?
Some insects are poisonous.	Do they smell with antennae?
Some help plants.	
Some insects eat plants.	
Some insects have stingers.	

Our study then began in earnest with observations of mealworms. We observed, sketched, and took notes on their behavior. Juan discovered in our second day of sketching that one of his mealworms was in the process of shedding its skin. Thus began the first in his series of meticulous sketches, both from live animals and from nonfiction books about insects. As a class, we spent the afternoons in the first week sketching, studying books and photographs, discussing entomological drawings by different artists, and observing the mealworms and caterpillars. On Friday we showed some of the sketches, and talked about what we were learning. The children were very impressed by the work, and those who hadn't been sketching asked Juan how he got so good.

"I practice a lot," he said, and our discussion continued about why we were sketching.

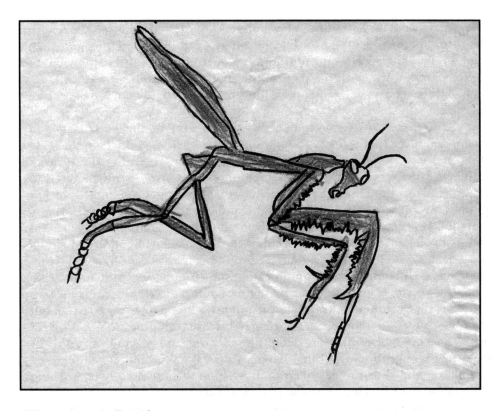

Illustration by David

David: I'd heard people talk about this thing. I think it was a praying mantis, but I didn't know what it was. So I looked at a book, and then I drew it, and then I knew what it was.

Juan: Or if you don't know what a wing is and how it's made you can draw it and then you know.

A few days later, Adam was seated by himself, trying to sketch a picture of a monarch butterfly from a book. Since September Adam had struggled with fine motor tasks, such as drawing, cutting, or construction, but he was so impressed with the work of other children that he had decided to try to do a sketch. As I watched, he was quite absorbed and had finished one wing, but the second wing was more difficult. He threw down his pencil, and I could see he was going to cry. "Don't stop, Adam," I said, and he nodded, wiped his eyes, and picked up the pencil.

Juan walked over to see what was wrong and offered a few suggestions. "You don't have to make it perfect today. Just draw it, then do more tomorrow." Adam went back to work. A few minutes later I saw him using the length of his forefinger to gauge how big the wingspread in the picture was. Juan came over to check, but said nothing. Adam continued until it was time to go home, and worked on the picture for another week until it was finished. He had done a beautiful, meticulous job, and he asked if I could make copies for the class to share.

It is intense artistic activity like this that begins in the early stages of learning and continues throughout a study that enables children to become immersed in a subject. The deep involvement in representing the form of an insect, whether it is one that has been observed or one only pictured in books, expands the child's basic knowledge of that organism and his or her ability to represent it both in thought and form. For Juan, visual representation is a natural process. It is his method for examining his world, as well as his means of externalizing what he is learning for others to share. For Adam, who excels in reading, writing, and abstract thought, but who often has a difficult time communicating and interacting with other children, the artistic process of drawing the monarch butterfly expands his own boundaries of symbolic representation and gives him a new way to reach out to other children. Adam often approached the learning process in a highly verbal and discursive manner, delighting in puns and playing on words or ideas in his speech and writing. These abstractions sometimes eluded his classmates, and thus the act of presenting himself in a visually compelling form became a new challenge for him as a learner.

One day early in our study, Carolyn made a special request. She had finished reading most of our nonfiction resource books, but she wanted to know if I had any poems about insects. I was sure I did, but I wondered why. She explained:

A poem is a little short, and it tells you some things in a funny way. But a science book, it tells you things like on the news. . . . But in a poem, it's more . . . the poem teaches you, but not just with words.

Carolyn, whom I would often find throughout the year alone in the coat-cubbies writing poetry on scraps of paper, had reminded me that I had constructed my plans and gathered my resources too narrowly. Throughout the year as a class, we had used poetry as a way to gain more insight into whatever subject we were studying. Carolyn began to collect poems to read to the class about insects, and I reconsidered the place of poetry in this study. Her interest in metaphoric ways of knowing is not an isolated one. Poetry sometimes provides children with a window of insight that is broader than that offered in even the best nonfiction resources. Poetic form is often more suited to the thinking and writing of children than prose; it is spare, yet rich with sense impressions. It is a medium in which the images of wonder, curiosity, and analogic thinking, which so often characterize children's language, can flourish.

In the next week, our observations of insects continued outside, where each child found an insect habitat, observed the insect, sketched the habitat, and wrote field notes. Upon returning one afternoon, we shared our findings and began to discuss the relationships between our classroom study and our outdoor explorations. Soon after, we read *The Inch Boy* (Morimoto, 1986), a Japanese folk tale that describes the experiences of a character who never grows larger than an inch tall. The children were fascinated by the notion of living in the world as a tiny being. Adam wondered out loud what the world might be like for a tiny velvet spider mite: he had made the connection that I hoped would occur.

Jeffrey offered, "Well, what you might think is a hill would probably only be a pebble or a big piece of dirt."

"And," added Carolyn, "you might never see the blue sky, only just green and green and you'd think the top of the world was green." These ideas produced a lot of commotion, and before we left the meeting I asked the children to write a poem in the persona of an insect that they had observed. Sean chose the ant:

> ANT
> *by Sean*
>
> I pretend I'm a ant
> running and dodging birds.
> Grass feels tickly under my feet.
> Big trees shade me.
> I climb a bush and I see buildings
> houses and even other bugs too.
> And then I see a watermelon seed
> and I go off to carry it away with my friends.

After two weeks, the mealworms and caterpillars were pupating, and these observations, together with our classroom research and outdoor experiences, offered an opportunity for us to compare the life cycles of several insects. Many children had gained a great deal of new knowledge about different insects and their habits, and their understanding had been shared in a variety of ways. I encouraged the children to relate and expand their knowledge through movement and dramatization. In small groups, they presented either the life cycle of an animal they had observed or one they had researched. Each group conferred, agreeing on an insect to present, and then after some rehearsal mimed the stages of that insect's life cycle. Sometimes each member of a small group enacted a different stage in that cycle, while in other groups the members played out the transformation in unison. Brian and Roberto lay on the floor, legs tucked against their sides, mirroring the slightly visible legs on the mealworm pupa. I was surprised when they portrayed the transition from mealworm to pupa with such accuracy that even the timing of the twitching of the pupa was realistic.

For Brian, who might easily be labeled "attention deficit" because of his constant motion and distractibility, the action and focus of the movement experience demonstrated how carefully he had observed and examined the mealworms, and it also showed that Brian has the ability to translate his ideas into a kinetic modality with great clarity. By offering him access to the arts of movement and enactment, I have been able to see Brian's strengths: how carefully he observes and analyzes every detail of the world around him, and how creatively he solves challenging problems. Those strengths are often obscured by his behavioral problems, but when Brian works through movement and drama, the behaviors that handicap him in one situation become his gifts.

One of the more difficult tasks that I face as a teacher is moving children like Brian beyond the level of acquiring new knowledge and ideas and asking them to synthesize and apply their ideas to new and different contexts. It would be easy for me to take a very basic approach to assessment and simply ask children to regurgitate what they have learned, and we would have reached our goals: "Tell me the facts of the life cycle of insects and label the stages on this diagram." Yet the act of moving beyond simple knowledge acquisition towards true assimilation of learning is the challenge for most children, and the process of assessing their learning in a way that stimulates that growth is my challenge. True knowing means transformation and change, and it is that level of learning that I hope for but often find difficult to offer as a possibility to the children.

Fortunately, however, when given the opportunity, the children will provide me with ideas to accomplish this goal. Sean, who is a talented artist, had become fascinated by the notion of relative size. He asked if he and Jeffrey could do a picture to go with his poem. They spent a week working on a huge mural, drawing towering blades of grass, large rocks, and giant sunflowers, then adding tiny insects trudging up the huge plants. Sean's fascination, like Carolyn's, expanded my ideas of what was possible both for these children to grasp conceptually and for all of us to achieve aesthetically. The union of critical and creative thinking that I had repeatedly observed taking place in the production of the mural, in Sophia's song about the struggle to complete a cycle, in Brian's translation of biological change into movement — this interaction that constantly occurs in the process of artistic activity is the key to an expansive curriculum.

Like the children, I must remain open to the potential of the arts to expand both my knowledge of the children I teach and my creative insight into the ongoing development of a curriculum. Many times I seem to miss opportunities to expand the children's experience because I am unable to see beyond the boundaries of my own goals for their learning. For example, Juan, our keen observer, in his careful scrutiny of all the pictures in our resource books, discovered a picture of a cocoon we had had in our room for several months but were unable to identify. The description in the book confirmed what we had observed in early May, when hundreds of tiny cater-

Detail of illustration by Sean and Jeffrey

pillars came streaming out of the cocoon and then promptly took up residence in our garbage garden. There they crawled through the planters and wrapped themselves in pieces of leaves and potato skins. We were astonished and puzzled. The little caterpillars were, we read, called bagworms. Alison, who had brought us the cocoon in late winter, was terribly excited about the discovery. For several weeks we watched the survivors grow amidst the potato plants, which they preferred. They continued to cover themselves in leaves and debris.

At the same time, eight children, including Alison, had become involved in reading and sharing different "why" and "how" stories, such as *Why Mosquitoes Buzz in People's Ears* (Aardema, 1975) and selections from the *Just So Stories* (Kipling, 1902/1978), which explained occurrences in the natural world. For me, Juan's discovery of the bagworm and its habits, which struck us all as ludicrous but wonderful, and the children's interest in stories that offered humorous explanations of animal adaptation seemed to mesh with our class discussions of how animals and humans adapt to survive in their environments.

My realization that these events coalesced also addressed the challenge of developing an integrated arts curriculum that provides a range of arts experiences that will offer opportunities for *all* children to communicate their new knowledge and expanded understanding of the world. Every child is not a visual artist, like Juan or Sean, though some are; every child does not find expanded meaning through the poetic voice like Carolyn, though many do; and every child cannot represent an idea in movement or sound, like Brian and Roberto. The challenge, then, is to ensure that the range of experiences is broad enough to reveal each child's voice, and that those experiences spring from events that all of the children have shared in common.

Alison, whose shy demeanor and sparse language gives an impression of austere silence, is, in fact, a storyteller. Storytellers are often unknowingly discovered (and then eschewed by teachers) in the daily classroom event of sharing time. Their talents are rarely recognized in a classroom, because talk and telling is generally dominated by the teacher. Yet storytelling, as we know from studies of culture and folklore, is a way to pass on knowledge and information, and is a dramatic event. Like drawing, music, and movement, it is also a preferred medium through which some children more adeptly clarify their relationship to the world and to their companions.

When I placed the challenge before the children of taking their new knowledge about insect life cycles and applying it to a different problem, Alison decided, with a few other children, that she wanted to make up a story to tell the class. Her story would explain how the bagworm came to carry the bag. At the same time, several other children decided to invent completely new insects based on their generalized knowledge of insects and draw or construct their imaginary habitat and life cycle. Alison proceeded to write a twelve-page story about the bagworm, which she edited and revised, realizing at one point that she had forgotten to explain allegorically that the female bagworm never comes out of the bag. When she finished, she told us a story in which the bagworm went from a tiny, unnoticed nuisance to a huge creature that ate everything in sight. In order to save themselves from the wrath of humans, the female worms decided to construct a bag to hide in, and they invited the males to join them. "But," said Alison in conclusion, "the males only stayed in the bags until they turned into moths, but the females were too scared to ever come all the way out, so they even laid their eggs inside of the bag, and then they died there." What Alison had described was the correct life cycle of those strange animals, but her vehicle for presenting it was entirely of her own invention. The story enabled her to transform her observations and study of insects, and her involvement with a new literary

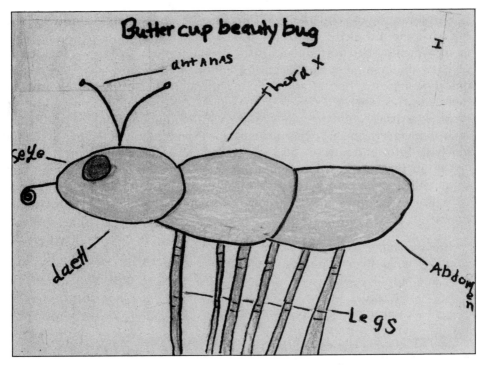

Illustration by Ronit

genre, into a unique language event. In effect, Alison was creating her own folklore about a phenomenon she had observed in the world.

As Alison finished her project, other children created insects that were adapted to completely unique circumstances. I observed Ronit drawing a picture of her insect. She had labeled it with two parts: "head" and "body." I saw this and asked her to rethink what body parts an insect had. She looked at her drawing and back at me, then got up and went to fetch her science journal, opening it up to refer to a diagram we had used a few weeks earlier when we observed the mealworm beetles. On a new piece of paper, Ronit correctly redesigned her insect to include three body parts, colored it in with a bright yellow crayon, and began a third drawing of the insect in its habitat. As she drew, she told me it was going to live in the grass when it was an adult, and that it would get its food from buttercups.

"This is the actual size of my insect," she said as she drew a line which was about two inches long. Then she stopped, her eyes widened, and she gulped.

"Oops, that's way too big," and she grabbed the eraser once again. After drawing a line that was much smaller, she continued, "Aren't I smart? 'Cause I was thinking of him in the buttercups, so I had to make him smaller, or someone would come along and be terrified."

For Ronit, the art experience at this time became an opportunity to find out what she did or did not understand and to rethink her ideas in a new form. Watching her work on an artistic problem, I was able to see that Ronit had not understood some basic information, but I could also observe her quickly correcting herself and thinking through the problems that are inherent in this type of activity. An extremely creative child, Ronit's love of drawing, writing, and language shows great flexibility of thinking and sensitivity to imagery. The art experience in this instance stimulated her to clarify her basic information while also engaging her aesthetic viewpoint.

Late in June, as we approached the end of school, we talked about our studies of life cycles. I asked the children to brainstorm with me about what they thought of when they heard the word "metamorphosis." Here is what they said:

Metamorphosis
egg — mealworm — pupa — beetle
egg — tadpole — frog
egg — caterpillar — chrysalis — butterfly
egg — caterpillar — cocoon — moth
egg — larvae — mosquito
seed — plant — flower — fruit
water — rain — snow — ice
wind — tornado — cyclone — waterspout
egg — dinosaur — reptile — bird
egg — baby — grownup — death — dirt

We gathered for a movement and drama session after this, and I asked the children to describe, through movement, a metamorphosis that they had thought about or seen. Most of the children presented impressions of one of the ideas listed above. Finally, Brian, Jeffrey, and Lea, who had asked to go last, took their turn. They began with Brian enclosed between Lea's and Jeffrey's arms, as if in an embrace. Slowly, Lea and Jeffrey opened their arms and lifted Brian above them with his arms outstretched. He stood there as long as they could hold him and then the three toppled over together, flattened against the ground. Brian leapt up, took out an imaginary pencil, and began to write on Jeffrey's stomach. The other children who had been mystified, jumped to their feet and shouted, "Tree! It's the life cycle of a tree!"

What we all understood by the end of this study was more than a collection of ideas about life cycles. What we understood from our experiences with the arts as subject matter and as inspiration was that knowing wasn't just telling something back as we had received it. Knowing meant transformation and change, and a gradual awareness of what we had learned. For both children and teacher, the arts offer opportunities for reflection upon the content and the process of learning, and they foster a deeper level of communication about what knowledge is and who is truly in control of the learning process. As a pedagogical standard, the integration of the arts offers a rich resource for educators to infuse the learning experience at all levels with expansive and challenging perspectives.

The arts make it possible for all children, regardless of their differences, to participate fully in the process of education. They transcend the limitations placed on those children, like Juan and Brian, whose language, culture, or life experience is outside of the mainstream of American schooling. They challenge children like Adam to expand their boundaries of personal expression and communication. They confirm the perspectives of children like Alison, Sean, and Carolyn, whose modes of communication and expression do not fit the predominant classroom discourse. They enable all children to recognize the breadth and depth of their learning.

REFERENCES

Aardema, V. (1975). *Why mosquitoes buzz in people's ears.* New York: Dial Press.
Kipling, R. (1978). *Just so stories.* New York: Weathervane Books. (Original work published 1902)
Morimoto, J. (1986). *The inch boy.* New York: Puffin.

Life after Death: Critical Pedagogy in an Urban Classroom

J. ALLEYNE JOHNSON

Recently I saw a dead boy. I don't know for sure if he was dead. He looked dead. He laid on the ground in fetal position. Blood oozed from beneath him slowly changing the color of his shirt. I was craning my neck through the car window to see why there were so many policemen on Redding Blvd., when I saw him. Four police cars, lights flashing hysterically, surrounded the stilled body. People were everywhere. I scanned the crowd for any familiar adolescent faces. I wanted to get out of the car and gather with the crowd. I wanted to see if the boy was dead. What happened? Did anyone see? I knew I'd hear about it tomorrow. My students all lived around here. In the hood. It could be family, a homey I saw lying on the ground. I hoped not. It would be hard enough as it was to insist that we get back to the math problems, world history, and lessons in sentence structure for English. (Journal entry, April 18, 1993)

When I wrote the above, I was a teacher of a combined seventh- and eighth-grade "special" class at Brent Junior High School in Northern California's East Bay area. I taught social studies, math, English, and physical education during the first four periods of each day. My students' experience with violence and death was one of the first insights they shared with me about their realities of living in, around, or near a poor neighborhood, one not unlike many others in urban areas across the United States.

All of my students know someone who was murdered. One recent death was that of a young man who had attended our school two years earlier. The

Harvard Educational Review Vol. 65 No. 2 Summer 1995, 213–230

day after his death, everyone was whispering about it. Although only one person in my class was actually related to this young man, the death was felt personally by many of them. Not only was he a former student, this young man was a "homey," that is, someone from the flatland neighborhood where all of my students — and most of the others who attended Brent — lived. Another student in my class had witnessed the actual shooting. After listening a while to their quiet murmuring, I respectfully asked, "Did someone die?" The young people confirmed the death without giving me the details I had gathered from just listening. I then asked, "When was the funeral?" They responded that it would be that afternoon. They asked me, "Why you ask, are you going?" I replied, "Yes." I introduced my lesson after a brief pause. I waited to hear a reaction to my attending the funeral. None came. I was thinking about the colors I had worn to school that day: a black-and-yellow African print blouse with a bright yellow silk skirt. These were not colors that I would normally wear to a funeral. As I looked down and frowned at my attire, the student who was a relative of the deceased quietly said, "It don't matter what you have on. Anybody who want to come, can come." She had answered my unstated question. I nodded, grateful for the reassurance as I began the world history lesson.

Later that day, in English class, we continued the lesson we had started the day before. I was teaching the students about different kinds of narrative paragraphs and assigned students to construct a first-person narrative. Students had to interview each other and write these paragraphs using the information they collected. From past experience, I knew students liked talking into a microphone, so I used a tape recorder and an outside mike to make the interview process more exciting for them and to enhance the interactive process of the assignment.

I had an interview topic prepared, but I told them they could choose their own. As I moved about the room, I noticed, not surprisingly, that in their interview groups a number of students wanted to discuss the recent death. Salima, the eyewitness to the shooting, ended up being interviewed by Tavia, a classmate whose brother had died in a similar incident a year earlier:

Tavia: On the day that Hasan died, what happened?

Salima: It was a large crowd of people. One of the males had a gun. Everybody start running when he pulled it out, except for Hasan 'cause he didn't have no reason to run. Me and my cousin ran across the street and we watch the shooting of Hasan. He got shot in the stomach and he got up start walking. Then the man shot him in the chest. He got back up start walking. He shot him on the side of the head. He got up start walking. And the man finally shot him in the back of the head and Hasan just laid his coat down like a pillow and he laid his head down on it. He started saying 'bye to everybody cause he knew he was gon' die.

But [then] I didn't hear nothing about it. The story was not printed in the newspaper. Hasan's funeral is October 7, 1992. It was a sad tragedy for a lot of people. I felt bad about it because he was a cool person. He was cool with me.

Tavia: After it happen, did it take long for the ambulance to come?

Salima: Well the police showed first. Then the ambulance come. I'll tell you like this: I felt like whupping them police A—, you know what. They just stood there you know, they just stood there for a little while watching him. If it was me, if it was me being a police officer I'd be trying to put him in my police car and try to get him to the hospital so he wouldn't die. He was just a cool person. I don't know why this man shot him and this man got life in jail. If that was me, the judge or the jury, I would kill that M—. You know what? I would kill him 'cause he don't have no reason to take nobody life. 'Cause if he got that gall to take somebody life, I'd take his.

Tavia: But don't you think that if he get killed, if we just kill him, if we kill the people that killing other people, that's all they gon' do is rest in peace, because they asking God for his forgiveness, we don't know if God gon' forgive them, but all he gon' do is rest in peace like everybody else resting in peace. 'Cause when the world end that's all God gon' look at, is our good side and our bad side. The guy who shot Hasan or whoever shot my brother, their good side probably be filled with good things and their bad side probably be filled with less and you know, they might just be resting in peace. It's good that he is suffering in jail and he gon' think about all what he did. I don't know.

We love him [Hasan] very much and you know we sorry for him to be dead. That's why we making this article like today, cause the damn newspaper people ain't doing nothing about it, so you know, we feel real sad about it, you know. We just love him. He gonna rest in peace.

Salima and Tavia finished their interview, but I did not immediately ask for the tape recorder's return. Later, Tavia spoke alone on the interview tape, recording some of her own thoughts about death and dying:

I just feel real sad that he's gone cause everybody's leaving like this. Because my brother died. Like A.B. that went to Harris Junior High. Like my cousin Shawn, Hario. Everybody's just dying like this. I just wish that I could be there for my cousin and everybody else that's gone. But he's going to be resting in peace now and we gon' let him go on and rest in peace. Because we do love him.

A year after the brutal death of her brother, Tavia still misses him and is struggling with the loss of an important influence in her life. Of her own volition, Tavia decided to give personal testimony about the frequency of death in her family and in her neighborhood. I did not know she had done this until I listened to the tape later that day.

Nationwide, nearly 7,000 people between the ages of ten and twenty-four died of gunshot wounds in 1991 ("Bleeding Colors," 1993). People, mostly men, specifically Black men, are being murdered.[1] This rising homicide rate is frequently mentioned in the news, and is usually followed by a more general report on violence, poverty, crime, unsafe neighborhoods. Occasionally, one hears about racism and the political, economic, social, and moral implications of these deaths. Rarely is it reported that someone's father or mother, son or daughter, brother or sister, aunt or uncle has been killed, or that the death has had a traumatic effect on the immediate and extended families. A family's trauma is especially silenced when the dead person was a "wrongdoer," someone who broke the law. Whether someone was a "gangsta" killed by cohorts or police usually receives more attention than whether someone was a "homey" — a friend, a loved one.

This 1993 release by the rap group GETO BOYZ acknowledges the death of all the homies:

> *Another homey got smoked but it's no surprise/ Everybody's trippin' cause the boy was too young to die/ A sad sight to see my homey take his last breath/ Everybody's trippin' 'cause they can't accept my homey's death/ Another killing was reported on the evening news/ Somebody's brother got killed behind a pair of shoes/ In the midst of all this shit I think about myself/ Wondering when somebody's gon' try to take me off the shelf. (© 1993 N-the-Water, Inc., ASCAP; Straight Cash BMI)*

The song reiterates the death and familial loss embedded in rising homicide rates in urban areas. It notes the mindless killing that takes place, and the trauma that family members suffer in the wake of personal tragedies. It also notes the questions faced by those in the midst of the violence about their own mortality. Death is at home, in the news, in the culture at large. And death is unquestionably in our schools.

EDUCATION: A MATTER OF LIFE AND DEATH

> Education as the practice of freedom — as opposed to education as the practice of domination — denies that man is abstract, isolated, independent, and unattached to the world; it also denies that the world exists as a reality apart from men. (Freire, 1989, p. 69)

The purpose of this article is to assert the need to make connections between the day-to-day realities of students' lives and the day-to-day process of teaching and learning that takes place in urban public schools across the United States. In the small city where I lived, we had twenty-one homicides by the middle of 1993. I realized that this homicide rate had an impact on my students' lives and also spoke to societal issues of power and oppression. As such, the need for a critical pedagogy is vital. Henry Giroux (1992) describes critical pedagogy as an educational process that integrates issues of power,

---

[1] See Wideman and Wideman (1984); McCall (1991); Blackwell (1985).

history, self-identity, and the possibility of collective agency and struggle. In this article, I tell the story of one classroom community in which teacher-student interactions formally addressed and acknowledged death as an important issue in the lives of the students. This acknowledgment enabled the teacher (me) and students together to find power for ourselves in disempowering circumstances through the employment of critical pedagogy. I describe my journey as I came to realize that connecting school knowledge with the students' real-life issues is essential in my classroom.

This article evolves from my concurrent experiences as an urban middle school teacher in Northern California and a graduate student at the University of California at Berkeley. The privilege of having time to write about my teaching is the result of my experience as a graduate student. In my writing, I struggle to combine several "languages": the language of my students, the language of secondary education teachers and schools, and the language of teachers and writers within the academy. The process of combining and balancing these languages as producers of different but equally important sets of knowledge is integral to my work, and represents the formation of my own critical pedagogy. Giroux (1992) points out that

> critical pedagogy needs a language that allows for competing solidarities and political vocabularies that do not reduce the issues of power, justice, struggle, and inequality to a single script, a master narrative that suppresses the contingent, the historical and the everyday as serious objects of study. (p. 75)

My struggle to combine these languages is also my struggle not to subsume the important issues related to my work. Issues such as the politics of authority and power (between, for example, university researchers and classroom teachers, teachers and students, etc.), class, and the "re-presentation" of race occupy my mind as I write this article.[2] Thus, I have carefully developed a language or re-presentation — written and spoken — that mirrors those languages utilized by my students and the teachers about whom I write. As Ngugi Wa Thiongo (1986) asserts, "From a word, a group of words, a sentence and even a name, one can glean the social norms, attitudes and values of a people" (p. 8).[3] The insistence, pervasive in university settings, on finding one voice, one definitive writing style is problematic in the face of my varied experience. I claim the languages of all those with whom I teach and work and study as a part of my own ethos and in my formation of a critical pedagogy.

---

[2] The writing of "re-presentation" in this way is a political act — creating an awareness of the politics of identity formation, particularly with regard to race, in the U.S. social context.

[3] Ngugi's (1986) comment refers specifically to African culture, but language as the most powerful bearer of a culture has been posited by social scientists for centuries. See DuBois (1961); hooks (1989); Smitherman (1986); Sanchez (1970); and Bernstein (1971).

Each of these languages speaks volumes on the state of U.S. schools, but unfortunately, conversations combining all three languages are rare. Across the nation, students who are failing or have "failed" at school can tell anyone who will listen why schools "didn't teach them anything." The "failing" students I have met and their parents are apt to point out the school's failure to educate all of its children. Practitioners struggle with the frantic rhythm of classrooms, which leaves little time to acknowledge or to record fleeting reflections on the act of teaching. In addition, in universities across the country, graduate teacher researchers like myself struggle to translate solutions often hidden in convoluted academic writings into daily practice. I hope that this article will illustrate the power found in merging the conversations of the students, of teachers and schools, and of the academy.

DEATH IN U.S. SOCIETY

Until recently, most discussions of death in the literature were of an existential nature; death was discussed only in relation to aging, terminal illnesses, or war, as opposed to death as a more general part of life, an everyday occurrence that threatens one's human existence. These limited discussions of death come, in part, from a fear of the inevitability of death (Corr & McNeil, 1986; Kubler-Ross, 1969; Schowalter, 1987). Partly as a way of coping, people subsume the impact of death in rhetoric about ageism, illness, violence, and moral issues. The view of death as oppositional to life, instead of as part of an inevitable, natural progression, makes it a difficult issue to discuss.

Discussions of adolescent death are even more complex and problematic. One significant factor is that the most common causes of adolescent death — suicide, accidents, and homicide — all occur unexpectedly (Schowalter, 1987). In addition to the shock of a loss, surviving adolescents often contend with the inability of the adults around them to discuss death. Audrey Gordon (1986) expands on this idea. She writes that

> at the point where the teen has a personal experience with the death of a significant person, all the [mainstream American] cultural messages about death as distant, violent or beautiful are challenged. Nothing in previous experience has prepared the youth for the feelings of rage, loneliness, guilt and disbelief that accompany a personal loss. (p. 22)

For young African American adolescents, the difficulties of dealing with death are even further complicated by the brutal nature of homicide, which is the main cause of Black adolescent death. Furthermore, the literature and media have generated certain perceptions of African American homicide. For instance, newspaper headlines scream: "MAN GUNNED DOWN IN . . ." — a headline that could describe an event in a poor neighborhood in any major U.S. city. Television shows like *Cops, Crime Stories,* and *Hunter* sensationalize such acts of violence. The music industry commodifies the "romance" of violence, frequently, but not only, in rap music.[4]

The response to the increase in deaths by homicide has been a public outcry for increased police surveillance, weaponry, and manpower, as well as prison construction. Embedded in this response is what many scholars identify as a racist notion; that is, that the violence occurring in Black, low-income neighborhoods is entirely the fault of the people in those neighborhoods (Baldwin, 1985; Blackwell, 1985; Brown, 1988; Jordan, 1977; Wilson, 1990; Wright, 1987). Amos Wilson (1990) provides a rich discussion of the racist underpinnings in perceptions of crime and violence in Black communities. He locates this bias in many aspects of crime and violence reporting, from FBI reports to general attitudes and responses toward "crime in the streets," as "an African-American monopoly" (p. 19). Wilson views criminal justice statistics as having much less to do with accurate reports of crime in the United States than with what he sees as a generally held belief about the violence-prone nature of Blacks. He quotes Evan Stark:

> [The] alternative view [to blacks being more violent-prone] is supported by national surveys of crime victims, a far more accurate source of information about crimes committed than arrest reports. According to the FBI, for example, the proportion of blacks arrested for aggravated assault in 1987 was more than three times greater than the proportion for whites. But the National Crime Survey, based on victim interviews, found that the actual proportion of blacks and whites committing aggravated assault in 1987 was virtually identical: 32 per 1,000 for blacks; 31 per 1,000 for whites. (Stark, 1990, quoted in Wilson, 1990, p. 25)

The tragedy of homicides among Blacks is negated in this suggested framework of crime and violence. Violence becomes the word that both subsumes one event (the tragedy of the victim's death) and qualifies another action (a brutal homicide). In addition, this framework defines the actors as potential menaces to society, thereby undermining any sympathy when lives are taken by an act of violence. As a result, the public feels a macabre sense of relief when it is reported that the "menaces" kill each other.

Death framed as violence begs the question, "Where is the tragedy?" This framework leaves no room to mourn a family member lost to a brutal death. On an even more insidious level, the "violent" framing of African American homicide incriminates both the assassin and the deceased. Looking at death only through a lens of violence generates silence around the issue of this death as loss. Thus, the tragedy and overall impact of death felt by surviving

[4] Rappers like Ice Cube, Too Short, Ice-T, and NWA (Niggas with a Attitude) made their mark on the music industry with a particular discourse of violence in their music. The irony of death in the African American community is sometimes played out in different songs from the same album. For instance, the GETO BOYZ's poignant rendering of death as a loss of a life in "Six Feet Deep" is followed by a rap tale justifying the murder of a Black woman.

African American adolescents is hidden by mainstream society's inability and unwillingness to deal with the issue of death or with the brutal way most Black adolescents encounter death.

In this harsh light and harsher silence stands the African American adolescent whose friend or loved one was gunned down. There are too few spaces where Salima and Tavia, the students quoted earlier, could deal with their emotions about witnessing a killing of a "cool person" or losing a sibling. Few are the spaces where Tavia could admit that she "just feel real sad that he's [her brother] gone 'cause everybody's leaving like this." Few are the spaces where the two young people can discuss different views of the tragedy. Salima's anger at her friend's death is directed at the policemen — their seeming lack of interest and their failure to act swiftly to save a life. She also expresses anger at the assassin and argues for his death. Tavia sympathizes with her friend, but responds to Salima's wish for vengeance by reminding her that "if we kill the people that killing other people, that's all they gon' do is rest in peace."

Tavia's and Salima's experiences with death reflect those of many African American students from low-income families living in poor neighborhoods across the country. The students at Brent are among these; therefore, I will examine how death entered my classroom. I am not referring to the rise in school crime and violence, but rather the long-term effects of experiencing frequent deaths on teaching and learning in urban classrooms.[5] I will show how I transformed the notions of teacher authority and legitimated knowledge within my classroom. Through my approach to teaching and learning, I acknowledged one of the most traumatic life experiences survived by my students — the trauma of death.

CLUSTER ACADEMY: ANOTHER KIND OF DEATH

Brent Junior High School has a population of approximately nine hundred students. In the 1992–1993 school year, 62 percent of the students at Brent were African American. Some of these students are bused from poor neighborhoods of the city to the middle- and upper-class neighborhood where Brent Junior High is located. As these minority students, mostly African Americans, leave the flatlands and come up the hill to the school, they yell greetings, friend to friend, that formerly blended with the morning rhythms of their neighborhoods, but sound harsh in the quiet neighborhood surrounding the school. Nothing affirms their presence in the hill neighborhood, not even their roles as students at the school. As a Black woman ascending the hill, I too feel some sense of displacement, but, unlike them, I ascend the hill to a position of relative power. I am a teacher there.

---

[5] For a critique of the impact of school crime and violence in urban schools, see Comer (1980).

In the 1992–1993 school year, the school district received Chapter One funding. With these federal dollars, they created Cluster Academies, which are classes that provide prevention/intervention services for students who have been promoted based on their age or retained in grades seven, eight, or nine. Each junior high school in the district had at least one Cluster Academy class. These classes are allowed to have a maximum of twenty-five students. Brent had only one Cluster class, which I taught. Twenty-one of my students were Black, two were Asian, and one was Mexican.

The general perception at Brent Junior High is that Cluster Academy is "a classroom for bad students" who are labeled "at risk," "learning disabled," "violent," "disruptive," and other debilitating terms, even by their own schoolmates. The general feeling around the school was that students who were placed in Cluster Academy could not function in regular classes, mainly because of "behavioral" problems, secondarily because of academics. My students were, in fact, the ones with the most reported disciplinary and behavioral problems in the school. Prior to being placed in Cluster, the best of these students averaged a C on their report cards, and many had received straight F's. By all of the school's indicators, any attempt to educate these students was hopeless. The Cluster teacher was not expected to make much headway with these students, and the students themselves were very aware of this. I once asked my students to write their perceptions of the school's view of Cluster Academy, and combined their individual responses into the following essay:

How People View Cluster

People look at Cluster as though we do not do anything, we are doomed, all we ever do is play, and we are bad all the time. That's how people look at Cluster. People say that Cluster kids are stupid. It's a class for dummies. Some people think that we are just dumb and just bad. I bet if we let someone from regular classes in for a day they would be shocked. Even a teacher. We do more work than in regular classes. People always pass judgment on each other and for what? Just to put someone down. To me it does not make any sense. Some people talk about the Cluster Kids every day, probably not just students. Maybe teachers. Maybe even the principal talk about us too.

People make it seem like we're those terrible kids. Every time we get sent out of class, they suspend us or give us SAC [suspension alternative class]. Some kids in regular classes are cutting classes and all they get is a note to get back to class. They don't even give the Cluster class a chance in the office. One time [counselor X] suspended me without hearing my side of the story. I think its because I'm in Cluster class. This counselor didn't used to act like that when I was in regular classes.

I think they look over us like we are bums in the street. I'll let them know how I feel about being looked over. I'm not saying that everybody looks over us. I'm saying that its people like [Mr. X (a teacher)] and a whole bunch of kids. I don't like when they say that Cluster is dumb. I get mad and curse and say "You dumb!" but I don't really mean it. I just get mad.[6]

Initially, the call for classes like Cluster Academy came from a desire of policy makers, school officials, and concerned parents to aid educationally disadvantaged students (Fine, 1991; Levin, 1971; Minow, 1990; Ravitch, 1983). However, clearly the euphemistic title of the class did not impress the students and did not hide the reality of their being framed as a certain type of student by being placed in Cluster Academy class. By perceiving the negative label and the subsequent negative treatment, Cluster students experienced another reality, one that contradicted the original intent of the formation of the class.

It was my challenge, then, to change the Cluster students' negative self-perceptions of the Cluster Academy class and to liberate them from their images as Cluster students. I began to reflect on how other parts of their lives might impact the roles they see for themselves as students. Although there were many times when my students would criticize the way the school community viewed them, their critique was difficult for them to maintain in light of so few school experiences that affirmed their abilities and competencies as students.

It was true that a number of students experienced difficulty in reading and math; difficulties that I now believe were exacerbated by the way teachers "taught" the subjects. For example, I started the year with skills and drills in math because I, to some degree, also bought into the view that students' difficulties were due to their lack of math ability, as opposed to a range of causes, not the least of which might be my presentation of the material and the teaching method. I noticed, however, math in operation on the P.E. field, when students were playing baseball, setting up teams, and keeping score; I saw it in money and candy exchanges and bartering. I decided, therefore, to risk seeing how much of their difficulty with math was contextual and situational, or presentational and procedural, according to classroom norms. I let them take one of the Friday math tests in groups of four students. Some of the test questions were created by the students themselves, submitted in advance. I also included an applied math problem I'd found about setting up a basketball tournament schedule. The students responded well to making up the test questions, and to having a problem on a familiar topic that they were interested in.

After this experience, I reflected on how well the students responded to acting as agents in their own learning process. This reflection was the avenue

---

[6] The students who wrote this essay are Sabrina Brown, Kevin Henderson, James Porter, Danny Simpson, Coral Wilson, Rodney Walker, Stacey Willis, RJ Johnson ("Rodney" in the text), and Damon Marshall.

through which the issue of death entered our classroom and the advent of my attempts to transform the structure of education in our classroom. In the process of being "students," these young people might also find power in being themselves: who they were outside the classroom and away from the school.

DEATH

I first realized how much death was on the minds of these young people when I let them draw during a "rained-out" physical education period. I encouraged them to draw whatever they wanted. I noticed that the letters "R.I.P" were in almost every drawing. In some, "R.I.P" and the name of the person or persons who died comprised the drawing. In others, the words were located in corners or at the bottom of the drawing.

When I looked at my students' artwork earlier in the year, the drawings didn't appear to me to have anything to do with death or resting in peace. One picture that especially impressed me was a detailed drawing of the artist's neighborhood. In the picture were two tall buildings, each with eighteen squares representing windows. A brick wall adjoined the second building. "R.I.P XIV" was drawn on the wall along with other graffiti. A "gangsta," wearing a XIV's hat ("XIV" is the name of a neighborhood gang), high-top sneakers, and a t-shirt with a marijuana plant on it, sat on the wall. An old car, its tires flat and the back window broken, was parked in front of the wall. Another homey, giving the peace sign, stood in front of the car. I was so impressed by the drawing's detail and depth that "R.I.P" initially seemed like only another detail. Yet as time passed, I noted that "R.I.P" was frequently scratched into the desks, and appeared in the young people's art and on their hats and t-shirts. I then began to acknowledge the presence of death in the classroom.

Later in the semester, my interactions with the students around the death of the former Brent student made it clear that I had to address the issue of death with my students. Something that mattered this much to them and was so prevalent in their thoughts could not be ignored. My challenge was to find a way to deal with death in the classroom.

Paulo Freire's (1989) work offered me ideas to begin the process of negotiating the issue of death in the classroom. Freire's "banking concept" of education critiques teacher-student relationships. The banking concept is the idea that "knowledge is a gift bestowed by those who consider themselves knowledgeable upon those whom they consider to know nothing" (p. 57). He describes the character of the teacher-student relationship as it traditionally operates in public schooling: "This relationship involves a narrative subject (the teacher) and patient, listening objects (the students)" (p. 57). As a person new to the role of teacher, I quickly realized that the burden of conveying specific information to the students is placed on teachers by the

117

structure of the schooling process. In California, for example, there are restrictive curriculum guidelines for every grade level in public schools. Covering all of the topics dictated by the guidelines is virtually impossible, considering the many interruptions that occur daily during school, where students exit and enter the classroom continuously. Neither administrators nor teachers logically expect to complete all of the requirements, yet students are held accountable based on state guidelines as they move from one grade level to the next. The goal of having the students present every day to receive this "gift" of knowledge seems an even more insurmountable task if one acknowledges the many outside disruptions, including those caused by the prevalence of death, in students' lives.

Moreover, Freire questions the relevance of the gift of knowledge to the lives of students. He notes that in using the "banking concept" of education "the contents, whether values or empirical dimensions of reality, tend to become lifeless and petrified. Education is suffering from narrative sickness" (p. 57). The symptom of this sickness in my classroom was the students' response to lifeless, disengaging material, their blank faces staring back as I lectured. No learning was taking place. It became obvious that the superficial nature of teacher as the "giver of knowledge," and students as the "patient," listening receptors needed to be transformed.

At one point, in a desperate attempt to ignite some excitement in my students, I stopped "teaching" and started to talk about possible field trips that might bring to life the importance of the material I presented. The shutters of disinterest on students' faces lifted momentarily. I went on about where we would go, what we would do, and how we would do it. As I paused to catch my breath and reign in my own excitement, one student packed a powerful punch, asking loudly, "Did you ask us?" I was stunned into silence and had no reply. I realized that, as hard as I had tried not to, I had fallen back into the trap of teacher as authoritative knowledge-giver. I had not engaged the students, or asked what they might like to do with my idea. I merely brainstormed in front of them about what *I* thought *they* would find interesting without asking for their input. Not only did I realize my failure to engage students with my curriculum, I also realized that I was ignoring other issues that were occupying their thoughts — such as death and dying — as shown clearly in their art and in the earlier taped interview.

I began to see that education, real education, as Freire states, must begin with a solution to the teacher-student contradiction — where the teacher is the only conveyer of knowledge and the knowledge brought into the classroom by students is unrecognized and negated — by reconciling the poles so that both are simultaneously teachers and students. Once again, my awareness of the importance of death to my students returned to me, but I had no idea where to start: How could I broach the subject? What part of the discussion might be culturally taboo? In what lesson would the discussion fit? How would I grade it? How would I make up the time I would lose in covering "school knowledge" (the curriculum) if I used class time to discuss death? The conflict between teaching a prescribed curriculum and wanting to respond to students' realities became unbearable — and so I sought their help.

RENEGOTIATING DEATH IN THE CLASSROOM

We were halfway through the school year, and things were becoming really stale in the classroom. In despair, I wrote and read a letter to my students. The following is an abridged version of the letter:

> Something's happened to me. What happened is that I lost it. I get discouraged trying to teach you. I get caught up in the everyday — giving out referrals, teaching at you, forgetting that I had a bigger picture when I came into the room. There's a certain number of black kids (and the number is growing) that come into schools and just don't make it the way the schools say that you should. They make it in other ways but the school and the teachers do not care. So these kids get placed in classes like Cluster and Opportunity. That's why I chose to teach Cluster. I felt that I could turn things around, that I could prove the school wrong about these kids.
>
> But then I get down here and I get discouraged but this is where I went wrong. I think I know what's best. I bring in all the ideas and just expect you to do them. I stopped asking you what you want to do, what you want to be taught. What do you think will help you the most in the long run? . . . Anyway I propose or put to you that we think of a project or something to end the semester with. My idea is to first get each of you to write about what troubles you the most about your life that you would like to change and then we decide as a class what out of those things we can try to start changing before the semester ends. But we must make a plan *together*. It will take time but I believe that we can do it. Some of the things I thought about are: going to high school next year, dying, getting shot, clothes, sex, parents, brothers and sisters, the police, the hood, gangstas. But I don't know that any of these things are the most important. Whatever we decide, we must also think up a plan.
>
> That was my idea but I truly want to hear yours so that we are doing this together. I recently read this essay that a black student at Clark High wrote. She wrote that one of her teachers "wallowed over the class like a bowl of jelly." I don't want to do that. I want to interact with you. I won't take people playing the fool, but I want to be sure I let everyone have a say in their education.
>
> Thank you for listening.

The young people did not comment on the letter, except to ask me to read it a second time for the latecomers, and again the next day for the people who had been absent. At first, I thought they only wanted to hear it again because the word "shit" was in it (original version), but then I saw other reasons: I asked for their input, and I acknowledged that I, too, got tired of school every day the way it was.

The process to become a community where knowledge is expected from and acknowledged by all members, although trying at times, is one from which my students and I hoped to extract some value. I was attempting to undo or at least challenge a multiplicity of hegemonic processes in the classroom simultaneously. In the weeks after I read my letter to the students, I allotted two English class periods per week to discuss the end-of-semester project. There was a lot of classroom conversation that did not necessarily include me, and I eventually had to "join" with the various groups to have a voice in the discussions.

The class eventually voted to create a newspaper. Students decided that anyone could write as many articles in as many sections as they wanted. I arranged time in one of the school's computer rooms so that students could type in their contributions. The students read and critiqued each others' writing for spelling and grammar. I did not impose any spelling or grammatical rules, but checked with individuals to verify that their use of other than standard English was a personal, informed choice. The first paper took about four weeks to complete, taking up all of their class periods in the last week for final editing changes and production.

The students became very involved in the process; everything started to matter, from how many pages the newspaper would be, to what color paper to use, to how it would be distributed. During the process of constructing the newspaper, I noticed that the students became less afraid of being vulnerable with me and with each other and of challenges they were initially hesitant to face. The writings for the "Special Memories" section brought out a lot of personal and sad exchanges in the classroom. I learned a lot about coping with the stresses of day-to-day living from these young people. They also showed me humor in the worst situations. A camaraderie grew between me and my students that extended into other class periods when we were not working on the paper.

This interaction resulted in the creation of the *Cluster Chronic*. The students decided to share their newspaper with the rest of the school community. In the first year, we distributed two editions and completed a third that was distributed only to members of the class. Creating this newspaper was powerful on many levels. First, I saw a change in how my students felt about Cluster Academy. For example, they decided to include the collaborative essay, "How People View Cluster," adding the following ending paragraph:

It's alright being in Cluster. Some teachers, they woo [say] "Cluster is so nice. They do all their work." This makes me feel very happy. People look at Cluster like its a messed up class but its not. It's a good class for me. Who puts on all the shows and do newspapers? Cluster kids are getting talked about because we made a newspaper and no one else did. We did a concert. I don't feel we get enough props [validation] for the things we do at Brent School and that's all I have to say.

Second was the response of the rest of the school community to the newspaper. Cluster students distributed the newspaper during their lunch break to students in the rest of the school. Teachers received any copies that remained. The following excerpts from my field notes illustrate the magic of the moment of distributing the first edition:

> We distributed the newspaper 4th & 5th period lunch to the students of the school. I announced it over the intercom that we were going to be doing this. It was great! The students were reading it. Some had it on their laps, reading it while they ate their lunch. Some were in the lunch line reading it while they waited to go in. GP [a security guard] sat down and read the whole thing. I did not see any papers thrown anywhere although D [the custodian] said that he picked up a few. Ms. M. [a teacher] came into the class for a copy. She said "the kids are all reading it." Ms. S. asked for a copy. Ms. H. [the vice principal] asked for 2 copies to take to the district office.
>
> My kids were walking tall when they distributed the newspaper. At first I kept a few copies for the teachers but the kids kept asking for them to give to other students. I ended up with only two copies for the teachers' room. M. immediately took one up as I put them down.
>
> One English teacher stopped me and told me how she enjoyed the paper. She said that she was an English teacher and she agonized about letting the kids write slang words. She said, "the kids would put slang words into the computer and the spell check would go crazy! Because she was an "English Teacher" the slang words worried her so much. Yet she recognized and appreciated the emotion, the realness in the kids' writing. (Journal entry, April 1993)

The act of creating a newspaper that was widely read by their peers in the school was empowering for the young people.

Finally, the most powerful experience for all of us in writing the newspaper was while revisiting the topic of death. To give respectful mention and remembrance to their loved ones who had died, the young people created a "Special Memories" section in the first edition of the newspaper. There were six articles in this section. In addition, the "Street Life" section, which included opinions on events that occur in students' neighborhoods, had two articles about death. In all, eight contributions in the *Cluster Chronic* discussed death in the young people's lives. Below are three of the eight:

SPECIAL MEMORIES

In Loving Memories

I love my cousin Trevel Jamison
He was one of the best
R.I.P. David Rogan and Hasan Bess
To all the birds we have to feed
Rest in peace Andre Reed
And all the ways we have to go
R.I.P. Gizmo

written by Sabrina Brown

James Roberts — Dec. 10, 1974 to Aug. 29, 1991

In loving memories of James Roberts. He attended Clarke and Brent Middle Schools and Sojourner High School. He loved to go fishing and riding around in his car. He was 18 years old when he died. He left us his beloved kids James Jr. and Jamilah. He loved football. He departed this life August 29, 1991. I really do miss him. We had our ups and downs but he still told me what was right from wrong.

I was hurt when my brother left me because he was my mother's only son. Now I don't have a big brother but its going to be all good, because he's going to see me again in the next life. We really do miss him.

written by Tavia Keller

STREET LIFE

My Opinion

There are more than two-hundred people getting killed because of gun wars. People are getting shot by mistake. More people should start a crime watch in their neighborhood. Some people are being killed over a word. Sometimes there are fights but mostly threats. A man was beaten to death with a baseball bat because of the part of town he lived in. I think this stuff is wrong because brothers are killing each other and by the year 2000 there will not be enough black men to communicate with.

written by Willis Irwin

On the day of the first edition, I made the following field note: "We talked about dying and family. Rodney, me, Damon, and some others said we did not know what we would do if our Moms died" (Journal entry, April 1993). I asked no questions about death, but instead shared my feelings about the subject. This enhanced my relationship with my students, as we acknowledged our whole selves, not only the roles of "student" and "teacher." It was also a relationship where knowledge was not mine alone; everyone gave and everyone received.

As I struggled to deal with death in the classroom, I gained clarity from another teacher's experience, which was less successful than mine. The following tells of this teacher's attempt to negotiate the issue of death without changing the operating norms and behaviors in her classroom, and emphasizes the difficulty of this endeavor as well as its necessity.

CRITICAL PEDAGOGY: NO TEACHING AS USUAL

The day after the funeral of the student mentioned at the beginning of this article, I made copies of the funeral program for the students who had known the deceased but had not attended the service. Another of my students' teachers took one of the funeral programs and copied only the picture of the deceased. The following day, she handed out copies of this picture to her class, asking students to write a letter of condolence to the mother of the deceased.

The young people's reaction was swift. The girl who was related to the deceased screamed obscenities at the teacher, burst into tears, and ran out of the class. Other girls also cursed the teacher as tears fell from their eyes. Paralyzed with confusion, this well-meaning teacher dropped the subject and barely managed to get through the rest of the period. She was still shaken by the experience as she related it to me the next day.

Later, feeling more comfortable with the students after working with them on the first issue of the *Cluster Chronic,* I ventured to ask them what had occurred that day with the other teacher. Their indignation was still apparent in their responses:

She had the nerve to copy his picture on a ditto!

Coral ask her "why you put his picture on a ditto and ask us to write his momma a letter when his momma is having a hard time as it is, you stupid-ass b-t-h?!"

A school ditto! A school activity!

Don't nobody wanna keep feeling those memories!

It's like she making his death a joke.

It seemed that this teacher had assumed she had to "teach" the students how to cope with death. She had assumed the role of "knowledge-giver," and these students were not about to be "told" how to handle death. They coped with death on an almost daily basis. They and their communities were already coping the best way they knew how. These students were not about to compromise a lived experience to the banking concept of knowledge transference. The students' response was passionate, with the intent to hurt and insult the teacher the way they'd perceived themselves to be hurt and insulted. This well-intentioned teacher omitted an important part of the negotiation. She didn't ask them.

CONCLUSION

Death is one example of students' life experiences that enters the classroom whether a teacher chooses to acknowledge it or not. It is also one of many student experiences that debunk the notion of classroom teaching and education as neutral spaces or endeavors. It is important to find a way, with the help of the young people, to connect teaching in the school with life outside of school and, as Freire suggests, to find space for the emergence of teacher-students and student-teachers.

Although the classroom I share with the young people has come a long way, there are still days when education suffers from "narrative sickness," but now there are twenty-six of us acting as doctors on call, so diagnosis is possible. Cuban and Tyack (1989), who wrote a historical perspective on schools and the students who don't fit them, make two suggestions for policy reform relevant to this discussion. They state that "as hard as it may be to change the school to match the students of an 'imperiled generation,' it is a more promising strategy than trying to fit the student to the school" (p. 29). They propose further "to undertake comprehensive changes that take no features of schools for granted" (p. 29).

Our classroom is now an exciting place where learning and teaching take place, bringing life to a usually lifeless curriculum. We've become a community of student-teachers and a teacher-student. We are a community of learners. Students have opinions about what they would like to get from their education. I have found that it is important to start from where they are. I ask them.

In this article, I attempted to demonstrate how our class moved from traditional one-way teaching to an interactive teaching and learning environment. I no longer want to acknowledge students only to the extent of how well they fulfill my expectations or their response to a prescribed, petrified curriculum. I believe that it is not effective or responsible to teach on a day-to-day basis as though nothing that happens outside of the school building impacts on the act of teaching. My students were empowered through the acknowledgement of knowledge acquired as a consequence of their lived experiences. They also taught teachers the benefits of respecting and incorporating students' knowledge into their classroom pedagogy. Whether we as teachers choose to address it or not, students' lives come with them to school, death and other aspects of students' realities come into our classrooms. Instead of wishing for other students, let us gear our work towards the students we have.

APPENDIX

Following are the three other articles from the *Cluster Chronic* that deal with death:

In Loving Memories of Omont L. Wilson

Omont was a proud young man. He stayed in J.F.K. manor. Omont had two brothers by the names of Marvin Wilson and Kiniko Wilson. Omont departed this life a few days after Christmas. He left behind loving memories of what he and his family used to do together. He left behind good and helpful friends that hang inside of "Easter Hill" on South 26th Street. Omont liked to ride bikes with me, Ree-Love, Ghetto "o", and other friends. Omont is badly missed by family and friends. May He Rest In Peace.

written by RJ Johnson

In Loving Memories Willie L. Bowie

On March 20, 1991 Willie L. Bowie departed this life leaving behind two little boys of his own by the names of Kamari and Larry Bowie. His family was badly hurt when they found out this tragedy. R.I.P. B-40.

written by RJ Johnson

In Loving Memories — Dameion D. West

In loving memories of Dameion. I love him from the bottom of my heart. He means something to me more than some of the other people I know. I know and you know that Dameion was a young, Black, intelligent teenager. Before he got laid in his grave he came over to my house and kissed my momma and everything, and then the next day his first cousin came over to my house and told my momma that Dameion just got killed. He said that he was out there fighting with his friend and his friend got beat up. After the fight was over the boy told Dameion that he was going to get killed. At the time Dameion wasn't tripping, because as I said before, Dameion was a young, loving Black boy. That boy just looked back and shot him. I'm glad that Dameion didn't have any kids because now they would be without a father and that's not what we want. Everyone needs a father, especially these little kids nowadays that don't have a mother, so you know they need a father.

written by Coral Wilson

REFERENCES

Baldwin, J. (1985). *The evidence of things not seen.* New York: Henry Holt.

Bernstein, B. (1971). *Class, codes and control.* New York: Schocken Press.

Bleeding Colors. (1993, September 26). *West County Times* (Special Report), pp. 1–18.

Blackwell, J. E. (1985). *The Black community: Diversity and unity.* New York: Harper & Row.

Brown, R. L. (1988). *The state of Black America.* New York: National Urban League.

Comer, J. (1980). *School power: Implications of an intervention project.* New York: Free Press.

Corr, C. A., & McNeil, J. N. (Eds.). (1986). *Adolescence and death.* New York: Springer.

Cuban, L., & Tyack, D. (1989). *Mismatch: Historical perspectives on schools and students that don't fit them.* Unpublished manuscript.

DuBois, W. E. B. (1961). *Souls of Black folk.* Greenwich, CT: Fawcett.

Fine, M. (1991). *Framing dropouts: Notes on the politics of an urban public high school.* Albany: State University of New York Press.

Freire, P. (1989). *Pedagogy of the oppressed.* New York: Continuum.

Giroux, H. A. (1992). *Border crossings: Cultural workers and the politics of education.* New York: Routledge.

Gordon, A. K. (1986). The tattered cloak of immortality. In C. A. Corr & J. N. McNeil (Eds.), *Adolescence and death* (pp. 16–31). New York: Springer.

hooks, b. (1989). *Talking back: Thinking feminist, thinking Black.* Boston: South End Press.

Jordon, W. D. (1977). *White over Black: American attitudes toward the Negro, 1550–1812.* Chapel Hill: University of North Carolina Press.

Kubler-Ross, E. (1969). *On death and dying.* New York: Macmillan.

Levin, H. (1971). A decade of policy developments in improving education and training for low-income populations. In R. Herman (Ed.), *A decade of federal anti-poverty programs* (pp. 123–188). New York: Academic Press.

McCall, N. (1991, January 13). Dispatches from a dying generation. *Washington Post,* p. C1.

Minow, M. (1990). *Making all the difference: Inclusion, exclusion and American law.* New York: Cornell University Press.

Ngugi, W. T. (1986). *Decolonising the mind: The politics of language in African literature.* London: James Currey.

Ravitch, D. (1983). *The troubled crusade: American education 1945–1980.* New York: Basic Books.

Schowalter, J. E. (1987). Adolescents' concepts of death and how these can kill them. In J. E. Schowalter, P. Bushman, P. R. Patterson, A. H. Kutscher, M. Tallmer, & R. G. Stevenson (Eds.), *Children and death: Perspectives from birth through adolescence.* New York: Praeger.

Smitherman, G. (1986). *Talkin and testifyin: The language of Black America.* Detroit: Wayne State University Press.

Wideman, J. E., & Wideman, R. D. (1984). *Brothers and keepers.* New York: Henry Holt.

Wilson, A. N. (1990) *Black-on-Black violence: The psychodynamics of Black self-annihilation in service of White domination.* New York: Afrikan World Infosystems.

Wright, J. B. (1987). *Black robes, White justice.* Secaucus, NJ: L. Stuart.

Writing Workshop as Carnival: Reflections on an Alternative Learning Environment

TIMOTHY J. LENSMIRE

or Russian literary theorist and philosopher Mikhail Bakhtin, the carnivals and popular festivals of the Middle Ages and Renaissance were extremely important alternative social contexts that could teach us much about how to bust open and transform traditional, closed discourses. Bakhtin championed carnival because he saw it as a social sphere that embraced freedom and equality, and that created possibilities for learning and positive change. In this article, I use the lessons of Bakhtin's carnival to examine critically a progressive, alternative learning environment found in schools — the writing workshop. My strategy is to portray writing workshops as a form of carnival. This helps me to articulate problems that have not been confronted in the how-to books of workshop advocates or in research on the teaching and learning of writing. At the same time, the portrayal of writing workshops as carnival enables me to affirm what I take to be the core of workshop commitments — a vision of children writing themselves and their worlds on the page, within a classroom setting that liberates student intention and association.

BACKGROUND AND CONTEXTS

Throughout the 1989–1990 school year, I taught writing five days a week in Grace Parker's third-grade classroom using a writing workshop approach, and I also researched teaching and learning in the workshop context as a

Harvard Educational Review Vol. 64 No. 4 Winter 1994, 371–391

participant observer.[1] As a teacher, I wanted my students to "come to voice" (hooks, 1989); that is, I wanted them to explore and order their experiences as an expression of a unique self, as well as to participate in the cultural work of naming and renaming the world and their places within it. As a teacher-researcher, I wanted to study what happened when my students and I went about teaching and learning writing in ways that transformed typical classroom social relations and work. I brought qualitative research assumptions and methods (Bogdan & Biklen, 1982; Erickson, 1986; Hammersly & Atkinson, 1983) to this work and collected the following types of data:

Fieldnotes. These included detailed descriptions of classroom life, as well as reflections on specific pedagogical and methodological problems and issues.

Teacher and classroom documents. These included lesson plans, lists of rules and procedures for the workshop, forms, and notes to students and parents.

Audiotapes. Starting in October, I taped class sessions and writing conferences with children in order to analyze discourse closely in various workshop situations.

Student interviews. Twenty-four of twenty-seven children in the class participated in interviews conducted at the end of the school year by outside researchers. Interviews focused on the sense students were making of the writing workshop, and explored children's relations with one another and with their teachers, as well as how these relations influenced their writing.

Student writing. Throughout the year, I photocopied students' written work. I found these texts essential for analyzing the topics and genres children pursued in their writing, as well as for examining how topics and genres were related to the immediate social context.

I taught in a school that served a largely middle-class, suburban community. Also attending the school were children who lived in a nearby trailer park inhabited primarily by working-class families. As I worked with my students throughout the year — and watched them play on the playground, vote for student council representatives, decide whom to sit by in the cafeteria — I began noticing patterns of association among children that divided them along gender and social-class lines (if we take the wooden fence separating the children living in the trailer park from those living in the surrounding community as a rough social-class line).[2]

---

[1] I have used pseudonyms for all children, staff, and parents who appear in my text. I have also used pseudonyms *within* children's texts when those texts name other children or staff from the school. I have also done some minor editing of children's texts (mainly of spelling) when presenting rough drafts.

[2] Lines did not appear to be drawn by race/ethnicity: The four African American children in our classroom, and the one whose parents were from India, did not form a subgroup — each of them worked and played primarily with White children within gender boundaries. Because I was mainly

In previous work, I focused on how this divided, stratified peer culture asserted itself within our workshop and shaped the production and sharing of children's writings (Lensmire, 1993, 1994; Lensmire & Beals, 1994). I drew on the language and literary theories of Bakhtin (1981, 1986) and Kristeva (1986) to examine children's texts in relation to the social contexts of their production. According to Bakhtin, texts are "dialogic," in that they respond to preceding and anticipated texts and are sensitive to audience and social context. In my analyses, I developed interpretations of children's work in which peers as well as teachers were important audiences, and in which children drew not only on their conversations with teachers and their readings of books, but also on the words, meanings, and values of their peer culture, to construct their texts. These readings of children's texts enabled me to examine how peer culture intersected with the official work of the writing workshop.

In these earlier explorations of workshop life, my primary concern was to describe my own and my students' experiences and activities in this third-grade workshop — our hopes, our relations, our struggles with teaching, learning, and writing. In this article, my subject is the critical examination of writing workshop approaches as an agenda for writing classrooms. To accomplish this, I turn to Bakhtin's analysis of carnival — especially as developed in his *Problems of Dostoyevsky's Poetics* (1984a) and *Rabelais and His World* (1984b) — in order to identify crucial problems and issues attending such literacy practices in schools.

BAKHTIN ON CARNIVAL

Bakhtin repeatedly characterized carnival as a "second life" of the people. For Bakhtin, the carnivals and popular festivals of the Middle Ages and Renaissance conferred "the right to emerge from the routine of life, the right to be free from all that is official and consecrated" (1984b, p. 257). This second life of the people was both unofficial and antiofficial — unofficial because the playful, fearless spirit of carnival loosened the grip of established norms and relations and allowed alternatives to emerge in their place; antiofficial because this same carnivalistic spirit engendered and supported the criticism and mockery of the official social order and ideology.

I emphasize four features of Bakhtin's carnival.[3] The first is the *participation of all* in carnival. Carnival, for Bakhtin, is not a spectacle, not something

---

concerned with the inclusions and exclusions children made as a result of their decisions of whom to work with in the workshop, and because race/ethnicity did not appear to be important to those decisions, my analyses in Lensmire (1994) do not explore in any depth the meaning of race/ethnicity in the lives of children in this workshop. This does not necessarily mean that it was unimportant (see, for example, Lensmire, 1994, pp. 63–65).

[3] A brief treatment of Bakhtin's writings on carnival is difficult, because, as Gardiner (1992) notes, "It is often difficult to disentangle what Bakhtin takes to be some of the more salient features of carnival,

performed by some and watched by others. Instead, the line between spectator and performer is blurred, as in the 18th century Roman carnival described by Goethe (1970) in his *Italian Journey*. During carnival, participants move in and out of processions, games, mock battles with confetti, verbal duels, and exaggerated reenactments of the body's struggles with birth and death. For Bakhtin, it is only later, with the encroachment of the state on popular festive life and the movement of festive life from the marketplace to the private household, that the people's participation in carnival shifts toward spectatorship — carnival becomes a parade, and the carnival spirit is "transformed into a mere holiday mood" (1984b, p. 33). The full-bodied carnival that interests Bakhtin features active, universal participation, and is a "play without footlights" (p. 235): "Carnival is not contemplated and, strictly speaking, not even performed; its participants live in it, they live by its laws as long as those laws are in effect; that is, they live a carnivalistic life" (p. 122)

One of carnival's laws — and for Bakhtin perhaps the most important — is the seeming obliteration of the official, established social order, and "all the forms of terror, reverence, piety, and etiquette" connected to it (1984a, p. 123). In the second life of carnival, behavior, gesture, and discourse are freed. With the suspension of social hierarchies and conventions, a joyful "disorderly conduct" flourishes:

> Members of all social strata mix, joke and cavort in a mood of carefree abandon and "universal good humour." . . . Young men and women, each dressed in the clothes of the opposite sex, interact in a scandalous and provocative manner. Mock officials parade through the crowd, accusing people of horrible crimes and threatening them with arrest and punishment, which only elicits howls of laughter from the populace. (Gardiner, 1992, p. 44)

Carnival is life turned inside out and upside down. This disruption of life's routine, and especially the temporary abolition of powerful social hierarchies, allows participants to experience relations with each other and the world that are unavailable to them in everyday life.

A second important feature of carnival, then, is *free and familiar contact among people*. Physical and social distances between people are suspended in the jostling crowds. Constrained, coercive relations give way to ones based in freedom and equality. For Bakhtin, carnival is a context in which people

---

insofar as it constitutes a complexly interconnected and 'organic' whole" (pp. 45–46). My characterization is based on Bakhtin's (1984a) own summary of carnival in *Problems of Dostoyevsky's Poetics* (pp. 122–126). I omit discussion of what Bakhtin calls a "special category of the carnival sense of the world" — eccentricity — which permits the "latent sides of human nature to reveal and express themselves" (p. 123). Eccentricity is closely connected to two other features of carnival that I do discuss: free and familiar contact among carnival participants and a playful stance to the world, both of which function to liberate individual behavior and talk. Other helpful depictions of carnival are provided by Gardiner (1992) and LaCapra (1983).

take up and work out, even if only temporarily, new relations with others. Participants experience "in a concretely sensuous, half-real and half-play-acted form, *a new mode of interrelationship between individuals,* counterposed to the all-powerful socio-hierarchical relationships of noncarnival life" (Bakhtin, 1984a, p. 123; author's emphasis).

But it is not only social relations that are transformed in carnival, not only people who get mixed and combined in disorderly ways. For Bakhtin, a "free and familiar" attitude spreads over everything, as values, ideas, events, and things are wrestled from their ordinary places in thought and practice, rearranged, and perceived anew. Carnival participants take up new relations not only with the people around them, but also with their world. A third feature of carnival, then, is a *playful, familiar relation to the world.*

This playful stance is signaled in numerous carnival practices, such as clothes being worn inside out, or underwear as outer wear; countless gestures, such as walking backward, standing on your head, showing your backside; the use of spoons and pots and other household objects as weapons of war in mock battles; and the creation of useless objects, such as buckets and barrels without bottoms. Bakhtin warns against passing too quickly over these seemingly frivolous activities, and sees great import and possibilities in carnival's playful manipulation of the everyday world:

> It is a gay and free play with objects and concepts, but it is a play that pursues a distant, prophetic goal: to dispel the atmosphere of gloomy and false seriousness enveloping the world and all its phenomena, to lend a different look, to render it more material, closer to man and his body, more understandable, and lighter in the bodily sense. (1984b, p. 380)

As the weight of the established social order and official ideology is lifted in carnival, unofficial and antiofficial discourse and activity emerge. The fourth feature of Bakhtin's carnival is this strong antiofficial current in the carnival sea — what Bakhtin calls carnival abuse, or *profanation* — which is expressed in the loud blasphemies, obscenities, and parodies that sound in the carnival square. Bakhtin emphasizes that carnival abuse is not personal invective aimed at other individuals. Instead, profanation has as its target the system of practices and ideas that oppress the people. Carnival abuse is directed, by the folk, at traditional authority and its "old truth," which are represented by "a Mardi Gras dummy, a comic monster that the laughing crowd rends to pieces in the marketplace" (1984b, p. 213).

The purpose or project of carnival abuse, however, is not purely negative. For Bakhtin, profanation is profoundly ambivalent — that is, both negative and positive, both destructive and regenerating. Carnival abuse kills the old so that the new can be born. This ambivalence is clearly seen in one of the most important rituals of carnival — the mock crowning and decrowning of the carnival king. In this ritual, a carnival king is crowned, only to fall prey later to carnival abuse in the decrowning, as he is stripped of his regal vestments, crown, and other symbols of authority, and subjected to ridicule and beatings:

> The ritual of the decrowning completes, as it were, the coronation and is inseparable from it (I repeat: this is a dualistic ritual). And through it, a new crowning already glimmers. Carnival celebrates the shift itself, the process of replaceability. . . . Under this ritual act of decrowning a king lies the very core of the carnival sense of the world — the pathos of shifts and changes, of death and renewal. Carnival is the festival of all-annihilating and all-renewing time. (Bakhtin, 1984a, pp. 124–125)

This, for Bakhtin, was the lesson taught in carnival: things change. In carnival, the people laughed at ideas and practices supposed to be universal and eternal and saw them for what they were — partial and contingent. And for the folk, for everyday people worn down by oppressive conditions, this was a hopeful lesson.

The carnival features of active participation, free and familiar contact among people, and a playful, familiar relation to the world are also prominent and positive features of writing workshops. Profanation, however, is not a prominent characteristic of workshops. Carnival abuse is muted in the writings of workshop advocates and is redirected, in sometimes disturbing ways, by children in their texts. I discuss these variations later in the article, when I examine shortcomings in the theory and practice of workshop approaches.

WORKSHOP AS CARNIVAL

Affirmations

The active participation of both students and teachers is a prominent theme in workshop literature (Atwell, 1987; Calkins, 1986, 1991; Graves, 1983; Murray, 1985).[4] In the opening sentence of one of the classics of workshop advocacy, Graves (1983) asserts: "Children want to write. They want to write the first day they attend school" (p. 3). The problem, according to workshop advocates, is that traditional school practices do not encourage and sustain this active engagement with writing. In fact, traditional practices actually deny participation, demand passivity, and produce student resistance. Thus, workshop approaches emphasize the need for teachers to provide students with the opportunity to explore and learn about writing by writing. The primary strategy of these approaches is to grant students increased control (or "ownership") over their own literate activities. According to Graves, writing workshop teachers

---

[4] I will emphasize active student participation, since students have traditionally been put in relatively passive roles in classrooms. But workshop advocates emphasize an active role for teachers in the workshop as well — see, for example, Calkins (1986, pp. 163-165).

want the child to control, take charge of the information in his writing. Their craft is to help the child to maintain control for himself. That is the craft of teaching. They stand as far back as they can observing the child's way of working, seeking the best way to help the child realize his intentions. (1983, p. 6)

In writing workshop theory, students' increased control over their work helps them regain their interest in and commitment to expressing themselves in print.

In the workshop I set up with my third graders, this active participation — as well as the second feature of Bakhtin's carnival, free and familiar contact among people — can be seen in the primary activities of different parts of our daily routine.

Our workshop had a three-part routine. The first part — *the opening meeting* — lasted approximately 5-10 minutes and was modeled after what Calkins (1986) calls mini-lessons. I used this time to teach, usually in a whole-class situation, the procedures and norms of the workshop and aspects of the craft of writing. This part of the routine placed students in a fairly traditional, passive student role. Interestingly enough, once students got used to the relative control they exercised in other parts of the workshop routine, they actively resisted the opening meeting. They persistently complained about it, claiming that it wasted *their* writing time; they called the opening meeting, among other derogatory things, the "opening infinity." Students even circulated a petition in the workshop that called for the opening meeting to be shortened. By March of that school year, we were calling the opening meeting the "opening minute," and I was consciously working to keep it short (Fieldnotes, 3-12-90).

The second part of the routine, lasting approximately 30 minutes, was *writing time.* This was the part of the workshop where children exercised the greatest control over their own work and movement. Children used this autonomy to engage in topics and stories that they found meaningful and to engage their peers and me in ways and at times that suited their work and the problems they faced as they wrote. If children needed to talk with someone about ideas they had for revisions of their stories, for example, they had the freedom to do so. They could go to their peers, or to me, if I was not talking to another child at that moment, or to Grace, the regular classroom teacher, who often worked with us in the workshop. Primary activities for children during this time included brainstorming, drawing, drafting, revising, and editing texts; holding conferences with peers and the teacher; publishing selected texts; and reading. Children made choices during this time as to what they wanted to work on, with whom, and for how long. My primary activity was to help the children identify important stories, revise their texts, and get their drafts ready for typing and publishing.

The final ten minutes or so of the workshop routine was *sharing time* (modeled after Graves and Hansen's [1983] "author's chair"). Sharing time was one of two primary ways for children's texts to "go public" within the class-room, to reach a larger audience than those in teacher and peer confer-ences. (The second was our workshop "library" — a few shelves at the back of the room where we housed children's published pieces.) Children do-nated the books they wrote to the library for certain amounts of time so that other children could check them out and read them during writing time and other parts of the school day. During sharing time, one or more children read their texts in front of the class, after which classmates and adults in the rooms shared their responses. Sometimes children shared finished pieces, which they typed, illustrated, and bound between cardboard covers. Other times, they used sharing time to get help with planning or revising earlier drafts of texts.

Unlike traditional classrooms, our writing workshop did not lock children into passive spectator roles. Like participants in carnival, children experi-enced a blurring of performer and spectator roles in the workshop — "ac-tive" producing authors were not separated from "passive" consuming read-ers. Instead, children moved in and out of the roles of writer and audience. In both sharing time and the workshop library, child writers and their texts occupied spaces typically reserved for adults and official texts: in sharing time, the storytelling child replaced the teacher at the front of the room; in the workshop library, the child's book replaced the adult authored and se-lected book. And, in contrast to traditional seating arrangements that bind children to desks and constrain peer relations — relations that flourish only at the edges, or in the absence, of the teacher's gaze (Erickson & Shultz, 1992) — writing time permitted movement and allowed children access to each other. At any given moment during writing time, children were clus-tered around desks, huddled under the bookshelves, or on the move to a conference with friends. Children could draw close to one another and en-gage each other in less constrained ways.

Writing workshop approaches encourage free and familiar contact among children. They also seek to lessen physical and social distances between teachers and students. As was suggested above in my discussion of our work-shop routine, the teacher in the writing workshop is often *among children,* rather than in the front of the room.[5] In addition, workshop approaches encourage transformed teacher-student relations in their conception of teacher response to children's texts. A major concern of workshop advocates

[5] I regularly wrote in my fieldnotes about how different children's expressions of affection and trust touched me. As an example, I made the following comments about Rajesh when he came to talk with me about trouble he was having with some classmates:

Rajesh told me he had something "very important" to talk about with me. He said the words with feeling, and his voice broke several times. It didn't seem easy for him to talk to me about what he wanted to tell me.

I like Rajesh a lot. He was one of the first kids I really started liking in the class. He was the first one to play with my long hair and tell me I should put it in a pony tail. He used to come over by me and sit on my leg while I talked to someone else at the table. So seeing Rajesh

is helping teachers avoid falling into a typical classroom discourse that affirms the traditional social hierarchy between teacher and student, and silences students (Cazden, 1986).

Workshop approaches emphasize that teacher response should not simply evaluate student writing for grading purposes, but should seek to help students realize their own intentions in text. The teacher, once the sole initiator and audience/evaluator of student writing, now follows the child (Graves, 1983, p. 103), watching carefully for ways to encourage, support, model, and coach, at appropriate times, through oral and written response. Calkins (1986) would have a teacher draw close[6] to students and become a genuine audience for them, an audience that is interested in what young writers have to say:[7]

> Our first job in a conference, then, is to be a person, not just a teacher. It is to enjoy, to care, and to respond. We cry, laugh, nod, and sigh. . . . Sometimes that is enough. Sometimes the purpose of a conference is simply to respond. Other times, if the moment seems right, we try, in a conference, to extend what the youngster can do as a writer. (p. 119)

In addition to transformed social relations, writing workshops support the active engagement of children with writing through the transformation of school writing tasks. And in this transformation of task, writing workshops, like carnival, encourage participants to adopt a playful, familiar relation to the world. In at least three ways, workshop approaches support this playful stance by young writers.

First, workshop approaches reject traditional school writing tasks: they reject the grammar and usage textbook with its gloomy exercises, as well as tightly controlled teacher assignments. Second, writing workshops grant students the freedom to determine the topics, audiences, purposes, and forms of their texts, and also support students in their choices. Rather than confront an alien, imposed world, children are asked to explore their own familiar worlds, and to do so in their own language; workshop advocates want "the schoolyard talk of children to become the poetry and prose of the

---

hurting hurt me too. But there was also a strategic, serious aspect to his words and tone. It seemed he felt he needed to persuade me of what he was saying. (Fieldnotes, 2-23-90)

I am not arguing that writing workshops are the only places such interactions can occur. Rather, I am arguing that the relative openness of the workshop creates more opportunities for such interaction during class itself than does traditional pedagogy.

[6] Graves (1983) even attempts to represent workshop commitments to "drawing close" to students graphically, in a diagram of alternative roles that can be played by the teacher in writing conferences. Graves affirms the role of "advocate," which teachers embrace when they sit "next to the child" and position themselves so as to be "as close to equal height as possible" (p. 98).

[7] This does not mean that workshop teachers are necessarily successful. A number of studies have indicated that it is actually quite difficult for teachers and students to break out of more traditional school discourse patterns. See Florio-Ruane (1991) and Ulichney and Watson-Gegeo (1989) for helpful discussions of this problem.

classroom publishing house" (Willinsky, 1990, p. 200). As Atwell (1987) notes, workshop approaches have strong student-centered commitments in that "individuals' rigorous pursuit of their own ideas is the course content" (p. 41). But this "rigorous pursuit" is not necessarily "gloomy" or "serious": what are brainstorming, friendly conferences, and Elbow's (1973) "free writing" but strategies for replacing an all too serious school approach to ideas and work with a playful, familiar one?[8]

Finally, writing workshops support children's playful, familiar stance to the world by bringing *writing itself* close to students and demystifying it. Rather than experiencing the typical, alienating school task of producing texts for evaluation purposes, children experience what it means to engage in the craft of writing, continuously and close up. They explore their experiences and world through drafting and revision, through seeing the effect of what they have to say on multiple audiences in the workshop. In the writing workshop, the process of writing and the role of writer are not kept at a distance, not denied children. And through writing, children begin to give shape and order to their world: "By articulating experience, we reclaim it for ourselves. Writing allows us to turn the chaos into something beautiful, to frame selected moments in our lives, to uncover and to celebrate the organizing patterns of our existence" (Calkins, 1986, p. 3).

In support of children's active engagement with writing in the classroom, writing workshops encourage a free and familiar relation to the world by child writers, as well as free and familiar relations among workshop participants. Thus, it seems reasonable to compare writing workshops to carnival — a reasonableness that is only strengthened if you have ever actually experienced the noise, laughter, and incessant movement of active children in a writing workshop. Having made this comparison, however, I must immediately admit that if workshop is carnival, it is a rather pale and subdued one: a carnival without bite, without the critical, radical edge of Bakhtin's carnival. In the following section, I contrast workshops to carnival.

An Orderly, Individualistic Carnival

Bakhtin emphasizes that a central aspect of carnival is its struggle against the official social order, its attempt to meet and disable established social relations and ideas with laughter, frank speech, and, especially, carnival abuse or profanation. Bakhtin's carnival has a strong antiofficial commitment that is simply absent from the writing workshops promoted by Graves (1983), Calkins (1986, 1991), Atwell (1987), and Murray (1985). These workshop advocates *do* provide important critiques of traditional school practices, but they seldom link these critiques and their proposals for classrooms to

---

[8] I emphasize playfulness here because of Bakhtin's (1984b) continued association of certain forms of seriousness with the official ideology — an ideology that worked, in part, through inspiring fear: "In the eyes of Rabelais seriousness was either the tone of that receding truth and doomed authority, or the tone of feeble men intimidated and filled with terror" (p. 285).

broader societal problems and struggles for change (Berlin, 1988). Workshop advocates make the teacher responsible for sharing curriculum with students that is aimed at supporting and enhancing children's writing processes. The content of children's writing is left up to individual children. Thus, any carnival abuse that does occur — and it does (I share some examples below) — is incidental, and represents individual students' decisions to challenge, parody, or criticize aspects of their worlds. But there is no systematic commitment within workshop approaches to the development and support of such critical practices by students.[9]

The bite of carnival is blunted in writing workshops, at least in part, by the guiding visions workshop advocates have put forward.[10] In contrast to Bakhtin's images of a subversive, popular carnival, workshops have been guided, in the theories of workshop advocates, by visions that are neither playful and critical enough nor collective enough to sustain profanation. As Willinsky (1990) has noted, workshops are often portrayed in ways that recommend them as effective preparation for an official, corporate, workaday world, rather than as carnivalesque breeding grounds of playful, critical dissent and liberatory alternatives:

> [Workshops] would, after all, encourage independent and collaborative projects while drawing on peer support networks and conferencing with professionals to enhance the production values of the final and literate product. It can all sound and seem very marble and glass, office-tower work. While the editorial meetings at the classroom publishing house may not be a training ground for the leveraged buy-out artists, neither is it so removed from hustling projects and prospectuses for tomorrow's Wall Street jungle. (p. 19)

Bakhtin's carnival took place in the medieval market square, a site that shared something of the hustle and excitement, I suppose, of Wall Street. But Bakhtin's carnival was animated by a desire for freedom and equality, and celebrated a shared, communal abundance, rather than individual selfishness and greed.

For Bakhtin, profanation was a collective, critical response to an oppressive official world. A second aspect of workshop visions that undermines

---

[9] In future research, I hope to figure out what a commitment to carnival abuse in the workshop might entail. Work on critical pedagogy (which has been extremely important to my own thinking about the goals and practices of school writing) will be helpful, even though I worry that such approaches might not be playful enough (in Bakhtin's strong sense of the word) and that we might miss the liberatory aspect of playing with ideas and practices. Davies's (1993) writing on her attempts to help children "disrupt the dominant storylines through which their gender is held in place" (p. 1) will certainly influence this future work.

[10] In the following discussion, I concentrate on the writing of workshop advocates and how they have conceived of workshops. I do not confront institutional aspects of schools and classrooms that undermine transformed social relations and tasks. Schools are not necessarily conducive to the sort of "adventurous learning" (Cohen, 1988) we might expect in more carnivalesque workshops, largely because of the pervasive demand that students be controlled and "orderly" within them.

profanation, then, is their almost exclusive focus on and concern with the individual writer. Workshop approaches, as Dressman (1993) puts it, "lionize lone wolves." The goals of workshop approaches are conceived in terms of supporting individual children's intentions for writing, and they project a vision of empowerment that is at odds with visions, such as Bakhtin's, that conceive of positive social change as the product of individual *and collective* struggle.

Workshop advocates have embraced an individualistic, Romantic rhetoric that abstracts writers and their texts from social context. Berlin (1988) argues that this rhetoric, represented most ably by writers such as Murray (1985) and Elbow (1973), *does* provide a powerful "denunciation of economic, political, and social pressures to conform" (Berlin, 1988, p. 486). The problem for Berlin is that while this rhetoric champions resistance to dehumanizing forces and conditions, it is always (and only) individual resistance:

> The only hope in a society working to destroy the uniqueness of the individual is for each of us to assert our individuality against the tyranny of the authoritarian corporation, state, and society. Strategies for doing so must of course be left to the individual, each lighting one small candle in order to create a brighter world. (p. 487)

It is not that individual children do not try to light a candle every now and then in the writing workshop, for they do. There is carnivalesque student writing in the workshop that targets aspects of the official world and submits them to a playful disrespect and abuse. A fairly direct example comes from one of my students, Rajesh, who made his gym teacher the main character of a story he wrote. This gym teacher was almost uniformly disliked by children in our workshop — according to them, he was quite mean. In his first draft, Rajesh used the teacher's actual name in the story; later, Rajesh changed the character's name to "Jud Coat." Rajesh's story:

> Far far away in the milky way galaxy there was a planet called MEAN. The things that lived on it were called Tickyes.
>
> One of the Tickyes came to our planet earth. Now, Tickyes can change shape. So it changed into a man called Jud Coat. He got a job at Clifford School. Jud was very mean! When anybody said Hi to him he would beat them up! And the worst thing was he kept multiplying. So somebody was going to have to get rid of him.
>
> And so I, Rajesh, stabbed him in the brain. ["the heart" in another version]

In his story, Rajesh targets an authority figure for criticism — "Jud was very mean!" — and abuse — "stabbed him in the brain" (a rather severe form of "uncrowning"?). Within the logic of the story, Rajesh's abuse clears the way, presumably, for a better world, one without the mean and multiplying Tickye, Jud Coat. Thus, in addition to the criticism and abuse of a powerful figure in Rajesh's official school world, the story has something of the ambivalent quality (both destructive and regenerating) that Bakhtin claims characterized carnival abuse.

Other examples from our workshop were less direct, and seemed intent on testing implicit teacher and school definitions of acceptable topics for student writing. James, for example, told me on one of the first days of school that he was going to write about vomit (Fieldnotes, 8-30-89). Later, he and Ken wrote a story in which the two main characters, Kurt and Lisa (both named for children in this third-grade classroom), went to bed together. (Grace made James and Ken remove this event from their story before they shared it with the class.[11])

I point to these examples of carnivalesque writing because they employ — even if without the conscious intention of the authors — one of the main strategies of carnival abuse that Bakhtin (1984b) examines in *Rabelais and His World*. Within the system of carnival images, both the earth and the lower body (the belly, bowels, and reproductive organs) functioned as a grave for the old and a womb for the new. In carnival abuse, then, a common tactic was to bring the high "down to earth" or *into contact or association with the lower body*, where the old would be killed, and then transformed and reborn. For example, one of Rabelais's characters in *Gargantua and Pantagruel* says that the shadow cast by a monastery's belfry impregnates women. This bit of carnival abuse works by associating the high, the church tower, with the low, the human body (male penis and pregnant women). Bakhtin argues that this abuse is not directed solely (or even primarily) at somewhat less than abstinent monks. Instead, "the monastic belfry, uncrowned and renewed in the form of a giant phallus . . . uncrowns the entire monastery, the very ground on which it stands, its false ascetic ideal, its abstract and sterile eternity" (1984b, p. 312).

James and his friends made the carnivalesque move of taking up as topics, within their official school writing, functions of the human body usually censored out of elementary schools or at least tightly controlled within them (as in sex education). They were young Rabelaises, with the similarity in strategy explained by the continuity of what they and Rabelais were up against — a Western tradition that separates mind from body and that asks its students to "look higher" to the things of the mind. As James explains in his interview, he liked to "make serious things funny when the day's kind of going slow, and it's really not going, nobody's really having any fun" (Interview, 5-24-90). If you want to have a little fun, then one thing you can do is "look lower."

We can even hear echoes of carnival in an official workshop story told by Calkins (1991). When consulting with a school district on workshop ap-

---

[11] See my extended discussion of this story, and the two sequels it inspired, in chapter three of Lensmire (1994).

proaches, one of her colleagues was met at the airport by a group of teachers who said that they were relieved that she had come, for they had embraced the writing workshop dictum that children could choose their own topics, and it had led to a problem. The problem? All over the school, students were writing about farts. Calkins's colleague told the teachers to tell the students to stop it, and the teachers responded with surprise — they could do that in a writing workshop approach? Calkins (1991) concludes: "We laugh and think, 'How silly.' But it's not silly. It's sad. The problem is not that kids are writing about farts but that some of us have lost confidence in our ability to think for ourselves within the writing conference" (p. 228).

This is a fair enough moral to the story, especially given the larger context of low teacher status in our country and continued attacks on teachers and schools for putting the very survival of our nation at risk. But there is another moral, another problem lurking in Calkins's story. For me, the problem is that workshop approaches have an impoverished view of the ends toward which children might put their writing.

Workshop approaches have traditionally emphasized personal narrative. Children's writing remains cozily wrapped in a romantic rhetoric that portrays it as "the innocent perceptions of children making individual sense of the world and their role in it" (Gilbert, 1989, p. 199). Rajesh, James, and the children writing about farts were pushing writing in another direction that sought to upset and challenge aspects of their world — a direction that might, with support, grow into mature forms of parody or criticism.

I am sure that the students who were writing about farts were just "having fun." But surely part of the fun was knowing that, within the relative freedom of the writing workshop, they had found a topic to write about that made authority figures nervous. Writing workshops created a small space for expressing a part of life that is traditionally closed off in school, and the kids exploited that space. Calkins's colleague suggested that these children should just stop it. Maybe so. But the responses of Calkins and her colleagues suggest to me that workshop advocates assume that once traditional social relations and school tasks are transformed in the writing workshop, students will have nothing left to challenge, criticize, and abuse. These advocates tend not to consider the broader social, cultural, and political aspects of children's present and future lives, and pay scant attention to the benefits for children that might come with helping them oppose and criticize aspects of their world (Lensmire, 1994).

For Bakhtin, carnival abuse represented an explicit collective struggle against an oppressive social order. At best, writing workshops, as currently imagined, might allow individual dissent. At worst, they might shut down even this, because their guiding visions provide no real resource for making sense of and responding to student resistance and opposition.

I have argued that writing workshop life contrasts to the "second life" of Bakhtin's carnival in its lack of profanation, even as individual students sometimes push their writing toward such an "abusive" end. In the next section, I conclude my examination of workshops by articulating a problem that is common to both the writing of workshop advocates and Bakhtin's writing on carnival. Carnival abuse, it turns out, is not the only sort of abuse that is possible within the relative openness of carnivals and writing workshops.

A Shared Uncritical Populism

When the restraining hand of traditional authority was loosened during the actual carnivals of the Middle Ages and Renaissance, it was not only powerful groups and the official ideology that were open to abuse and mockery. Burke (1978), for example, tells of a London festival in 1512 that became the occasion for the massacre and expulsion of foreigners. In certain instances, powerful groups used the openness of carnival to their own advantage; in others, relatively powerless groups *turned against even more powerless groups.*[12] Thus, even as carnival provides opportunities for freedom and equality and a protected space for antiofficial activity and discourse, it also "often violently abuses and demonizes weaker, not stronger, social groups — women, ethnic and religious minorities, those who 'don't belong'" (Stallybrass & White, 1986, p. 19).

I have been similarly concerned with how children treat one another in the carnival atmosphere of the writing workshop. Workshop advocates have assumed that the classroom communities students and teachers create for themselves in writing workshops will be supportive and productive *for everyone.* Dressman (1993) points to increasing concern by educators and researchers that this is not the case, especially for minority, working-class, and female students. Thus, an important criticism that Stallybrass and White (1986) and others level at Bakhtin's work on carnival — namely, that it embraces an uncritical populism — also holds for the writing of workshop advocates. Although these advocates are concerned that teachers take action to help students interact with each other in supportive ways — and their books contain helpful suggestions toward this end — ultimately workshop advocates overestimate (as I did) the effectiveness of such teacherly interventions. They also overestimate the goodwill and openness that students have toward one another, especially across lines of social class, gender, and race.

My characterization above of free and familiar contact among children in the writing workshop was quite similar to the portrayals of peer relations in workshop literature. Atwell (1987), for example, who writes from her experiences as a teacher of eighth graders, asserts that

> within the structure of a writing workshop, students decide who can give the kind of help they need as they need it. . . . Small groups form and disband in the minutes it takes for a writer to call on one or more other

---

[12] See Gardiner (1992, p. 182) for a brief overview of historical studies of carnival.

writers, move to a conference corner, share a piece or discuss a problem, and go back to work with a new perspective on the writing. (p. 41)

My worry is that this openness and fluidity is only apparent, that beneath it are more stable patterns of peer relations among children that divide them, subordinate some to others, and routinely deny certain children the help and support that others receive from peers.

In our third-grade workshop, when given the choice, girls worked with girls, and boys with boys. And the boys and girls who lived in the trailer park were at the bottom of informal peer hierarchies of status and power in the classroom. The experiences of Jessie — one of the children at the bottom of the peer pecking order — help us understand what is at stake here and suggest the importance of considering seriously the peer relations that children work out with increased control over their own work and lives in the workshop.

Jessie was the classroom's "female pariah," ostracized by nearly everyone "by virtue of gender, but also through some added stigma such as being overweight or poor" (Thorne, 1986, p. 175). Jessie was not small, and she came from the trailer park. Nearly everyone in the class, in their interviews, said that she was the least popular person in the class and the least desirable to work with. Bruce, for example, called her "idiotic, dumb," John said that she stank, and Mary said that Jessie never brushed her teeth. Only a few children said that they had worked with her in the class.

Grace and I often intervened in verbal fights between Jessie and other children. For example, when I arrived at school one Wednesday morning in February, I saw Robert and Suzanne, among others, yelling at Jessie, calling her "zit face."[13] I told them to stop it and made a point to walk up to Jessie

---

[13] Oral abuse using "zits" — in the form of "zit face" and "zit man" and "zit fit" — worked its way into several children's writing (see Lensmire, 1993). Thus, children's social relations were expressed not only in their talk and actions within and without the workshop, but also in their texts. An example is provided by Sharon and Carol, who described how certain boys used writing to tease girls in the class:

Sharon: They used girls' names that, that liked other boys.
Interviewer: Oh, and if-
Carol: I think they used me with David, I'm not sure.
Sharon: They used me with um, Ken.
Interviewer: How do you feel about that?
Sharon: I didn't like it.
Interviewer: Why?
Sharon: Because you don't like somebody to use your name.
Interviewer: What can we do about that to change that?
Sharon: I told them not to write it and I told them, and they, they kept on writing and then I told Mrs. Parker and they erased my name out of it. Then they would write the story, they kept on saying that, um, that somebody in the story liked another person. (Interview, 5-30-90)

Boys wrote stories that named Sharon and Carol as characters. Within these stories, Sharon and Carol were supposed to like other boys in the class. In her study of gender relations among elementary school children, Thorne (1986) found that teasing such as "Carol likes David" was a "major form of

and say good morning. Jessie paused long enough to say hello before continuing her own verbal defense and attack.

These verbal fights continued over the next few days. I wrote in my notes that "Jessie has been doing battle with Mary, Suzanne, Carol, and even sometimes, it seems, her friends Karen and Janis. But primarily with Suzanne and Mary" (Fieldnotes, 2-9-90). That Friday, I discovered that attacks on Jessie had found their way into print. When the children left for lunch, I noticed a child's text in the wastebasket. It was a story entitled, "The Killers in Mr. Lensmire's Class":

> When we got into the classroom on Monday morning we heard singing. It was Jil, Jessie, and Paul. They were singing a dumb song that went like this: Let's get together, ya, ya, ya. Mrs. Parker was out of the classroom. Then Lisa shot Jessie in the back. AAAAAH! Jessie said with a scream!

I do not know who the author was, or why he or she threw it away, but Jessie was being attacked both in real life and as a fictional character.

In her interview, Jessie said that she had only a few friends in the class — Janis and Karen (both from the trailer park) — and a few students in the other third-grade class. She said she sometimes had conferences with Janis and Karen and shared her finished pieces with them, but usually she kept her work to herself. Although she published four books during the year, she did not share them either during sharing time or in the writing workshop library. She often had conferences with me, Grace, and the teacher aide. In contrast to many of her classmates, Jessie looked almost exclusively to adults as audiences. When asked if there were things about the workshop that she did not like, she said, "Sometimes I didn't like it was when Mr. Lensmire couldn't get to me [for a writing conference]. I didn't like that" (Interview, 5-30-90).

There were other children who seemed to prefer adults as audiences over peers, but most children in the workshop enjoyed and valued conferences with classmates, and shared their work with the class in sharing sessions. In fact, because they valued their interactions with peers, the opportunity to have conferences and share their work with classmates was one of the most positive aspects of the workshop for these third graders.

But not just any peers. Children in the workshop *sought and avoided* specific peer audiences in their daily interactions in the classroom. Children accomplished this by selecting with whom they held conferences and collaborated on their texts.

---

teasing, which a child risks in choosing to sit by or walk with someone of the other sex" (p. 52) and that such teasing functioned to emphasize and maintain gender boundaries.

In the workshop, children created stories that teased other children by associating them, as story characters, with members of the other sex. They created stories that drew on gender arrangements (as well as social-class differences) for their meaning and impact.

In general, *children worked with friends within gender boundaries.* All children identified other children with whom they did and did not want to have conferences — in other words, they made inclusions and exclusions, and these differentiations were often associated with social class and gender differences. Karen, for example, spoke for boys and girls in the class when she stated that "the boys like the boys, but the girls like the girls" for peer conferences (Interview, 5-21-90). In Mary and Lori's interview, Mary was quite explicit (as were most boys and girls) about whom she did and did not want to work with: "I like working with Carol, Lisa, Marie, Sharon, Emily, Julie, and Suzanne. And I don't like working with the boys" (Interview, 5-31-90). Mary's list of girls, except possibly for Emily and Julie, is a fairly complete naming of the most popular girls in the class. She was also forthcoming about girls with whom she did not want to work and why. Mary said that "some of them had lice, they stunk," and she did not like their "styles" or their personalities.

> *Mary:* Most of them, and some of them are from the trailer park and I don't like working with people who are from the trailer park. . . . Like at first I thought that Lori was from the trailer park before I went over to her house the first time.
>
> *Lori:* Thanks a lot.
>
> *Mary:* Well I did.

Jessie was from the trailer park, and she decided that it was too risky to share her stories with peers. After identifying children with whom she did not want to have conferences, Jessie described how she would feel if she were forced to do so:

> *Interviewer:* What would they do with your writing? How would you feel if you had to conference with them?
>
> *Jessie:* I would feel like a jar of slime. Being sat on.
>
> *Interviewer:* So maybe they don't treat you very well?
>
> *Jessie:* Yes. No, like getting cut in half. (Interview, 5-30-90)

Later, she said that she never shared in front of the whole class because they would make her feel the same way in that situation. She declined my numerous offers to have her share with small groups of classmates.

From the beginning, I worked to make the writing workshop, and its conferences and sharing times, a safe place for children to write and share their work. We did many activities to help children respond to each other's writing in helpful, respectful ways. Obviously, these "teacher" efforts by Grace and myself were not enough to make the classroom a safe place for Jessie to share her work with peers. When asked why other people felt comfortable sharing their stories in front of class, Jessie said, "Because they have lots of friends."

One of the consequences of Jessie's relations with her peers was that her writing was never shared publicly in the workshop. Most children never encountered Jessie's retelling of "Sleeping Beauty":

> Once upon a time there was a beautiful princess, and her name was Jessie. One day, she was sleeping, and she heard a noise so she got up and went upstairs to the room upstairs. When she opened the door she saw a spinning wheel.
>
> When she was spinning at the spinning wheel, she poked her finger. Suddenly she fell asleep, and everyone fell asleep too. Just then a prince came.
>
> He snuck into the castle and found the princess and kissed her. And suddenly everybody awoke and the prince became an empire.

Bruner (1990) believes that the stories we tell and write "mediate between the canonical world of culture and the more idiosyncratic world of beliefs, desires, and hopes" (p. 52). If I understand him correctly, Bruner is saying that our stories represent a sort of compromise between privileged versions of how the world is (given to us in the "canonical world of culture") and how we, as individuals, would like the world to be. When we tell stories, we draw on given, cultural narratives about the world and our place in it, and we manipulate and twist these narratives in ways that express our "idiosyncratic worlds."

The twists Jessie gave to a more canonical version of "Sleeping Beauty" (from the Grimms [1883], for example) are charming, and suggest self-importance, youth, and movement. Her crowned princess is named Jessie, instead of Rosamond. Jessie, the author (as well as Jessie the princess), avoids altogether the angry witch who casts a death spell on the young princess, and the good witch who transmutes that spell to sleep. Jessie seems impatient with sleep, so she has her princess "suddenly" fall asleep, only to be awakened almost immediately by a prince who "just then" arrived. In the Grimm version, the two live happily ever after together. Jessie's princess and prince may do likewise, but Jessie leaves this open. Jessie, however, is not content with some sort of romantic bliss for the two. Her version ends with the rise to power of her prince: He became an empire (sic).

Jessie's story may also be read against another "canonical world of culture" — the peer culture in which Jessie participated. The rift between the canonical peer world and Jessie's more idiosyncratic one is wide, and leaves the peer world looking anything but charming (in fact, a little grim) for Jessie. In the peer culture, Jessie was not beautiful in the stories others told and wrote about her. She labored to avoid those who would cast spells to "cut her in half" or turn her into a "jar of slime." The school year was long, and she had little chance of association (nor did she say she wanted it) with the powerful.

Jessie wrote herself and her vision of the world on the page, but others seldom heard her voice or saw her vision, at least not in the public spaces the workshop provided. Jessie thought that those spaces were for people with "lots of friends."

Most children had enough friends to make free and familiar contact with peers at least a mixed blessing. But there is an underside to children's relations that workshop advocates have not confronted. As in carnival, workshop participants sometimes use the free and playful space not to work out humane new relations, not to lampoon and discredit an unjust, official order, but to reassert and reinforce ugly aspects of exactly that same unjust, larger society. Abuse in carnival (and the writing workshop) is not, as Bakhtin wanted it to be, solely aimed at worthy objects of uncrowning. Some targets are chosen because they are easy targets, because already uncrowned, never crowned.

CONCLUDING COMMENTS

I have examined writing workshops as a form of carnival in order to highlight important, liberatory aspects of workshop life, and to identify problems that threaten to undermine its positive force. I have pointed to active participation, free and familiar contact among people, and a playful, familiar relation to the world as positive features of writing workshops that we should affirm. And I have questioned the individualistic and uncritical visions that guide current workshop approaches — visions that provide precious few resources for understanding, supporting, and criticizing the diverse ends to which children might put their talk and texts in writing workshops.

In future work on writing workshops, at least three broad topics need critical examination and development: student voice and self-expression, the teacher's role and responsibilities, and workshops as communities for writing and learning.

The writings of workshop advocates are replete with romantic portrayals of innocent, straightforward children pursuing individual writing projects within the workshop. Such portrayals help workshop advocates ignore serious problems and issues that attend workshop commitments to student self-expression and control — for example, the problem of children pursuing questionable intentions and material in their texts, such as when a violent, sexist story (with thinly veiled attacks on a female classmate) represents the "authentic voice" of a group of boys during sharing time (Gilbert, 1989). What if, as Willinsky (1990) asks, the "self finally expressed in student writing is not the one we were hoping to see emerge" (p. 94)? An alternative conception of student voice is required — one in which finding your own voice is not (as in the romantic version) burrowing to some authentic nature, but appropriating the myriad voices and words surrounding you, and forcing them to your own purposes (Lensmire, 1994; Ritchie, 1989).

An alternative conception of student voice and expression also requires revisions of current conceptions of teacher practice in writing workshops. Workshop advocates have consistently criticized the traditional, controlling, fault-finding writing teacher, and promoted instead a supportive teacher who finds meaning and who shares the craft of writing with students. The role they have imagined for teachers, however, assumes that teachers will never have to take up a critical stance in relation to children's work and, consequently, drastically underestimates the sort of intellectual, moral/political, and aesthetic influence and leadership actually required of writing teachers if they are to be responsible in their work with children.[14]

Finally, the examination of workshops as communities of writers and learners is crucial. My students and I created a community within the writing workshop, and children's writing emerged from and contributed to that community. The classroom community we created was important for the experiences and learning of the children, Grace, and myself. If, as Harris (1989) asserts, we "write not as isolated individuals but as members of communities whose beliefs, concerns, and practices both instigate and constrain, at least in part, the sorts of things we can say" (p. 12), then we had better pay attention to the communities we create in writing classrooms.

With the help of Bakhtin's work on carnival, I have tried to pay attention. Writing workshop approaches have the potential to contribute to the creation of more humane and just forms of life in school and society — a potential grounded in workshop commitments to help students engage in meaningful activity and take up open, learning relations with each other and the world. The absence of Jessie and her Sleeping Beauty from the public spaces of our workshop, however, reminds us that transformed peer relations represent both promise and problem in our progressive pedagogies. In the open, engaging, laughing, playing workshop-carnival, students have something to say about who speaks and who is heard. We ignore what they are saying at our children's and our own peril.

REFERENCES

Atwell, N. (1987). *In the middle: Writing, reading, and learning with adolescents.* Portsmouth, NH: Boynton/Cook.

Bakhtin, M. M. (1981). *The dialogic imagination.* Austin: University of Texas Press.

---

[14] I sketch a possible direction for a revised teacher practice in workshops in the final chapter of Lensmire (1994). I argue for an engaged, pluralistic classroom community, developed from work on American pragmatism by Bernstein (1988), and propose two changes to workshop approaches that I think would help create and sustain such a community: 1) a critically pragmatic (Cherryholmes, 1988) teacher response to children's texts that concerns itself with, among other things, the rhetorical play of children's texts in the classroom community; and 2) an increased curricular role for teachers in the workshop, in the creation of collective writing projects that would help children work critically with texts.

Bakhtin, M. M. (1984a). *Problems of Dostoyevsky's poetics.* Minneapolis: University of Minnesota Press.

Bakhtin, M. M. (1984b). *Rabelais and his world.* Bloomington: Indiana University Press.

Bakhtin, M. M. (1986). *Speech genres and other late essays.* Austin: University of Texas Press.

Berlin, J. (1988). Rhetoric and ideology in the writing class. *College English, 50,* 477–494.

Bernstein, R. J. (1988). Pragmatism, pluralism, and the healing of wounds. *American Philosophical Association Proceedings, 63*(3), 5–18.

Bogdan, R. C., & Biklen, S. K. (1982). *Qualitative research for education: An introduction to theory and methods.* Boston: Allyn & Bacon.

Burke, P. (1978). *Popular culture in early modern Europe.* New York: New York University Press.

Bruner, J. (1990). *Acts of meaning.* Cambridge, MA: Harvard University Press.

Calkins, L. M. (1986). *The art of teaching writing.* Portsmouth, NH: Heinemann.

Calkins, L. M. (1991). *Living between the lines.* Portsmouth, NH: Heinemann.

Cazden, C. B. (1986). Classroom discourse. In M. C. Wittrock (Ed.), *Handbook of research on teaching* (3rd ed., pp. 432–463). New York: Macmillan.

Cherryholmes, C. (1988). *Power and criticism: Poststructural investigations in education.* New York: Teachers College Press.

Cohen, D. (1988). Teaching practice: Plus ça change. . . . In P. Jackson (Ed.), *Contributing to educational change: Perspectives on research and practice* (pp. 27–84). Berkeley, CA: McCutchan.

Davies, B. (1993). *Shards of glass: Children reading and writing beyond gendered identities.* Cresskill, NJ: Hampton.

Dressman, M. (1993). Lionizing lone wolves: The cultural romantics of literacy workshops. *Curriculum Inquiry, 23,* 245–263.

Elbow, P. (1973). *Writing without teachers.* London: Oxford University Press.

Erickson, F. (1986). Qualitative methods in research on teaching. In M. C. Wittrock (Ed.), *Handbook on research on teaching* (3rd ed., pp. 119–161). New York: Macmillan.

Erickson, F., & Shultz, J. (1992). Students' experience of the curriculum. In P. Jackson (Ed.), *Handbook of research on curriculum* (pp. 465–485). New York: Macmillan.

Florio-Ruane, S. (1991). Instructional conversations in learning to write and learning to teach. In L. Idol & B. Jones (Eds.), *Educational values and cognitive instruction: Implications for reform* (pp. 365–386). New York: Erlbaum.

Gardiner, M. (1992). *The dialogics of critique: M. M. Bakhtin and the theory of ideology.* London: Routledge.

Gilbert, P. (1989). Student text as pedagogical text. In S. deCastell, A. Luke, & C. Luke (Eds.), *Language, authority and criticism: Readings on the school textbook* (pp. 195–202). London: Falmer Press.

Goethe, J. W. (1970). *Italian journey* (W. H. Auden & E. Mayer, Trans.). London: Penguin.

Graves, D. (1983). *Writing: Teachers and children at work.* Portsmouth, NH: Heinemann.

Graves, D., & Hansen, J. (1983). The author's chair. *Language Arts, 60,* 176–183.

Grimm, J., & Grimm, W. (1883). *Household stories* (L. Crane, Trans.). New York: R. Worthington.

Hammersly, M., & Atkinson, P. (1983). *Ethnography: Principles in practice.* London: Tavistock.

Harris, J. (1989). The idea of community in the study of writing. *College Composition and Communication, 40,* 11–22.

hooks, b. (1989). *Talking back: Thinking feminist, thinking Black.* Boston: South End Press.

Kristeva, J. (1986). Word, dialogue and novel. In T. Moi (Ed.), *The Kristeva reader* (pp. 34–61). New York: Columbia University Press.

LaCapra, D. (1983). *Rethinking intellectual history: Texts, contexts, language.* Ithaca, NY: Cornell University Press.

Lensmire, T. (1993). Following the child, socioanalysis and threats to community: Teacher response to children's texts. *Curriculum Inquiry, 23,* 265–299.

Lensmire, T. (1994). *When children write: Critical re-visions of the writing workshop*. New York: Teachers College Press.

Lensmire, T., & Beals, D. (1994). Appropriating other's words: Traces of literature and peer culture in a third grader's writing. *Language in Society, 23*, 411–426.

Murray, D. (1985). *A writer teaches writing*. Boston: Houghton Mifflin.

Ritchie, J. (1989). Beginning writers: Diverse voices and individual identity. *College Composition and Communication, 40*, 152–174.

Stallybrass, P., & White, A. (1986). *The politics and poetics of transgression*. Ithaca, NY: Cornell University Press.

Thorne, B. (1986). Girls and boys together . . . but mostly apart: Gender arrangements in elementary schools. In W. Hartup & Z. Rubin (Eds.), *Relationships and development* (pp. 167–184). Hillsdale, NJ: Lawrence Erlbaum.

Ulichney, P., & Watson-Gegeo, K. (1989). Interactions and authority: The dominant interpretative framework in writing conferences. *Discourse Processes, 12*, 309–328.

Willinsky, J. (1990). *The new literacy: Redefining reading and writing in the schools*. New York: Routledge.

I would like to thank Diane Beals, Mary Ann Dzuback, Jane Lensmire, and Lauren Sosniak for their encouragement and responses to early versions of this article. I gratefully acknowledge the support of The National Academy of Education and its Spencer Fellowship Program.

Mathematics Workshop as Carnival?
A Response to Lensmire

To the Editor:

I note that you encourage responses to articles that have appeared in the *Harvard Educational Review* and would like to respond to Timothy Lensmire's article, "Writing Workshop as Carnival: Reflections on an Alternative Learning Environment," in the Winter 1994 edition.

Lensmire's Carnival analogy is both interesting and productive in yielding insights into writers' workshops. I should like to extend it. Given the anti-establishment orientation of Carnival, one might speculate as to why the medieval authorities tolerated it. However, Carnival was, in fact, only superficially anti-authoritarian: Although it took an anti-establishment form, its effect was, in fact, supportive of the status quo. For Carnival happened for a fixed period only, and was bracketed by normality, so its function was cathartic rather than transformative. This explains why ridicule of authority figures was often imprecisely directed and therefore innocuous, whereas the tendency, which Lensmire notes, for the weak to assail the weaker was much more personally targeted. For once Carnival was over, the powerful resumed their power, and the possibility that the face behind the mask might have been glimpsed was sufficient disincentive for too personalised an attack. On the other hand, the license to rub in the mud the faces of those at the bottom of the pile only served to reinforce the hierarchy through the year.

This raises two key questions for writers' workshops: First, how are the excesses of personal attacks on the weakest members of the class to be circumvented? Second, are writers' workshops to remain isolated oddities where the normalities of schooling do not apply, or to become a means of transforming the realities of the pedagogical relationship?

My tentative solutions to both these questions are based on several years of teaching writers' workshops with seven- to ten-year-olds. Rather than accepting at face value the claims of Donald Graves and the other "romantic" proponents of writers' workshops, I have felt the need, like most practitioners, to adapt them.

Educators working on anti-racist initiatives have found that it is not enough to seek to create a micro-culture where the trappings of racism are not countenanced. Racism in the wider world has to be identified and acknowledged; only in this way can it be countered. Similarly, it is not enough in writers' workshops just to say to students, "Here's the power. You take it." The relationship of teachers to power in a school is bound to be different from that of the students; the teacher cannot get rid of it or wish it away.

Harvard Educational Review Vol. 65 No. 4 Winter 1995, 668–680

Writers' workshops allow a wonderful opportunity for raising the issues of power with children. By allowing them access to the power of the word, you are changing the balance, but they have also to realise that there is no power without responsibility and that what they take has to be negotiated for. In practical terms, this means using sharing sessions as a springboard for discussion of issues such as the effect of writing on different audiences, the difference between fiction and lies, the meaning and consequences of the terms libel and slander, and the power of fantasy. These discussions may lead to agreed guidelines such as, "You cannot name anybody you know without their consent," as well as to the more co-ordinated projects, mentioned by Lensmire in his footnote where the whole class collaborates on a project such as a collection of folk tales from a different perspective.

If the benefits that writers' workshops provide in student motivation and independence are to be properly exploited, then ways must be sought of allowing the relationships which develop between the students and between teacher and children to continue in other contexts. This calls into question the whole organisation of the classroom — what does a mathematician's workshop look like? Once again, the key to this process is negotiation based on the principle that teachers and pupils do have different agendas and that both are in different ways accountable.

The idea of writers' workshops as Carnival is helpful in thinking through some of the issues, but if this approach to learning is to be fully exploited, then we need to see how the lessons of the few mad days of riotous colour can be used to brighten up the sombreness of the rest of the year.

JOHN PRYOR
Research Fellow
Teacher Assessment at Key Stage One
Institute of Education
University of Sussex
Falmer, Brighton, UK

Transforming Pedagogy — Classrooms as Mathematical Communities: A Response to Lensmire and Pryor

Advocates of writing workshop approaches seek to move traditional writing instruction in school away from an emphasis on mechanics and form and away from teacher control of topics. The problem, as writing workshop advocates see it, is that school writing inhibits children and that children lack opportunities to develop voice and to play with language and text. According to Lensmire, "with the support of the teacher and numerous opportunities to collaborate and share texts with peers, children (in writing workshop classrooms) are supposed to gradually become more and more able to realize their intentions in text" (1994a, p. 3). A romantic image is of children writing about topics, ideas, and experiences that matter to them. Unfettered by teacherly control, young writers are freed to express themselves, to explore, critique, and remake their worlds, to play with language and form. Teachers serve as interested audience to their students' work, seeking to understand children's projects, and offering help and advice in support (Roosevelt, in press).

With classrooms more open to student voice, the cacophony is not always pleasant, however. Some students produce texts that are troubling, and for which teachers feel unprepared: Roosevelt (in press) describes his struggles with a young boy's violent story, filled with blood and horror, and Lensmire (1993) exposes and explores his experience with children using their writing to hurt or demean classmates along class and gender lines. Teachers are in the difficult position of trying to understand whether their young authors are calling for help, seeking to tantalize and shock, or critically challenging the world they see around them. As teachers open their classrooms to the world, inviting students to engage in meaningful work, the world creeps into school. It is a two-way street. This connection, envisioned and promoted by John Dewey over seventy-five years ago, is one about which we still have a lot to understand as we develop our visions of what we want schools to be places for (Dewey, 1900/1956).

Watching all this in his own classroom, Lensmire draws on Bakhtin to propose a view of writing workshop as carnival, a space and time within the institution of school in which young people can freely play, turn the world upside down, and experiment. Yet, as he points out, "the bite of carnival" — its potential to use expression to challenge larger societal problems and to seek change — is "blunted" because the writing workshop vision, as promoted by its vocal advocates, contains no such political agenda (Lensmire, 1994b, p. 379). Choices of content or intention are left to individual child-writers, while the focus of pedagogical change is on the more structural and relational issues of children's control over time, purposes, and interactions. Lensmire wonders how to develop the writers' workshop to become a deliberate forum for collectively engaged social critique and change. He envisions projects in which children might jointly examine, challenge, and change the texts of the worlds they inhabit. His questions point the development of the writing workshop explicitly outward, toward *society*.

Pryor, too, wonders — but differently — about the extension of the writing workshop. He turns the issue on its side, observing that if writing workshops are to leverage significant change, they must be used to transform schools beyond the teaching and learning of writing. While Lensmire seeks to use writing workshop as a forum for children to read, write, and rewrite the *world*, Pryor seeks to use writing workshop as a lever for a broader reconstruction of *school*. He asks what mathematics class might look like, for example, were it to be remodeled in the spirit of writers' workshop. How could the possibility and spirit of the workshop inspire wider change in *school*?

As is the case with traditional school writing, school math is also a target of complaint. Consider what is typical in most U.S. mathematics classes: children spend their time practicing procedures presented by teachers, performing calculations, and going over homework; the mathematics in which children engage consists of algorithms, procedures, and terminology; teachers show and tell, but students are only expected to copy and practice. Math classes have not typically abounded with language, aims, or imagination. Although many students have found it difficult, for too many, mathematics has not been the challenging, exciting kind of difficult. Additionally, school mathematics has served as a barrier for many groups of students. The image of a math classes inspired by greater connection to the real world and greater personal sense of student ownership seems both reasonable and appealing.

Paradoxically, in either writing or mathematics, a first step seems to be to get a solid pocket of activity where the tasks, the discourse, the relationships, and the climate are different from those that characterize either the rest of school or the outside world. The writing workshop has succeeded as a function of its novelty; indeed, Lensmire's view of the workshop as carnival, a world apart from the routines of school life, reveals it as a space where a relaxation of "the grip of established norms and relations" allowed a productive freedom to be, think, and act (1994a, p. 373). Still, as both Lensmire and Pryor point out, life within the protected pocket can remain detached from the larger realities of school and society.

The very thing that has made school math the target of critics — that it is disconnected from the everyday worlds and realities of children — has, however, made it a more protected pocket of the school day. Less dependent on unevenly distributed cultural capital, mathematics has often been a path for working-class students to break academic barriers. It has been an arena in which a limited English speaker could participate successfully. To make mathematics more connected to the surrounding world may increase interest, but ironically risks lessening access.

In my own teaching of young children, I have seen this risk as a dilemma inherent in the work of reconstructing the context and content of school math. The school in which I have taught for over fifteen years is diverse culturally and linguistically, with a multinational population, including students from countries in Africa, the Middle East, and the Far East. The U.S. students are from all over the country, and almost half of them are children of color. Although over half the class qualifies for free lunch, they are mostly middle class. Their parents are enrolled at Michigan State, either in the English Language Center or in undergraduate or graduate programs. There is a high mobility rate in this school, and students arrive and leave all year. Few students remain in the school for more than two or three years.

In this setting, mathematical work situated in the everyday worlds of my students sometimes divides and differentiates in ways that can lose the mathematics. Take the following incidental, but telling, example: It was the first day of school. As students introduced themselves, I asked them to tell what year they were born. Using the year, I asked the class if they could figure out how old the child was. Cassandra, a tall African American girl, offered 1979 as her year of birth. When children clamored that she was ten, she shook her head. Born in December, she was still nine in September. The mathematical puzzle of it all was engaging to some of the children. How could Cassandra be nine and yet be born in 1979, ten years earlier? A few worked to solve the mystery. But some students also sneered. How could Cassandra not even know how old she was? Cassandra stood in front of her classmates silently, and I cringed. The resource of the children's everyday real interests and needs was intertwined with the students' accustomed out-of-school relations and ways of knowing. Familiarity brought with it, insidiously, patterns I wanted to deconstruct.

Across time, I observed that using the outside world as a context for my young children's mathematical development at times invited in that world in ways that seemed, paradoxically, to deflate the transformative possibilities of our pursuits. Sometimes it was because personal examples and contexts created arenas for meanness or disrespect. At other times it was that concrete contexts were unevenly familiar or interesting to boys and girls, to international and U.S. children, to children with big families and children with no siblings living with a single parent. As a result, the children were distracted or confused, or the differences among them were accentuated in ways that diminished the sense of collective purpose and joint work.[1] Whether or not using such everyday contexts is wise is not the right question. Using school to explore, analyze, and challenge differences makes sense. However, whether situating mathematics in the everyday world is the best way to transform mathematics in school is a question worth asking. And, given the status of mathematics in our society, whether it is the best way to gain access to the power of mathematics for all children is also worthy of attention.

What else might a mathematician's workshop be? How might the practice of mathematics animate a different kind of mathematical work for children in school? What might be its nature? What might be its purposes? Over the past fifteen years, I have repeatedly been impressed with the fascination that "pure mathematics" holds for young children from diverse cultural backgrounds. Unlike the parade of drill worksheets, and similarly unlike the applied problems of "everyday situations," theoretical explorations often intensely engage young children. Rarely do I see students become as engrossed as when they are debating whether zero is an even or an odd number, what a sensible answer might be to $6 + (-6)$, or from which bag one would be more likely to pull a green chip:

[1] See Buchmann and Schwille (1983), and also Floden, Buchmann, and Schwille (1987).

2 green chips   3 green chips
2 yellow chips   4 yellow chips

Theoretically, none of these relies directly on students' outside experiences. Not necessarily reliant on or connected to the outside world, these investigations often seem paradoxically more inclusive. And, with theory and abstraction central, they provide opportunities to engage fundamental aspects of mathematics that comprise some of its unique contributions to human experience and interpretation.

Take an example from later in the same school year of the birth date discussion. The third and fourth graders (many of the fourth graders were students I had taught the previous year) were holding a "meeting" — a joint discussion for which both classes had prepared — about whether zero was an even or an odd number. A brief glimpse of the discussion offers a view of the intensity with which the children were exploring the nature of zero, and what it means for a number to be even. The first position argued was by Arif, an Iraqi fourth grader.[2] He argued:

> I think zero's *even* because, take an even number like, maybe 10 and if you keep on going down to like, 8 is even, and 6 is even, and if you get like to zero, and I don't think it's odd or a special number because like, negative 1 is odd, and 1 is odd, so in between that I think it should be *even.*

Valerie, a White fourth-grade girl, offered a different perspective:

> I'm going to argue that, um, zero isn't even or odd. It's special . . . I think um, zero is special because zero's kind of like, nothing. There was not really even or odd. Um, because it's just there, it's not really anything. When you go through the numbers you hit zero and it's kind of like nothing. So, it's just, I think it's special because you can't really even or odd because it's nothing.

This generated a bit of discussion. Sipho, an African American fourth grader, asked Valerie if she was arguing that zero was not a *number*. "Well, it's a number, but it isn't even or odd. It's just nothing, but it really is a number," she replied thoughtfully. I asked the class if there were questions they wanted to ask Valerie. Tembe, a Black third grader from Kenya, said there were "other zeroes," and gave as an example, the number 50. He wanted to know if she thought 50 was nothing, too, since it had a zero in it. Valerie did not quite seem to understand what he was raising:

[2] Note: children's names are pseudonyms.

Oh, no, 50 is *something*. 50, like, you can have 50 things, but if you have zero things there's nothing.

Riba, a third-grade girl from Egypt, picked up on Tembe's point and connected it to something another child had said:

Is, that's the same thing Sean brought up, like um, everybody, well, most people think um that if zero isn't anything, then 50 shouldn't be a number because if you took off the zero it would just be 5.

Valerie was beginning to get it:

I'm not really sure. I think it's just the zero afterwards is to show that you don't have like 51 or something yet. I think it's just to show that you've got a 10 and you've got no ones yet.

Scott, a White fourth grader, raised his hand and said, "I agree because zero is like trapped in between the negative numbers and the normal numbers, so I don't really think it's nothing. I don't think it's even or odd."

Ball: So you're agreeing with Valerie?
Scott: Yeah.
Ball: Tembe?
Tembe: I think I'm going to agree with Arif.
Ball: Do you want to say why?
Tembe: I agree with Arif because, if you go 10, 9, 8 and you get to 1, then it would be odd, then if you go one more it would be zero and it would be even. So I agree with Arif.
Ball: Sheena?
Sheena: I think I agree with Valerie because I sort of think that zero isn't an even number or an odd number, it's kind of there when you need it. It's like you don't need it all the time, but it's there when you need it.

The discussion continued. Students clarified what particular students had said, agreed and disagreed with previous speakers, added to previously made comments, and introduced new points. Agreeing on the definition of even numbers ("numbers you can split in half without having to cut anything in half"), students nonetheless reached different conclusions:

Bob: If you take like, say 2, you can split that in half to make one on each side, but if you have zero there's nothing to split on each side.
Riba: This is what Betsy said last time. She said that, um, if you have zero things on each side you cut it in half and there's zero on each side.

Students changed their minds as they listened. They worked at understanding what others were saying, listening generously and curiously.[3] At no time was anyone openly disparaging or disrespectful of others' ideas. The level of engagement was intense; indeed, getting them to end the discussion and go out to recess was difficult. And this discussion was no anomaly in the class. Few topics interested the children as intensely as number theory, about which they had many ideas and theories: Are negative numbers the same as zero? How many numbers are there? Is six both an even and an odd number since it has three groups of two, and three is an odd number?[4]

Three points stand out here, one about the content, one about the discourse, and a third about the culture of the classroom. First, the students were attracted to an esoteric bit of mathematics, filled with the fascination of the number zero and the orderliness and patterns of definition. Nothing about the content or the task related to the students' everyday lives, or to a "real world." Neither useful or practical, it was nonetheless engrossing. And so engrossed, their activity was as much play as intellectual pursuit. Zero appeals to children's fancy, not unlike the appeals of magical characters in fiction they read and write. Exploring what zero might be capable of being and doing is an activity of imagination for eight- and nine-year-olds.

Second, they were participating in a mathematical discourse, considering arguments, relying on previously agreed-upon definitions, wrestling with consistencies and contradictions, and changing their ideas. They were trying to push what they thought and understood about the topic at hand. At one point, Bob suggested that the class ask a mathematician. David was skeptical that this would tell them much:

David: Um, just because you ask a mathematician doesn't mean that you . . . that the mathematician is going to be right all of the time, because mathematicians are people . . .

Bob: I know, but I never said that they always were right.

David: I know, but you said if you ask a mathematician, you said you'd have to ask a mathematician . . .

Bob: Well, I mean, maybe they might not.

David: Nobody knows.

A couple of months later, a professional mathematician visited the class. Almost immediately, several of the children demanded to know if he thought zero was even or odd. Although he responded that zero was an even number, this assertion did not satisfy those who believed it to be a special number. Weeks later, Betsy reminded the class about this at one point as a demonstration of the fallibility of mathematicians, and of the children's own relative reliability.

[3] See Jardine (1990, p. 2). Jardine describes the "following along behind" others' thinking in the effort to understand.
[4] See Ball (1993) for an extended analysis of children's engagement with such ideas.

Third, although these students had plenty of playground and neighbor-hood fights, in a mathematical discussion such as this one, those out-of-school relations seemed to have been left outside the classroom door. The children used tools and resources they had been developing together across the year; their interactions were shaped by norms of the math class. They listened to and tried to understand what others were saying, referred to one another's ideas, took positions, and also kept an open mind. These norms were special to school, inside the constructed pocket of the math class. It seemed a change turned inward rather than outward: inward on themselves as thinkers, and inward on the class as a special kind of community. Inside that pocket, the children had opportunities to participate in unaccustomed ways — to experience a kind of thinking, sorts of intellectual inquiries and playful pursuits. They played in and with qualities of relation not part of their everyday worlds.

The special pocket, within school, is a radical challenge to both school-math-as-usual and to much of the current move to situate math in real-world contexts. What has typically constituted mathematical work in schools is one aspect of the challenge. A second challenge is to the individualistic tradition of math class, reinforced by the individualism of testing. Collectively engaged with a mathematical question, children as diverse as the ones in this discussion met on a common ground. It was not the outside world that breathed life into the "mechanical, dry space" (Lensmire, 1994a, p. 153) of math class; it was the intellectual excitement of a little piece of number theory. Engaged together, the children's differences were woven into their collective pursuit.

The title of Joseph Schwab's (1976) famous essay, "Education and the State: Learning Community," highlights the double meaning of "learning community." Community — collective engagement, interdependence, and respect among diverse people — is something that can — indeed, must — be *learned*. And, learning is a *communal* endeavor: Knowledge is the product of communities, and communication about knowledge draws on the representations and modes of discourse of different communities. Schwab saw these two meanings of community intertwining in practice:

> The propensities that constitute community are learned only as we undergo with others the processes through which we learn other things. Meanwhile, the support, communication, and example that make it possible to learn these things become accessible and acceptable to us only as our propensities toward community develop. (p. 235)

Like Dewey, Schwab envisioned a balance between the centrifugal force of the home and the centripetal force of the public common school. Balancing the two, he believed, could allow room for diverse voices, habits of mind, perspectives, and ideas to found a rich common ground for collective engagement. This, he thought, could enhance both the community and the individual. Schools could serve as places where children would learn to engage in and *practice* a "discourse of exchange" through which they, in the heterogeneous environment of the public school, could learn to understand and learn from one another in ways that would support joint action and mutual concern.

A mathematics class in which children have opportunities to practice a civilized discourse, to engage with diverse others in pursuit of a common mathematical problem, issue, or fancy, may not be barricaded from the outside world, or from school, after all. What seems like a protected pocket of activity suspended from larger realities of school and society might be a medium for the development of new relations, habits of mind, and perspectives. What seems like more abstract mathematics, unconnected to the real world, may be one step toward the reconstruction of mathematics as common property and pursuit. Rather than seen as an escape from realities of everyday life as in carnival, the mathematics class might be deliberately repositioned relative to ideas, relations, discourse and community, and serve as an agent of change, not an intellectual retreat from it. Understanding whether and how this inward turn can effect change in school and beyond is a question well worth our collective effort and attention.

DEBORAH LOEWENBERG BALL
Michigan State University

REFERENCES

Ball, D. L. (1993). With an eye on the mathematical horizon: Dilemmas of teaching elementary school. *Elementary School Journal, 93,* 373–397.

Buchmann, M., & Schwille, J. (1983). Education: The overcoming of experience. *American Journal of Education, 92,* 30–51.

Dewey, J. (1956). *The school and society.* Chicago: University of Chicago Press. (Original work published 1900)

Floden, R., Buchmann, M., & Schwille, J. (1987). Breaking with everyday experience. *Teachers College Record, 88,* 485–506.

Jardine, D. (1990). On the humility of mathematical language. *Educational Theory, 40,* 181–191.

Lensmire, T. (1993). Following the child, socioanalysis, and threats to community: Teacher response to student texts. *Curriculum Inquiry, 23,* 265–299.

Lensmire, T. (1994a). *When children write: Critical re-visions of the writing workshop.* New York: Teachers College Press.

Lensmire, T. (1994b). Writing workshop as carnival: Reflections on an alternative learning environment. *Harvard Educational Review, 64,* 371–391.

Roosevelt, D. (in press). There the kid was, stranded in a car: Dilemmas of teacher responsiveness in a writing workshop. *Curriculum Inquiry* .

Schwab, J. (Ed.). (1976). Education and the state: Learning community. In *Great ideas today.* (pp. 234–271) Chicago: Encyclopedia Britannica.

Lensmire Responds to Pryor and Ball

Before anything else, I want to say that I am grateful to be in such generous, thoughtful company. Thank you to John Pryor for initiating this exchange, and to Deborah Ball for joining us.

Pryor's response has helped me clarify my own sense of carnival and writing workshops. I interpret the carnivals and festivals of the Middle Ages and Renaissance as *potential,* as *sites of possibility.* That is, I treat them as social spaces that offered possibilities for learning and change not found in other contexts. Now, Pryor reminds us that there are no guarantees that good things will happen within, or emerge from, such spaces. Indeed, for him the historical record suggests that carnivals were "only superficially anti-authoritarian," and that they functioned to support the status quo by being "cathartic rather than transformative" and by reinforcing hierarchies through "the license to rub in the mud the faces of those at the bottom of the pile." By extension, we should worry that writing workshops may serve a similar function within school and society. I agree.

Still, Gardiner (1992) reminds us that "carnival did occasionally make the transition from ritualistic theatre (which was easily co-opted or manipulated by the ruling groups) to actual revolutionary upsurges, whatever their ultimate outcome" (p. 182). And Pryor, like me, sees workshops as sites of possibility. His concern is that we direct this possibility toward democratic ends.

I couldn't agree more with his suggestion of how we might do this: Make the powers and responsibilities of writing an explicit part of the workshop curriculum and the focus of deliberation and negotiation among teachers and students. To Pryor's suggestion, I would only append two cautionary notes.

First, as we up the ante of our goals for workshops (as we must), I worry that we might lose sight of essential conditions for their realization. In this case, I am thinking of two important features of Bakhtin's carnival — a playful relation to the world, and free, familiar relations with others. And laughter. Sometimes, seriousness of purpose leads to somberness, tightening up, a fearfulness of failing in an important endeavor. As we become more "serious," we risk undermining the sort of joyful, playful relation to the world and each other that would actually allow us to look fearlessly at the world and tell the truth about it, as best we can. In other words, in order to criticize and rewrite the world and texts in the workshop, we and children will need to play (with ideas, with each other) in order to experience and imagine something better — a something better that throws the present's shortcomings into bold relief. Seriousness can undermine truthfulness, and criticism may require child's play. I've always liked Grumet's (1988) call for us to look to our "daughters' lies," their fantasies of how things could be, for help in redeeming our own and our children's lives:

In showing us the world as they would have it, they reveal the world that we fled because we were not brave enough to pitch our tents and raise our flags there. Their lies can become our knowledge. (p. 162)

Second, living out Pryor's suggestion would make for better workshops. But that doesn't mean that the teaching and learning would be easier. In fact, it would be harder. As we make workshops into places of serious moral and political deliberation — as questions hit "close to home" and teachers and students sometimes affirm and sometimes criticize meanings and values "held dear" — the work of writing workshops will become worthier, as well as more difficult and riskier.

Ball certainly does not see "greater connection to the outside world" — the world of children's everyday lives — as some sort of quick, easy fix to our educational woes. Indeed, for her, such connection sometimes introduces unnecessary complications and strife that "deflate the possibilities" for meaningful work in mathematics. And conversely, a seeming disassociation from the surrounding world sometimes enhances possibilities. Ball notes, for example, that she has "repeatedly been surprised by the fascination that 'pure mathematics' holds for young children from diverse cultural backgrounds." A solid moral, then, that Ball helps us draw: The call for meaningfulness is not exhausted in the appropriation of children's everyday lives for the curriculum.

But if we push at this a little, I think that another moral might emerge. The opposition Ball sets up between math class as "protected pocket" and the everyday world — and between "pure mathematics" and children's everyday lives — seems fairly unstable (at least in Ball's examples here — and of course, Ball soon undoes the opposition herself). I can imagine one of Ball's students yelling "Bingo" when a green chip is pulled from the bag. In other words, the exploration of probability may echo everyday games of chance — a roll of the dice in Monopoly, picking a lottery number (results televised each night). Furthermore, games of chance are used as metaphors to express the uncertainties of life. How do we draw the line that divides the study of probability from wondering about life, when "life's a crapshoot"? And while number theory may be an "esoteric bit of mathematics," numbers are certainly an ubiquitous part of children's lives. Children try to figure out, play with, and take joy in the language around them — the patterns of rhyme, the orderliness of narratives. Is the pursuit of number theory in a classroom like Ball's something similar for children? A chance to grab hold of, manipulate, wonder at the numbers they see around them everyday in the real world? A second moral, then, that Ball helps us draw: When looking to connect children's lives in school to the real world, in the name of relevance or meaningfulness, don't reduce the real world to that which is useful or practical.

With this second moral, the question of whether or not to bring the everyday world into the classroom is transformed into: What in the world (yes, this can be said with exasperation) should be taken up in the classroom with children? Ball reminds us that the call for meaningfulness, relevance, connection is only the *beginning* of an answer to the question of what to teach, not the end of it.

At the end of her text, Ball undoes the separation between math class and real world by suggesting that her math class might be "one step toward the reconstruction of mathematics as common property and pursuit" and a "medium for the development of new relations, habits of mind, and perspectives." Amen. But I'll quibble with her characterization of carnival as an "escape from the realities" of the real world and an "intellectual retreat from it." I have been attracted to the metaphor of workshop-as-carnival, in part, because Bakhtin envisioned carnival as a social context that was in relation and in interaction with another social context (see LaCapra, 1983). He didn't conceive of carnival as a total social environment, a utopia. Carnival was seen as in relation to the workaday world, a workaday world that — while improvable, while capable of transformation — would always be with us as we labored to feed, clothe, reproduce our bodies/selves.

In my article, I located carnival in the writing workshop — a workshop imagined in response to traditional classrooms. But we might locate carnival differently. Perhaps we should think of carnival as a moment in learning. There's hard work in learning, and a bowing to others and their ideas, but there also n eds to be a moment of play, fearless criticism, re-creation. Or perhaps — and the discussions of both Pryor and Ball suggest such a move — we should im. gine schools as carnival. Schools as the "second life" of the people — a life momentarily removed from the demands of reproducing material existence, but a life that *also helps us see and live in the other one differently.*

Schools as carnival. Such a vision certainly does not get us everything we want or need. It may need to be tempered by a little Deweyan soberness (or, conversely, Dewey may need to be goosed by a little carnival). Dewey (1922/1983) called on schools to "cultivate the habit of suspended judgment, of skepticism, of desire for evidence, of appeal to observation rather than sentiment, discussion rather than bias, inquiry rather than conventional idealizations" (p. 344):

And when they do? When this happens schools will be the dangerous outposts of a humane civilization. But they will also begin to be supremely interesting places. (p. 344)

TIMOTHY J. LENSMIRE
Washington University
St. Louis, Missouri

REFERENCES

Dewey, J. (1983). *The middle works, 1899–1924: Vol. 13. 1921–1922.* Carbondale: Southern Illinois University.(Original work published 1922)

Gardiner, M. (1992). *The dialogics of critique: M. M. Bakhtin and the theory of ideology.* London: Routledge.

Grumet, M. R. (1988). *Bitter milk: Women and teaching.* Amherst: University of Massachusetts Press.

LaCapra, D. (1983). *Rethinking intellectual history: texts, contexts, language.* Ithaca, NY: Cornell University Press.

A Teacher Learns
in the Context of a Social
Studies Workshop

GINNY SEABROOK

I had taught at the same private, independent school for seventeen years when, in September 1989, I began a year of "teacher research." Although I continued in my role as a teacher, I also engaged in my own form of research: While still immersed in the details of day-to-day teaching, I wanted to step back and reflect on what was happening in my seventh-grade Social Studies classroom and observe the effects of various changes I hoped to implement.

Over the previous two years, I had reorganized my English classes into a "workshop" format in which the students were the center of the class and I was the facilitator of their learning. This format had proved to be an exciting and effective way to teach English, and I was eager to see if I could similarly redesign my Social Studies class. I wanted both to change my role in the classroom from that of a mere dispenser of information and to encourage my Social Studies students to take more responsibility for their own learning. I hoped to stir their imagination so that they could picture another time and begin to make connections between their own world and the past. I could not have predicted the surprising connections I made to my students, nor could I have known, as I prepared to change my class, that I, myself, was necessarily going to change.

The school where I taught enrolled approximately two hundred students in grades K–12. The seventh grade consisted of eighteen students, eight girls and ten boys, ten of whom I taught the previous year in sixth-grade Social Studies. The other eight students were new to the school. The seventh-grade class was mixed in terms of socioeconomic status (some students were from

Harvard Educational Review Vol. 61 No. 4 November 1991, 475–485

affluent families, while others, attending on scholarships, were not), ethnicity (nine of the seventh graders were Caucasian, eight African American, and one Latino), and ability (the school did not use any system of tracking).

I saw the seventh-grade students twice each day, once for Social Studies and once for English. I had begun teaching English in the form of a workshop in 1987, after reading Nancie Atwell's (1987) *In the Middle: Writing, Reading, and Learning with Adolescents.* The workshop Atwell had created with her eighth graders seemed to offer solutions to problems with which I also struggled: how to teach one class containing many individuals with different interests and abilities, and how to give students more choice and responsibility for their learning. Following Atwell's model, I made my English students the center of the class, and redefined my role as a teacher to become more of a facilitator. I arranged the room as a place to read and write, and I expected students to do a great deal of both. Once I had built the framework of the class, the students had many choices about what to study, what books to read, what topics to write about, and what kind of help they needed. I encouraged them to think independently and respond to the ideas of other students. My job was to listen as their ideas took shape, help to fill in the gaps in their knowledge, urge them to think again, and confirm their successes. I had to know my students well in order to follow their thought processes and adapt my teaching to their needs. It was an exciting way to teach.

Compared to the English workshop, my more traditional Social Studies class seemed inert. The textbook and I supplied information; I conducted class discussion, presented films, showed slides from my travels, and assigned daily homework. Yet, despite my efforts, the Social Studies students remained uninterested in the Middle Ages, even those who, as sixth graders, had been fascinated by ancient history. I decided to adapt the workshop format I had found so successful in my English class to my Social Studies class, in the hope of changing my students' attitudes toward history. I planned to use a variety of teaching techniques in my new Social Studies workshop: mini-lessons, journal writing, sustained silent reading, student-selected books and research topics, and frequent student-teacher conferences. As a teacher/researcher, I hoped to observe whether these changes would help shape positive attitudes towards history.

As I thought about how to adapt the English workshop to Social Studies, I was immediately confronted with a much larger and important question: How could I teach Social Studies content within a workshop format? I wrestled with that question for most of the school year. Originally, I thought I could answer one question at a time in an orderly way, but before I had a hint of an answer to one question, another would draw my attention. As the year progressed and I sought a path through the growing pile of questions, I remembered Heracles and his eleventh labor: Heracles needed to get directions to the Garden of Hesperides from Nereus, the old man of the sea, but Nereus was as elusive as water. When Heracles grabbed hold of him,

Nereus kept changing his form — to a roaring lion, a serpent, a blazing fire. As the year went on, I knew how Heracles felt, although my struggle ended somewhat differently.

Obstacles arose as soon as I attempted to adapt my English workshop to Social Studies. In the English workshop I did not use a textbook, and students chose the novels they wanted to read. To avoid using only a textbook and myself as sources of information about the Middle Ages, I needed appropriate books for students to try free-choice reading. I ordered every book about the Middle Ages I could find, but when they arrived I was disappointed. The books were expensive, and there were not enough for free-choice reading more than once a week. As I checked out every book on the Middle Ages and Renaissance available from the library, I wondered what we would do during class time.

Nevertheless, I was determined not just to stand in front of the students and talk each day. If we couldn't do as much free-choice reading as I had hoped, I would find other sources of information. Two techniques that I had found successful in the past, even in traditional classes, were reading stories aloud and asking students to write journals. So on the first day of class I brought with me a beautifully illustrated book of Chaucer's *Canterbury Tales*. To encourage the students to begin to form pictures in their minds, I showed them the elegant illustrations and read "The Nun's Priest's Tale." I wondered rather anxiously what seventh graders would think of a tale about a talking rooster who was bullied by his wife after he had a frightening dream, but I need not have worried. My students had something in common with people of the fourteenth century: they loved a story.

On the first day, the students wrote their responses to Chaucer's story in their journals, some of which they later read out loud:

> I liked the description of the male rooster and the lady hen. The colors sound so beautiful. I felt sorry for the rooster. Dreams can be scary. Anything can happen to you and it all seems so real.

> I was not particularly impressed by that story. There was barely any action, too much description, and the story had no particular interest. I personally like stories with a more gripping plot. Sorry, old priest, I didn't like it.

I asked for the students' opinions to the story, and they responded honestly. I wanted them to know that they could safely express their ideas, whatever they might be. I accepted positive and negative responses equally, as their comments were valuable and provided a basis for further discussion. As we began our Social Studies workshop, I realized that I was charting a course into unknown water. I knew I didn't want too much reliance on a text or too much talk from the teacher, but I wasn't yet sure what I *did* want. While I thought I was progressing slowly, one step at a time, relying on past teaching successes, I did not realize that I had drifted from the shore and might, at any moment, lose sight of land.

As the days went by, the students and I let a "text" evolve from discussions and journal writings. When we made lists of what we could learn about people of the Middle Ages from hearing Chaucer's story, I was amazed at their contributions. The students were clearly forming pictures of the Middle Ages in their minds; they were seeing through Chaucer's eyes. They listed the following:

Always suspect treachery under the face of flattery.

Good guys always win.

Crime does not pay.

Towns have gates.

Never sleep in an oxen stable.

Don't trust women.

Don't believe everything you hear.

Dreams may teach you something.

Strangers shared rooms in inns.

People were superstitious.

People were naive.

It was easy to be a thief.

Stories were told for amusement

Lots of farms.

The topics of one class led to the next day's activity. One day I brought in a bag containing things a pilgrim would not have taken to Canterbury: sunglasses, credit cards, paperback books, and sneakers. We then discussed what they *would* have taken, whether people used money, how they travelled, and what had been the purpose of the trip. The last point led to a discussion of the importance of religion in the Middle Ages.

At first I felt uncomfortable because I did not know the answers to some of the students' questions. Since I didn't know from one class to the next what topics would come up, I could not prepare myself with the answers. I didn't know much about money in the fourteenth century, and I wondered along with my students how many bags of heavy coins the pilgrims might have carried. When I stopped relying on a text, I cut off the history teacher's oxygen line — the fact supply. I became, in fact, more like my students; much to my surprise they didn't seem to mind. And they didn't look to me for answers.

When I began the class, I had no idea how much unlearning I would have to do. First, I had to unlearn my "teacher behavior." Even though I realized I didn't know all of the answers — and sometimes even said so — my behavior had given a different message. Without a textbook, I had to think about what I wanted to teach and why it was important, and these changes enabled me to think about my teaching in a different way. In both of my workshops

I had to unlearn how to talk and learn how to listen. Though I had always been interested in what students thought, the framework of my traditional teacher-centered class had not provided enough time for listening and thinking; the new class format changed that.

One of my fears about changing the way I taught was that my students would not learn enough. "Learn enough what?" I then had to ask myself. Did they need to understand feudalism and chivalry, or were other concepts equally important? Were there certain things about the Middle Ages that students *had* to know at the end of the year? If so, what were they? If they hadn't learned a core set of facts, had I failed to teach them the history of the Middle Ages? I thought there must be essential facts they should learn, but I wasn't sure which were the most important.

As I look back, I believe that I was afraid to ask myself these questions or take them seriously because I didn't know the answers. In school I learned that teachers *must* know the right answer, and so for years had relied on a textbook to tell me what I ought to teach. I thought that I needed an expert to tell me what I should teach and when I should teach it; I thought that the students would not learn unless I motivated or forced them. As I began to think more under the new structure, the students followed and at times even outdistanced me. Perhaps they did not have as much to unlearn as I.

Though I should have been prepared, I was baffled by the unexpected. On a day when a double period gave me over an hour with the class, I experimented with free-choice reading. I placed the books around the room so the class could browse. There were books about the Crusades, William the Conqueror, and medieval medicine, as well as stories about a medieval monk and an Irish pilgrim. Each student chose a book and sat down.

I was surprised when they did not open the books and immediately start reading, as they had in English class. Instead they looked at the pictures, thumbed through the pages, and started reading in the middle, a little here and a little there. I was frantic. I thought, "They aren't reading. They won't learn anything." Since I did not really understand what was happening in my class, I tried to be patient and watch.

Later I reflected on what had happened, and realized that the students had done exactly what I would do if I were picking out a nonfiction book on an unfamiliar topic. I would read the contents, check the pictures, and read a few random sections. In my anxiety, I had forgotten to look at the situation through the students' eyes. Because the Middle Ages was not familiar to them, they needed time to find a topic that held their interest.

Since I continued to worry about whether the students would learn enough, I asked them to talk to each other about their reading. Someone who had read about castles could trade information with classmates who had read about monasteries and armor. But when I put them in small discussion groups at the end of the reading period, I had another surprise; they didn't know how to talk about their books. I wrote in my journal on September 15, "When I went around to listen, they sounded like they were giving each other book reports." Once again, my first impulse was to mistrust myself and the students. No one could tell me what I was doing wrong and what I was doing right; I had trusted Nancie Atwell's (1987) *In the Middle* when I tried the English workshop, but this time my instincts and thoughts were my only guide. I also had my students, but I hadn't realized their importance yet. Although I had once wondered what students knew about English and found out that they knew quite a lot, when I considered the Social Studies class, I forgot what I had learned with my English students.

After taking some time to reflect on my experience, it occurred to me that one reason students could not relax and talk to each other about castles and nuns was simply that they had never done it before. They had never been allowed to choose a book, and I had certainly never said to a class of seventh graders, "Now turn around to your friends and talk." I had spent twenty years saying, "Be quiet. Don't talk to your friends in class."

Though I knew the students and I needed time to get used to this new kind of class, I was impatient and could not resist stepping in to teach them how to do things right. I chose two students to talk with me, but neither would say anything; consequently, I did all of the talking. The rest of the class waited patiently while I talked, and then they formed their groups. When the bell rang, they groaned, "We didn't have time for everyone in our group to talk." They may not have been doing what I thought they should, but they liked what they were doing.

Not knowing what else to do, I left the students alone and just watched. Some began to take notes on what others in their group were saying. They were doing what they had always done in school — if someone talked about history, they wrote it down. I didn't want them to "teach" each other, but I did not correct them because they were trying very hard to be "good students," to figure out what the teacher wanted. Soon they discovered on their own that it took too long to write down everything another student said; if they wrote too much, there was not time for everyone to talk about what they had read. Consequently, they began to jot down brief notes instead. I had intended to set up a situation in which students could learn content from each other; much to my surprise, they had learned how to take notes as well.

I read their accounts of group discussion in their journals:

> I learned from Karen's book that if you commit a crime in the monastery, like in Karen's book a monk accused a boy of stealing a silver bowl, that you would have to stand outside with your shoes and socks off and your legs showing. There would be a slave standing by to tell people why you are there because you can't speak. How come in a monastery it was a crime to show your legs?

And another student learned about listening:

> Nuns had cats so they would kill the mice. Andy, Carly, and I told about our book and then the bell rang. Too bad! I liked telling about my book

because everybody seemed so interested. It really makes you feel good when you know other people are listening.

By the middle of October the students were quite enthusiastic about the Middle Ages, and I was not sure why. Though I was gratified by their enthusiasm, I felt disconnected from them. I didn't know all of the things they were learning, and I hadn't yet answered those initial questions about which ideas were important. I was insecure, and I wanted to be part of the group.

Nevertheless, I had the impression that this class had learned more about the Middle Ages by mid-October than my former students had learned all of the previous year. Could that be true? I needed some proof, some tests to show myself and others that my students really were learning. When the teacher is the center of the class, evaluation is easy: the teacher can give a test to see how well the students' knowledge matches hers. But I was not the center of the class, and I was becoming increasingly uncertain about which facts were most important. My students were learning things about the Middle Ages that I did not know, and because they were learning different facts, I could not give tests. I barely stopped to think that they were learning *without the threat of tests*. My students remembered what they read and heard in group discussions, and often mentioned these things in class. They also wrote about them in their journals. For example:

> I remember what Lina said about the pictures in the church and how the people could look at them because they could not read. Also I remember what Sham said about where the people were buried.

> Eugene's paper made me realize I made a mistake on my paper. The mistake I made was that the reason for the trip was for gold, jewelry, and silks and not to fight.

> I told about amusements in the Middle Ages. I told that kids learned to swim by jumping into the lake with a bale of hay in their arms. The hay would float for a few minutes and then begin to sink. They would dry it out and start again.

The journals clearly showed that students were learning. In a summary of her group talk on September 19, one student wrote, "The haircut men got before they became a monk is called a tonsure." On September 26 she wrote, "Irish monks had a different tonsure than other monks."

In order to evaluate what each student had learned, I asked them to do individual research projects. This would provide concrete evidence of what they had learned, while still allowing for individual interests and talent. I had gathered ideas about individual research from an article in the edited volume *English Teachers at Work*, in which Cora Five (1986) described how she guided her students through individual reading and research to produce a written report. I decided, however, to allow students who were not good writers to develop alternative ways of showing what they had learned. The

171

class discussed some possibilities for projects, and I listed their tentative choices on the board so that students having trouble thinking of something to do could get ideas. I also asked students to write as they worked — about the progress they were making, the problems they were having, and what help they might need. To my surprise, the projects arrived on time and were very well done. Lina wrote a report about religion. Richard made a cardboard model of a castle with a see-through wall in one of the towers, an idea he got from a picture in one of the books in class. Ken drew graph-paper floor plans of castles. Kacy made a peasant's hut, complete with furniture, food on the tables, and tools against the walls. Karen's report about how monks made books was written as an illuminated manuscript.

Although I did grade the students' projects, the most meaningful feedback came from their peers. The students were fascinated with their friends' work, applauded the presentations, and wrote a brief note to each presenter. They were eager to read the notes from their classmates, and I think those comments meant more than any of the grades I assigned.

About mid-year, I realized that I was enjoying myself and that I felt more comfortable with my new way of teaching. I wrote in my journal on January 9, "I do feel optimistic about the class, and I like what I have done so far. . . . I have given up on which facts they need to learn. I am flexible about that. And I am sure they have learned more because I have relinquished that control." January marked a turning point in my attitude: I felt I could trust my students, and I was also beginning to trust myself.

I wasn't teaching in the traditional sense; I was allowing something different to happen. I used to decide how many pages the class would "cover" and whether we would study the Crusades in January or church architecture in November. I decided when I would give a test. These were easy decisions that I could make by myself. In the Social Studies workshop, although I had assumed a different role, I still made many decisions. I decided how class time would be spent — how much time would be devoted to reading, writing, and talking — and I allotted time for cooperative learning and even some direct teaching. However, I also allowed the students to make more choices, and I set aside large amounts of time for thinking and working in groups. I was also taking more time to listen to students, and made their words and ideas the ones we discussed and wrote about. I had not given up responsibility, but I was allowing the students to assume more responsibility for the direction of the class. We needed a space in which to listen to each other. I had to stop talking so that I could listen to students and also hear myself think. I learned what Donald Murray meant when he wrote, "There is no silence when you listen, only silence when you talk" (1989, p. 80).

I was surprised to learn that I could step out of the center of the class and still find my place in the group. When I got out of the way, the students learned as much as they could as fast as they wanted without being limited by my knowledge and interests. I discovered that my students had interesting

ideas and that we had many things in common. For example, we all could
be touched by the beauty of words. When they wrote a response to a biography of Columbus that I had been reading out loud, many mentioned the
phrase "the green sea of darkness," the Arab name for the Atlantic Ocean.
Images, metaphors, and skillful use of words stirred our imaginations. I
found that I had not ventured into "the green sea of darkness" alone; the
students were with me. Even though I did not know exactly where we were,
we were not lost.

The atmosphere of the classroom was different from that of the year before. Students were talking more, asking more questions, and showing more
evidence of thinking. I believe that students who are thinking will express
opinions, make judgments, ask open-ended questions, see connections, and
synthesize information. In fact, these seventh-grade students often expressed
their opinions: "I think life in the Middle Ages was dangerous" or "Life was
boring. All they thought about was religion." Students thought things
through and made connections as they wrote in their journals, such as these
responses to an assignment to write about nobility:

> Well, I'm not quite sure what nobility means but I can tell about lords.
> They were in charge of manors and were men that worked for the king.
> Many fights started between lords. They had enemies and a few friends.
> Noblemen were people that worked at the same thing as lords. They got
> land from the king. That's it! Nobility might mean that you are privileged
> and royal.

> I think the eldest son got the land because he was more capable. The
> reason why girls were always the last to get the land was because they had
> to learn to cook, clean, and take care of their family. . . . Who do you think
> is more capable, a girl or a boy?

For some years, I have believed that students' self-generated questions
indicate that they are doing more than just absorbing information. Such
questions show that they are looking at the facts in new ways and rearranging
ideas in their minds. To show that I valued their questions, I had a bulletin
board on which I wrote down some of their interesting questions. Until this
year, they had seldom asked questions that did not have definite answers. In
contrast, the Social Studies workshop students raised a number of thought-
provoking questions:

> Why did medieval people fight so much?
> If the Crusaders learned so much from the Arabs, did the Arabs learn
> anything from the Europeans?
> Why didn't women travel?
> Were the people poor or rich or some of both?
> Why was land important?

Why are the countries of Europe so small and the countries of Asia so big?

When the Crusades failed, why didn't the people stop trusting in God?

Questions like these indicate thinking and learning that do not disappear shortly after a test is taken. Fortunately, I had given up trying to be the person with the answers! I couldn't answer these questions, and if five historians had come to the class, they would have offered us five or more answers for each. The class had the audacity to ask unanswerable, juicy questions and to let anyone tackle them.

I wanted to make students more aware of their own questions, so at the end of the first semester I asked the class to make up their own semester tests. I didn't require them to write answers; I felt their questions would show what they knew. As Donald Graves wrote, "The beginning of an answer, an understanding of the information, is contained in the formulation of a question" (1989, p. 89). Students were interested in different information, and making up their own tests allowed them to focus on their particular areas of expertise. We first brainstormed a list of topics. Then I told them to refer to the list in their journals and make up six questions each. I didn't want them to worry about how much time it would take to write an answer, so I told them that they did not have to answer the questions. As the students worked, I wrote on the board the first six questions that came to my mind. Next, they rated their questions from one to five, one being the easiest to answer and five being the more difficult. Then I asked them to explain in writing why they had rated their questions as they did. When I rated my own questions, I was surprised that I had not understood my own rating system until I explained it to the class. I gave ones to questions with short answers, as I thought a difficult question would require a lot of thinking and a lot of writing to explain, and thus deserved a five.

The students' perceptions were exactly the opposite of mine. From their point of view, the difficult questions were the ones they didn't know the answers to, and most of the examples they gave were short-answer questions that they would need to memorize. Those questions seemed easy to me, but the students explained that difficult questions were likely to involve something they hadn't heard in class or some seemingly unimportant detail that they might have missed in their reading — for example, "Who was the third son of the Duke of Monmouth?" I was not able to persuade most of my students that difficult questions took a great deal of thought. They enjoyed thinking, and, in contrast, they knew how they felt when they looked at a test question that could only be answered with one word — a word that they didn't know.

Clearly the students expected to be "tricked" by their teachers — a revealing glimpse of students' perception of their teachers that I found somewhat unsettling. I had intended to teach students about posing questions, but instead *I* learned about their image of teachers and tests.

As the year advanced, I began to wonder how my seventh graders would be able to handle the very traditional eighth-grade history class and its difficult text. I wanted to see if they could help each other understand the meaning of a difficult piece of nonfiction through group discussion. I made copies of an article about maps and fifteenth-century exploration, and told them to mark the parts that were puzzling so they could talk about them later. The students read the article, but they did not work well together in discussion groups. I was annoyed. Why wouldn't they learn what I wanted them to learn when I wanted them to learn it? They insisted that they had understood the reading, but I did not believe them. At first I wanted to ask some tricky questions to show that I was right, but I couldn't bring myself to do so. Instead, I told them to write what they remembered, which was not very much. I couldn't understand what had happened.

By the next period, I was no longer annoyed, just curious. When they came to English class, I asked some of the students if they knew why they couldn't remember the Social Studies reading. Without hesitation, they explained to me that I had told them to concentrate on the confusing parts, so they had focused on the parts that they didn't understand well. Thus, when I asked them what they remembered, they could not tell me. "We can't remember what we don't understand." Once again their logic was better than mine.

One student said that she understood what she had read, but that some of the parts had been boring. I asked her to show me the boring parts, and when she pointed them out, I could see that she had skipped large sections. I assumed that she had skipped the difficult parts — until I had a similar experience several days later.

The following Sunday, as I read an article in *The New York Times* about the Hubble telescope, I found that some parts were uninteresting. I realized that I had quickly formed an idea of what I wanted to know, and had skipped the parts that seemed irrelevant to me. I stopped short: I was doing exactly what my student had done. I am a good reader and I understood what the article was about; it was not difficult for me. However, I could not have passed a test on the information it contained, nor could I have explained it to someone else. My students and I had something else in common — we read alike.

Gradually, I noticed a more relaxed atmosphere in the class. Although I had not deliberately tried to create it, as I became more comfortable in my new role, I relaxed, and the students seemed to relax, too. This atmosphere helped me be a better teacher because it enabled me to be a more attentive listener and to think more clearly. In their journals, students often mentioned feeling relaxed when I read aloud to them, or when they were reading silently:

> I like having the teacher read because then I can just kind of relax and focus on what she is reading. If I had to read to myself I'd have to pay more attention because I'd be the one reading.

A student who is not a skilled writer recorded:

> When I know I will not have to write about something I read it like it is a
> book not a textbook. I then have more fun and sometimes even remember
> more. It sounds strange but I think this way students learn more. No one
> remembers what they read in their text books unless they study it.

Another told me about remembering what she reads: "I remember what is
interesting whether I need to know it or not."

I became increasingly curious about what students remember, about why
they remember certain things and not others. As a way to understand the
process, I began to think about how I remember. When I read, I use my
imagination to picture the story in my mind, and then I remember the pictures. When I read a nonfiction book about a medieval castle or the training
of knights, pictures take shape in my mind. My own reading experiences
correspond with those reviewed by Emrys Evans (1987), who discussed the
idea that writers leave spaces to be filled in by the reader's imagination.
Imagination seems to be related to memory; thus, teachers who can stir
students' imaginations will teach them how to learn. It is unfortunate that
many educators believe that creativity and imagination are subordinate to
reason and logic, and that creativity should be relegated to art class or to the
small "creative writing" portion of English classes. I believe that the use of
imagination is tied to memory and could be central to the learning process.

Frank Smith (1985) says that we understand what we read by relating the
information in a book to our prior experience. Since my students have told
me that they can better remember what they can understand, I believe that
prior experience is connected to memory. One day a student showed slides
of his trip to China to his seventh-grade classmates. At the beginning of the
next class period, I asked the students to jot down the first five things they
remembered about China. I expected them to remember the same things
and to remember at least some of the things I remembered. They did not.
To my great surprise, every list was different. The first five lists that were read
aloud had very little duplication. I immediately thought of Frank Smith's
comments on prior experience, and so I asked the students, "Why do you
think you remembered those particular things?" They answered, "We remembered them because they were important."

At first I was amused, and I thought, "Yes, everyone thinks what he or she
remembers is important." I uncritically assumed that what is important is
outside of ourselves, like Plato's ideas, floating around waiting for us to grasp
it. But when I thought more deeply, I realized that the students were right.
They remembered what was important to their own thinking and to their
own learning process.

Over the years, I had learned to rely on my intuitive understanding and
was sure I had a good relationship with my students because I had never
forgotten what it was like to be a student myself. I remember how it felt to
come to school without having done my homework, or to ask for help with

a math problem and still not understand after several explanations. When students sense that a teacher understands how they feel, they trust him or her, and I knew my students trusted me. Despite this knowledge, however, I felt that something was missing, that I was holding something back, and eventually I realized that I also had to trust my students, to expose to them the unfinished, imperfect, fragile ideas that were a part of my own learning process.

During a class discussion, I asked my students why they thought the monks in the Middle Ages kept a rule of silence in the monasteries. I was surprised when an active, robust boy replied, "To treasure their thoughts." I want to keep an open space in my classrooms in which I may treasure the thoughts of my students, as well as my own. At the beginning of the school year, I had simply wanted to create a Social Studies workshop. I had not foreseen that it would become a place where long-hidden thoughts would be formed into new ideas, where I would have to remember more than ever what it felt like to be a student, where I would create space for thinking and listening, and where I would learn how to learn once again.

REFERENCES

Atwell, N. (1987). *In the middle: Writing, reading and learning with adolescents.* Portsmouth, NH: Heinemann.

Evans, E. (1987). Readers creating texts. In B. Corcoran & E. Evans (Eds.), *Readers, texts, teachers* (pp. 22–40). Portsmouth, NH: Heinemann.

Five, C. (1986). History through a child's voice. In S. Tchudi (Ed.), *English teachers at work: Ideas and strategies from five countries* (pp. 120–124). Portsmouth, NH: Heinemann.

Graves, D. H. (1989). *Investigate nonfiction.* Portsmouth, NH: Heinemann.

Murray, D. (1989). *Expecting the unexpected.* Portsmouth, NH: Heinemann.

Smith, F. (1985). *Reading without nonsense.* New York: Teachers College Press.

SUGGESTED READING LIST

N. Atwell, ed., *Coming to Know: Writing to Learn in the Intermediate Grades.* Portsmouth, NH: Heinemann, 1987.

L. M. Calkins, *The Art of Teaching Writing.* Portsmouth, NH: Heinemann, 1986.

G. Chaucer, *Canterbury Tales* (B. Cohen, ed./trans.). New York: Lothrop, Lee & Shepard, 1988.

D. G. Dellinger, "Alternatives to Clip and Stitch: Real Research and Writing in the Classroom." In *English Journal*, September, 1989, pp. 31–38.

T. Fulwiler, ed., *The Journal Book.* Portsmouth, NH: Heinemann, 1987.

D. H. Graves, *Writing: Teachers and Children at Work.* Portsmouth, NH: Heinemann, 1983.

P. E. Greeley, "Historical Fiction: The Tie That Binds Reading, Writing, and Social Studies." In N. Atwell, ed., *Workshop I: Writing and Literature* (pp. 88–95). Portsmouth, NH: Heinemann, 1989.

NCTE Committee on Classroom Practices in the Teaching of English, *Focus on Collaborative Learning.* Urbana, IL: Author, 1988.

G. Soule, *Christopher Columbus on the Green Sea of Darkness.* New York: Franklin Watts, 1988.

W. Zinsser, *Writing to Learn.* New York: Harper & Row, 1988.

Elementary School Curricula and Urban Transformation

PAUL SKILTON SYLVESTER

66 "I want to get off welfare; I've been on food stamps all of my life!" Derek said to no one in particular. It was payday. Every Friday, each of my third graders received a paycheck or welfare payment. After cashing their checks at the classroom branch of the Fidelity Bank, they could spend their money, open their businesses, or report to work.

This was Sweet Cakes Town, a name chosen by students for the child-sized, red-brick neighborhood they created out of cardboard boxes in our classroom. (None of the students could explain to me why they seized upon one boy's odd suggestion for this name.) In this town, the businesses, government, and union were owned and run by the students. The economy of Sweet Cakes Town was not make-believe; Sweet Cakes dollars were legal tender for real goods and real services. Using money they earned from classroom jobs, students participated in the economy according to their individual interests. They could buy and manage businesses, rent a chess board at the toy store, rent paints at the Art Supply Store, borrow a book from the Free Library, plant seeds at the Wonderful World of Plants Store, sell one of their own paintings at the Art Gallery, rent an outfit at the Value Plus Clothing Store, get their hair corn-rowed at Shawntay's Beauty Salon, or feed the rabbit at the Sweet Cakes Zoo.

Derek's dilemma of finding a way off welfare was real both inside and outside the classroom.[1] The students' Philadelphia neighborhood had suffered the trauma of de-industrialization during the 1970s and 1980s, and 93

[1] Students' names have been changed for confidentiality.

Harvard Educational Review Vol. 64 No. 3 Fall 1994, 309–331

percent of our students were on public assistance (most recent figures available at time of writing) (School District of Philadelphia, 1991, p. 239). As in most eastern cities, factory closings compounded the historical effects of racial discrimination, leaving many African Americans and Latinos economically isolated.[2]

As an elementary school teacher attempting to engage my students in real social and economic issues, I needed clear illustrations of what critical pedagogy could look like in the mainstream, K-12 public school systems of this country. In reviewing the current literature on education for social reform, I found a great deal of information on the theory of critical pedagogy, including work in the fields of adult literacy, higher education, feminist pedagogy, international development, and education for employment. Unfortunately, most of this was written in an abstract fashion, with little explanation of how one could make it work in an actual classroom.

Educational anthropologist John Ogbu (1978, 1988) has shown how students' views about their chances in the economy affect their school performance. Ogbu has found that as some African American children grow older, they tend to engage in nonacademic activities and "become more aware of how some people in the community 'make it' without good school credentials or mainstream employment" (1988, p. 332). He has shown that such beliefs about success can lead to life strategies that undermine their school achievement. Similarly, in a study of twelve hundred Los Angeles high school students, Roslyn Arlin Mickelson found a significant relationship between the "economic returns" students anticipated from their education and how well they performed in school (1984, p. 112).

One could infer from Ogbu's findings that education cannot address the impoverishment in inner cities until changes have occurred in the economic opportunity structure. My own view, however, lies closer to that presented by Michael W. Apple and Lois Weis:

> If education can be no more than an epiphenomenon tied directly to the requirements of an economy, then little can be done within education itself. It is a totally determined institution. However, if schools (and people) are not passive mirrors of an economy, but instead are active agents in the processes of reproduction and contestation of dominant social relations, then understanding what they do and acting upon them becomes of

[2] Many of my assumptions about the causes of our urban situation come from the work of William Julius Wilson. Recently, he provided a concise summary of his landmark work: "I argue in *The Truly Disadvantaged* [Wilson, 1987] that historic discrimination and a migration flow to large metropolitan areas that kept the minority population relatively young created a problem of weak labor-force attachment within this population, making it particularly vulnerable to the ongoing industrial and geographic changes in the economy since 1970. The shift from goods-producing to service-producing industries, increasing polarization of the labor market into low-wage and high-wage sectors, innovations in technology, relocation of manufacturing industries out of the central city, periodic recessions, and wage stagnation exacerbated the chronic problems of weak labor-force attachment among the urban minority poor" (Wilson, 1990, p. 6).

no small moment. For if schools are part of a "contested terrain" . . . then the hard and continuous day-to-day struggle at the level of curriculum and teaching practice is part of these larger conflicts as well. The key is linking these day-to-day struggles within school to other action for a more progressive society in that wider arena. (Quoted in Erickson, 1987, p. 351)

In this article I describe one example of how education can address the inequality of a post-industrial society. I describe the evolution of a curriculum created with my students that involved the hands-on study of our neighborhood, as well as the creation of a child-sized model of the neighborhood in our classroom. I believe that the crucial element in the success of this curriculum was not in my personality as a teacher, but in the students' own creative power, which I tapped into by encouraging them to question, investigate, and interpret their experience of the world. As our classroom neighborhood evolved, it represented the opportunity for Derek and his classmates to imagine and actually live in, for a few hours a week, a future that defied the too-familiar statistics of their real-life chances.

In the second section of this article, I describe changes in the roles played by three students in the class. Finally, I discuss the implications of this curriculum for social transformation among the ghetto poor.[3] Overall, two questions guide this discussion: 1) How do we as teachers educate so that we do not replicate existing social inequalities? and 2) How do we avoid the twin pitfalls of a) stressing the obstacles to economic success, thereby encouraging defeatism, and b) stressing the possibilities for economic success and thereby encouraging the view that those who have not "made it" have only themselves to blame?

A CURRICULUM FOR URBAN TRANSFORMATION

Identifying the Problem and Becoming Part of the Solution

My interest in using education to address urban inequality began in the 1960s, as I was growing up in the suburbs of Detroit. I saw a city increasingly split between affluent suburbs where I saw only White people, and a run-down inner city where I saw mostly Black people. It was not until 1989, however, that I felt that I was making the least bit of progress in understanding what had been happening to Detroit. That year my parents gave me William Julius Wilson's *The Truly Disadvantaged* (1987) as a Christmas present, with the inscription " . . . that you may be part of the solution."

Wilson's *The Truly Disadvantaged* showed me our city through an economic lens in a time when much of the popular rhetoric blamed urban problems on the moral deficiencies of the poor (e.g., the need for "values"). Looking

---

[3] In response to Gans's (1990) suggestion that the term "underclass" is no longer useful due to the pejorative connations it has taken on through misapplication, Wilson (1990) has suggested the substitution of the term "ghetto poor."

at the problem from Wilson's perspective, I wondered what role, if any, an urban elementary school teacher could play in helping to create the solution.

I had recently completed my teacher training at the Bank Street College of Education in New York City where, in the tradition of John Dewey and the Progressive education movement, curricula are developed around in-depth studies of various aspects of students' experiences. I began to think that if students were to overcome the obstacles presented by changes in the economy — or better yet, to play a role in breaking down these obstacles — they would first need practice imagining how they might do it. I began looking for a way to bring together students' experience of the economic conditions Wilson described with the integrated, experiential education I learned at Bank Street.

Around the same time, I was getting my feet wet as a teacher new to Philadelphia. In a curriculum guide issued by the school district, I found the suggestion to pay students classroom dollars for being "good classroom citizens" (School District of Philadelphia, 1989, pp. 34–39).[4] In this curriculum, students were to fill in a pay sheet, deciding whether they should receive pay for fulfilling the responsibilities of attendance, homework, getting along with others, and other classroom "jobs" (p. 36). The writers of the curriculum pointed out that this project could be extended in endless directions.

What I liked about this idea was that it seemed to provide the possibility of bringing economic experience into the classroom. The problem I had was that in the real world, one does not get paid for being a good citizen, but rather for doing one's job; those who are richest are not always the best citizens. With this in mind, I reframed the economic system so that children were paid for "the job of being a good student" rather than a good citizen; I structured the classroom economy to run parallel to an experiential economic study of the outside neighborhood; and I used students' questions and experience about both economies to chart the direction of our study.

The Evolution of the Classroom Economy

When the classroom economy first began, all student jobs were "government work" and I, the teacher, was the only boss. I began paying students for the job of being students, which included classroom jobs (e.g., distributing corrected work), academic performance, behavior, and a personal goal of their choosing (e.g., "I will get a job"). Students voiced no opposition to the power I reserved, which might be attributable to the reality that teachers are always the boss. A job chart at the front of the room listed government jobs, their rate of pay, and the name of the person currently holding each position. I later added a second chart listing "private sector" jobs. To apply for a job,

[4] For other classroom uses of "micro-societies," see McCarthy and Braffman (1985), and Richmond (1989).

students filled out an application. On the job application, students gave reasons why I should hire them and included their previous work experience and names of references. I returned these applications with written explanations for their acceptance or rejection. Students became familiar with the boss's criterion for a strong application. They learned, for example, that last year's teacher made a better reference than one of their friends, and that it was better to cite one's success at the last job than to state that one needs money. I once observed a boy start an application, then crumple it up to start over, saying, "I forgot, neatness counts!"

Students designed the money that we used. On the different denominations we had pictures of Rosa Parks, "Homey the Clown," Don King, and a student's mother. We printed the money on different colors of paper using our hand-cranked xerograph.

In our class, the students' schedule was highly structured, with the basic subjects being studied at the same time each day. In some progressive classrooms I have known, activities tend to be "decentralized," with two or three different groups engaged in different lessons at the same time. One group might be reading with the teacher, another working on dioramas, and still another testing each other on their spelling words. In contrast, my students seemed to do best when working as a class. Although students' ability levels varied greatly, there seemed to be a feeling of momentum when the entire class worked on an exercise, with the faster or more advanced students tutoring the others. Within this rather traditional routine, students had a great deal of input into the curriculum, great flexibility in the approaches they used to complete their work, and great responsibility when they earned it. Academic work and social behavior became the basis for the ebb and flow of the responsibilities and trust earned by students. When a child was responsible, I hired him or her for the most important work, such as collating homework packets. When the class as a whole earned my trust, we took more ambitious walking trips, such as to the local pond.

In the last ten minutes of every day, each child evaluated his or her "job of being a good student" by filling out a pay sheet. On the top half of the pay sheet was a grid for the student to fill in, with one column for each day of the week and a row for each aspect of the "job of being a student": their school work, behavior, and "government" job. Based on their self-evaluations, students wrote in how much they should be paid. I provided some parameters, such as that school work paid a maximum of twenty-five dollars per day. At the end of each column was a row for them to total each day's pay. On the bottom half of the sheet was a space for them to write their personal goal for the day. On Friday afternoons, I paid the students. They then had the chance to use their money to buy the use of activities. Yet, before they could spend their wages, they were required to pay rent for their desk and taxes needed for municipal salaries. Students who were unable to pay rent or taxes went on welfare.

Each month I asked the students, "How can we make the classroom more like the neighborhood?" Their responses directed our explorations. The first time I posed this question, students answered that we should start stores in the classroom. When William asked how much a store costs, I turned this question back to the class by asking them where we might go to find the answers. In the discussion that followed, we decided that we would take a walking trip to the soul-food restaurant named "Ziggie's Barbecue Pit," which was located on the same block as our school.[5]

The next day, with Ziggie forewarned of the invasion, we set out to learn about starting a business. Ziggie's was a dimly lit, homey establishment, with hundreds of snapshots decorating its walls. With students and parent chaperons sitting on the stools at the lunch counter and on the seats from Ziggie's long-deceased Chevy van, the press conference began. The regular customers listened with curious attention as Ziggie patiently answered the questions students posed to him. After a half-hour of talking with Ziggie, we returned to the classroom, and I asked the students what they had learned. From our conversation with Ziggie they recalled: *start small and save; buy wholesale for cheap and sell retail for less cheap;* and the motto of the patient entrepreneur, *little by little.* The students' over-sized thank you letter is still hanging on the inside of Ziggie's door.

After talking about the goods and services already available in our classroom, the students discussed what stores we should have in our classroom economy. For example, because we used educational games and puzzles in our classroom, the students decided that we needed a toy store. Once we knew what stores we needed, student builders painted red bricks on boxes large enough to be used as storefronts. Using a razor-blade knife, I cut "windows" out of the boxes so that the merchants could stand behind them and sell their wares through the opening. Positioned around the perimeter of the room, these storefronts framed our carpeted area. Store names painted by students hung from the ceiling over each establishment. Two potted trees, donated by a company that rents large indoor plants to corporations, added to the realism of the "neighborhood."

In January, in my role as "the government," I auctioned off the Arts Supply Stores, Fidelity Bank, the toy store, Value Plus Clothing Store, an Art Gallery, and the Sweet Cakes Zoo. This "privatization" provided material for a lesson on the law of supply and demand. The students subsequently decided to add more businesses to Sweet Cakes Town. With each new proposal, we were propelled out of the classroom and into the neighborhood, visiting businesses and a factory, inviting visitors to be interviewed, collecting specimens from the neighborhood pond, and doing research at the public library.

---

[5] In many schools, the spontaneity of going on field trips is curtailed by the time it takes to issue and receive signed permission slips. The Philadelphia school system helps teachers to avoid this problem by issuing permission slips that allow children to go on neighborhood walking trips throughout the year.

After each trip, students drew in a few more neighborhood landmarks on a 5-foot-by-4-foot "working map" of the neighborhood that hung on our wall. Earlier in the year, students had made maps of our classroom, the school, and the area directly surrounding the school. Once we had some shared understanding of what the map of the neighborhood would look like, I laid out the larger street grid on our working map. Following each trip, two or three students would make additions to this map in pencil, then compare them to an aerial photograph of the neighborhood (purchased from the local regional planning commission) before making their additions permanent.

In January, when we first added stores to our economy, I created a form that asked students to subtract their rent and taxes from their earnings on their pay sheets in order to find their gross and net pay. From this point on, their paychecks included only the net figure. By gradually increasing the complexity of these forms, the students had meaningful applications of math problems at a level that was both challenging and attainable. I once overheard a boy say to himself after correctly filling out his pay sheet, "Ya, I'm all that."

Retail buying time on Friday afternoons was as exhilarating as anything I have experienced as a teacher. I watched in anxious amazement as students followed their own purposes, whether they were working at their store or spending their money. Without anything else to do, I might rent a hat at Value Plus, or go to the Men's Styling Shop, where Derek would spray water on my head, style my hair, and then slap the chair with a towel as I got up, as barbers often do. During this time, the zoo keepers even let Frances the rabbit wander about the classroom. The amazing thing to me was that usually retail buying time worked; that is, students went about their business and didn't require me to play the role of disciplinarian.

On those occasions when retail buying time did start to get wild, I followed the advice of a wise teacher trainer, Barbara Moore Williams, who once told me, "Don't lecture — let the kids tell you what the problem is. The kids know it all!" When it got too noisy, I would call things to a halt using the traditional hand in the air and a finger over my lips. The students would do the same, and pretty soon it would be quiet. Then I would ask, "Why did we have to stop?" One of the kids would explain, "Because Tyree was running." Then I would ask, "What's the matter with running?" Somebody would say, "It's too wild for the classroom." I would say, "What's going to happen if I see running again?" They would say, "We'll have to stop retail buying time." This generally worked for us.

After a few months of learning from people in the neighborhood, students wrote nominations for neighborhood citizenship awards (e.g., "My neighbor, Mr. Davis, watches over the children on the block to make sure they are safe. He is like a guardian angel."). We invited those people, as well as all those whom we had interviewed in our study, to come to the classroom to receive awards for their contributions.

Along with studying their neighborhood, the mandated curriculum called for third graders to study the city of Philadelphia, the state of Pennsylvania, the United States, and the world. We began to study the city after about four months of studying our neighborhood, and later, we studied the state. Our points of departure for both of these projects were first-hand investigations of other neighborhoods. We visited the outdoor Italian market as an example of the diversity of Philadelphia, and the community of Landsdale as an introduction to rural Pennsylvania. In both of these studies, we established correspondence between our class and third-grade classrooms in the other neighborhoods. Throughout these units, the Sweet Cakes Town economy continued to develop within our classroom.

Economics and the Classroom Neighborhood

I structured the Sweet Cakes Town economy to mirror some of the changes that had occurred in the economy of the students' neighborhood in North Philadelphia.[6] For example:

- I listed high-paying jobs, such as gerbil cage-cleaning, but then explained to the kids that this job had moved to a classroom in the suburbs. We talked about how many of the jobs that used to be in the cities are now outside the cities and the strategies that adults use for overcoming this problem.
- I hired fourth-grade students who would work for nothing just so that they could get out of their class. These were our immigrant workers. My students responded to this by encouraging them not to work unless they were paid.
- I sent one student a letter via Sweet Cakes mail relating the bad news that a great aunt had died. Enclosed was the inheritance check, which gave us the opportunity to discuss the fact that some people start off with more capital than others. Students reacted to this with quiet resignation.
- Students also dealt with recessions, layoffs, wage inequities, and alliances of capital.

Each of these obstacles was taken as a challenge to be overcome, rather than a defeat to be endured. After we read a biography of Cesar Chavez, student workers created their own union, which they named JBS Local 207 (standing for John Barnes School, room 207). It took a while for them to coordinate collective action. At first when I lowered their wages, one of them said, "I'm on strike," to which I replied, "OK, who wants her job?" At this point, many of the students raised their hands, and the striker backed down. Trying to make this as realistic as possible, I lowered their wages again and again. Eventually they realized that their individual good was dependent on

---

[6] Philadelphia, like most Eastern, industrial cities, had been decimated by the loss of manufacturing jobs in the last two-and-a-half decades. In the period between 1975 and 1979 alone, the city lost 128,000 jobs, or one out of six (Katz, 1986, p. 276).

each other, and except for two die-hard scabs, the workers waged a strike. The union leaders and I reached a bargain over lunch, and later the bargain was ratified by the rank and file.

Our classroom neighborhood study gave us an economic frame of reference for discussing a variety of real-life situations. For example, a work period was interrupted by two students yelling back and forth, "Your mother's homeless!" "No, your mother's homeless!" I intervened, and said that I was angry about their interruption and felt that we needed to discuss it as a class. We agreed that there were two issues at hand: one was that the two students were angrily arguing about something; the other was that homelessness was being used as an insult. I decided that the two students and I would discuss their dispute privately, but that the issue concerning homelessness would be addressed as a class.

I began this discussion by asking the students what kept people from being able to pay their rents. Jameel said, "They won't go out and get a job." We compared this explanation to what we experienced in our classroom economy, namely, the effects of intervening factors such as lay-offs, businesses relocating to the suburbs, jobs not paying enough, and people not having enough money to start a business. I emphasized that if a person is homeless, it is not something of which the person should be ashamed, but something of which our country should be ashamed. Individual students volunteered examples of honest and hardworking people they knew who were homeless. Only later did I learn that one of the students present for this conversation had recently moved to a homeless shelter with her family. I marveled at this, because even with such turmoil in her home life, she was excelling as a student, consistently making the honor roll.

It seems to me that impromptu discussions of economic issues complemented more structured discussions of inequality. For example, during the year, I used Margaret Davidson's (1986) biography of Martin Luther King, Jr., as one of our reading texts. In previous years, my students had always responded to King's fight against prejudice, but seemed to have trouble connecting their own lives with King's call for economic justice. This year, however, perhaps because of our classroom economy, students had an experiential vocabulary for talking about the economic factors behind inequality.

We also looked at language differences in an economic context. Knowing of the stigmatization of non-Standard English (NSE) in our society, I wanted to raise my students' awareness of the role that language differences play in social relations, but to do so in a way that did not demean the language style used in their homes. Assimilation was never the goal. Instead, I wanted them to see that one possible use of learning Standard English (SE) was *infiltration:* crossing over into a world where non-Standard English is not valued and using Standard English to achieve their own goals, while understanding that to do so need not mean giving up their identity as African Americans or their loyalty to their home communities.

I therefore initiated discussions of the relative effectiveness of SE and NSE in different contexts. Students identified quotes from poetry we had studied and speeches by African American leaders as "SE" or "NSE." Then we labeled quotes by students in the class in the same way. Finally, students identified a list of various situations with the type of English that would be most appropriately used there (e.g., speaking at home, writing a rap, asking for something from the principal, or applying for a job at a bank). I encouraged students to see language differences as options that could be invoked to suit their purposes in a given context, rather than as a once-and-for-all choice (Erickson 1987).

On a number of occasions, I saw informal evidence that these exercises might be raising students' awareness of their uses of language. For example, one afternoon as we were working on a science project, a boy with writing disabilities was dictating to me his observations about a snail that we had brought back from the neighborhood pond. The student said, "He ain't movin." As I started to write, he hurried to say, "He is not moving." I asked the boy if he was changing to Standard English and he looked at me perplexed. This suggested to me that while such labels as "Standard English" may have eluded him, this student had gained some practical awareness that he was able to switch codes and that he had knowledge of their appropriate contexts.

Democracy and the Classroom Neighborhood

As John Locke would have wanted it, the government of Sweet Cakes Town evolved naturally as problems arose between individuals. It seems that Lateef, the owner of the Value Plus Store, had been hiring new clerks each week rather than paying the old ones. Just when mob action seemed imminent, I separated the parties and suggested that we start a court. A judge was elected, jurors and lawyers picked, and for the time being, playground justice was held off. Before the trial, which was held a few days later, I invited an African American lawyer to coach both the prosecution and the defense. Witnesses were sworn in on a coloring-book Bible found in a student's desk. In lieu of the black robe, the judge wore a black velvet evening gown on loan from Value Plus. At one point during the defendant's testimony, Judge Jameson blurted out, "Oh, he is *so* guilty!" giving us a chance to explore the notion of "innocent until proven guilty." In the end, Lateef was convicted and forced to pay all back wages.

Occasionally an offense was committed without the perpetrator ever being discovered. On a day when I was absent and the students had a substitute teacher, someone scrawled graffiti across the red-brick front of our toy store. At the beginning of the following day, I asked the students to answer the following questions: "What feelings are people showing when they hurt the classroom neighborhood? Who does it hurt? Does it solve the problem? What are other possible solutions?" In this way, I tried to get students to see that destructive behavior, like doing graffiti, is sometimes an expression of misplaced feelings like anger, which could be better used to solve the problem. The effective uses of anger came up again in our discussion of the L.A. riots that followed the Rodney King verdict. "Solve the problem!" became our class mantra.

Another day, we had problems with loitering students starting trouble during retail buying time. I overheard one girl explain, "I don't want to shop. I'm savin' my money for a business." Some students decided that we needed a "no loitering" law and called for the election of a government. I suggested to the students that they conduct a poll regarding which citizens should be allowed to vote. The boys said that girls should not vote, and the girls said that the boys should not vote. I used these experiences to provide a meaningful context for discussing the women's suffrage movement and the history of African Americans' struggle for voting rights in the United States.

As a result of these history lessons, the class decided on universal suffrage. With signs hanging from the ceiling, they designated each group of desks as a different city council district. They elected a city council representative from each table group and a mayor for the whole town. I asked each student to submit ten laws to their city council person. Student suggestions included "No more pay increases for city council" and "No air pollution."

Once when I asked how we could make the classroom more like the neighborhood, students suggested that we add roads and garbage collectors. "Who's going to pay for all this?" asked one realist. I turned this dilemma back to them and asked, "Who pays for these services in the outside neighborhood?" We discussed this, as well as the local controversy over the privatization of municipal services.

To learn more about how tax money was used, two student delegates and I telephoned Philadelphia's City Hall. Afterwards we received a pie chart of the city's expenditures in the mail, which I simplified for use with the children. This provided the basis for a discussion of students' views on spending priorities for city governments. Students created their own pie charts showing how they thought Sweet Cakes dollars should be used, and these suggestions were given to the mayor of Sweet Cakes Town. In our discussions about public and private services, students offered a variety of opinions about which services should be paid for with tax money and which should be handled privately. Eventually, the government paid for roads made out of black contact paper marked with yellow lane dividers, and instituted trash collection.

The mayor of Sweet Cakes Town was popular for nearly a month, until students realized he had hired only close friends to fill virtually all the government jobs, with some friends holding four jobs. We talked about how this happens in real life and discussed what options voters have when they feel their elected officials are not acting on their behalf. The mayor was roundly defeated in his bid for a second term.

By the time students decided that the town needed a mayor, they were already in the habit of going to the source for their information. Philadelphia's Mayor Rendell graciously accepted the children's invitation and came to Sweet Cakes Town to be interviewed about his job. During his visit, students gave him a large bar graph showing the results of the poll they had conducted to survey their parents' attitudes toward the mayor (at that point, the mayor was enjoying an 80 percent approval rating). As a final gesture of thanks, the mayor of Sweet Cakes Town gave Mayor Rendell the papier-mache "key" to our city.

The final project the citizens of Sweet Cakes Town undertook was a community works project: the students agreed to address the problem of small grocers in the neighborhood selling "crack." By writing a newspaper about Sweet Cakes Town and selling it on the street, they raised money for DARE, an anti-drug group. This project had to be squeezed into a single week, as the end of the school year was closing in on us. Our last day of school was a triumphant one. We returned to the streets of our neighborhood to sell the *Sweet Cakes News,* telling stories from students' study of the neighborhood. The response from the community was tremendous: in about two hours we sold 250 copies of *Sweet Cakes News* at 25 cents apiece. The students also gave copies to the merchants who had helped them during the year.

At the end of the year I asked students to carry the storefronts of Sweet Cakes Town to the trash. They asked to keep them, explaining to me that, if I didn't object, they would like to use them to start concession stands in the neighborhood. I didn't object.

Student Experience and the Standardized Curriculum

A series of questions guided the Sweet Cakes Town curriculum. Each day, when students filed into the classroom, an "opening exercise" sheet awaited them on their desks. The opening exercise typically included a few problems reviewing yesterday's math lesson and a single question concerning the neighborhood study, such as, "What are some things that money cannot buy?" which did not have a single "right" answer. These questions formed the basis of our morning discussions. Sometimes they served an instrumental purpose ("What special rules will we need for our trip to the pond?"); other times, they prepared us for the arrival of a visitor from the neighborhood ("Write one question that you have about the job of a dress designer."). By linking the questions from one day to the next, we developed themes while keeping students' experience and opinions at the heart of our study. For example,

Monday: In the Sweet Cakes Town system of jobs, what leaves you feeling bad, sad, or angry?

Tuesday: In the outside neighborhood system of jobs, what leaves people feeling bad, sad, or angry?

Wednesday: In the outside neighborhood, what are some *bad* things some people do if they are having a hard time making money?

Thursday: In the outside neighborhood, what are some *good* things some people do if they are having a hard time making money?

After ten minutes devoted to this opening exercise, students had an opportunity to volunteer their answers, which I recorded on chart paper, and a discussion usually ensued. With this format, I found that students would listen to each other more patiently and give thoughtful responses based on their considerable life experience. I tried to let students' questions and interests guide our study as much as possible, but this was negotiated in the context of the requirements that I faced and my own beliefs about what should be taught. My principal gave me great support and flexibility, but also insisted that the objectives of the curriculum be met, and that students be prepared for the standardized tests. Unfortunately, a new standardized test was implemented during the study of Sweet Cakes Town, making comparison of students' scores to previous years problematic.

To keep track of what mandated objectives we had met, I kept a list of them in my planbook and marked each one as we studied it (Donnan, 1988, p. 3).[7] Topics from social studies, such as "interdependence in the community," arose relatively naturally. But when other required topics did not come up, I looked for opportunities to raise them during the course of our investigation. For example, students were not clamoring to learn about commas, so with Raquel's permission, we began a writing class with the question, "Where are commas needed in Raquel's thank you letter to the people at the clothing store?"

Overall, I found that some of the most difficult issues of our study came from the students' own experiences in the community. The proper response to violence was an issue that confounded my easy answers. After discussing problems of urban violence, Black-on-Black violence, and the uses of political nonviolence, and after doing countless role plays of conflict resolution, I would be reminded again of how complicated my students' lives were. In a bit of writing that makes me laugh even while it saddens me, Macio wrote:

> Being violent is bad to people. They steal from people. It is too bad that people are stealing from my mom. Me and my brother is going to kick some butts.

When I first began teaching in cities, I taught the gospel of nonviolence with less humility than I do today. Since then, I think that I have gained some understanding of my students' anger (and my own). I have a greater appreciation for how painfully difficult it can be to overcome anger and find solutions.

---

[7] See Elliot Wigginton (1989) for another framework for bringing together students' interests and mandated curricula.

STUDENTS AND CITIZENS

Our class had, on average, twenty-four students, which was typical for third-grade classes in our school but down from thirty-four children the previous year. (This reduction was due to a vote by teachers in our school to use discretionary federal funds to reduce class size.) During the year, six students transferred in and eight transferred out. Of the entire class, one boy was Latino, and all others were African American. While Sweet Cakes Town evolved, not only was there turnover in student population, but students' roles within the town changed. Most students switched professions every month or two. Workers quit or were fired. Partnerships came and went as easily as third-grade friendships. Everyone held a job for some period, and no one held only one job. I will now describe three children who seemed to benefit socially and academically from their experiences in Sweet Cakes Town. While some students showed less personal and academic growth during the year, the experiences of these three students were not atypical among the group.

Derek

Derek, the boy quoted earlier who wanted to get off welfare, was handsome, funny, keenly observant of social interactions — a gifted mimic. At the beginning of the year, Derek requested to sit alone; he told me outright that he did not get along with other children. He was vehemently protective of his work being seen by the other students, but had a habit of yelling out humorous commentary to those very peers he held at a distance. A burly eleven-year-old, he could read at a kindergarten level. Despite this, or because of this, he refused to see a reading tutor. In the early stages of our classroom neighborhood, Derek created the character of "Kool Homie." Homie had a haircut known as a high-top fade, a big gold chain around his neck, sometimes a hat, and the local expressive walk. Week after week, Derek would pay for the clothes to dress up as Kool Homie, and act out stick-ups and muggings.

It was during this time that I heard Derek pronounce that he wanted to get off welfare, and that he had been on it all his life. Since Sweet Cakes Town did not have food stamps, I believe Derek was expressing the connection he saw between his life outside of school and his role in Sweet Cakes Town. In an effort to get off welfare, Derek applied for the job requiring the highest skill and receiving the highest wage: the filer of corrected work. The job paid forty Sweet Cakes dollars per day. Because he lacked experience, he did not get the job. Later that day another boy told Derek to apply for another job paying only $10.00 per day. Derek replied, "Who wants some $10.00 job! I don't want to get off welfare. . . . I applied to be a filer. That shows I want a job. Now I'm stayin' on welfare for the rest of my life. . . ."

I discussed with Derek the fact that he had not gotten the higher paying job for which he had applied because he lacked experience. We discussed strategies that people use to overcome this problem in the outside world, and Derek decided to volunteer as a work distributor for a week before applying to be a filer once again. Though he didn't get the filing job, he succeeded in being hired to water the plants (a job that paid a moderate wage).

With the money that Derek saved from his job, he was able to start the classroom branch of the Fidelity Bank. Making the most of our trip to a neighborhood bank, occasional lunch meetings with me, and hypothetical banking problems in math class, Derek proved greatly successful as a banker. He offered checking and savings accounts, as well as high-interest loans. As his business increased, he took on two partners. At the same time, he showed marked increases in social and academic confidence. However, though he regularly completed his math work, being older and bigger than the other children and barely able to read, he rarely attempted any language arts work in the classroom for fear of losing face.

One day in April, the kids told me that Derek had sold the bank. Because of the success he had had with the bank, I wondered why. When I talked with Derek, he would give me no explanation. A former teller, however, confided to me that Derek had sold the bank because people were bouncing checks: Derek thought this meant that he was in trouble. With the money from the sale of the bank, Derek bought the Value Plus Clothing Store and ran it successfully until the end of the school year.

Later in the year, I recommended that Derek be evaluated by our school's instructional support team (IST), a cross-disciplinary team charged with finding remedies when the school was failing to meet a child's needs. Derek was said to have a normal IQ, but also deficits in information processing, perceptual organization skills, and fine visual-motor perception and integration. As part of the IST effort to find support for students with learning problems within regular education classes, Derek was given intensive tutoring, which — this time — he accepted. When this tutoring failed to help him, the members of the IST, of which I was a part, recommended that Derek be switched to a special education class the following year.

Shawntay

Shawntay was a quiet, amiable girl. She did not cause trouble or draw attention to herself, but often did not finish her work. I found that as a teacher, I needed to keep deliberate track of her progress. Shawntay had good social skills, but remained peripheral to the social network. Moreover, I worried that her academic progress was hindered by low self-esteem. Like Derek, she too had been "held back" in first and second grades and now, in third grade, she was developing as an adolescent. In the early part of the year, the school psychologist found that Shawntay was dyslexic, but it was decided that she should remain in our classroom, where she seemed to be making progress.

Shawntay was the student who bought the bank from Derek. After the purchase, she found herself having great responsibility, but lacking a good understanding of how to run a bank. When people came to her asking for "their money," she neglected to keep track of how much she was giving out. When we realized the problem, she arranged to pay Derek to take time out from his new business to train her in banking (our first highly paid consultant). Although Shawntay learned to run the bank, she never really seemed to take a liking to it. She sold the business after a few months.

With the money she made from selling the bank, Shawntay opened a beauty parlor in May. Here she thrived. Shawntay's Beauty Parlor offered hair braiding, manicures, and make-up consultation. She did a brisk business, and soon her idea for a beauty parlor was copied by Tyree, who began a styling salon for "men." Shawntay's business career proved to be a springboard for political life; now, as an esteemed leader among the girls, she was elected to a seat on the city council. In the process, she showed marked improvement in her math skills, going from B's to A's.

William

William was a thoughtful, quiet boy who was well-liked by his classmates. In reading and math he performed on grade level. He had gotten an A in reading for the previous year, even while getting an F in behavior. My journal notes from the beginning of the year describe William as "sullen" and "sulky." Sometimes, William would become emotionally removed and perform a "go-slow" for an afternoon. William occasionally gave me a glimpse of the experiences he was having outside of school that might be draining his vigor. In response to a homework assignment asking students to write a true story about their neighborhood, William wrote the shortest of stories, but one that told volumes:

> One day on a weekend my best friend's dad got shot. I didn't know that he would get killed because he was good to people.

Despite such troubles, William came alive when we started the classroom economy. He was the first to apply for a job and the first to hold more than one government job at a time (at one point he held four). During this time William saved his money, keeping it in a big "knot" in his front pocket. It was he who inquired how much a business cost and, not suprisingly, he was the first to buy a store of his own.

Over the course of the year, William demonstrated a great entrepreneurial spirit. William's first store was the toy store, for which he hired his long-time friend Tyree as manager. With their profits, the two bought the Art Supply Store and hired Ray as a manager. William was the town's first mayor (it was his fall from power that I mentioned earlier). William's first appointment was again his friend Tyree. On Fridays, William and Tyree stayed in the classroom during recess to calculate revenues and expenditures for that fiscal week. Eventually, William and Tyree completed them on their own. One day when they requested to use silent reading time to finish their calculations, I heard William say to his buddies, "Don't bug me — I'm busy!" As he left that day I told him that he had done a good job on the budget. He grinned from ear to ear as he walked out through the gate of the schoolyard.

After William was defeated in his bid for re-election, he returned to running his businesses with Tyree. In the springtime, they started a plant store where students could plant seeds and then pick up their plants a week or so later.

LEARNING FROM SWEET CAKES TOWN

In this section, I return to the first of the questions with which I began this article: How can we teach children so that we do not simply replicate the existing social inequalities? Following are the seven primary insights I gained from my experiences with my students in our development of Sweet Cakes Town.

— Creating opportunities for repeated, meaningful applications of academic skills

As has long been recognized by educational advocates among the poor, "self-efficacy" is a hollow term when one lacks the skills necessary to accomplish one's goals (Freire, 1993, p. 59; Lukas, 1986, p. 36). But, too often, "skills" and "knowledge" have been dichotomized, as if the two needed to be taught separately, as if the meaningfulness of a task could not increase the process of skill acquisition. Besides running counter to empirical research (Sticht, 1987), this dichotomization contradicts the common experience many of us have of learning deeply and quickly something that we care about.

Sweet Cakes Town involved students in what I call "meaningful drill." For example, at the end of each day, students computed their daily pay using multiplication and addition with carrying. At the end of each week, they also calculated their weekly pay, using addition with carrying and subtraction with borrowing. This was not math taught as practice for some task that the students might face in future years, but real math applied to make things happen in their present lives. Traditionally, most of what are called "applications" of math skills, such as story problems, ask students to pretend that they are using skills in a real situation. Unfortunately, it is all too possible for a student to go from kindergarten through twelfth grade and never use math for a real purpose. In Sweet Cakes Town, the calculations were as real as the privileges that the students could buy with their money. Similarly, I believe students' involvement in issues that mattered to them dramatically enhanced their acquisition of hard skills in reading, writing, science, and geography. It seemed that students learned skills faster in Sweet Cakes Town because they needed them, and they routinized their new skills by using them every day.

— Providing opportunities for students to imagine themselves in new roles

For years, sociologists have told us that schools prepare lower socioeconomic status (SES) students to become lower SES adults, and upper SES students to become upper SES adults. Though this problem is partly a sin of omission, there are other dimensions to it that I will address later. Schools have failed to broaden their students' range of possibilities, leaving students to choose from the limited options that they see around them.

Options that Derek saw were playing "Kool Homie," standing on the street corner, or being a thief. Though Derek was not satisfied being on welfare, other options did not seem accessible to him. There were obstacles in his way, such as his lack of experience, the lack of role models to teach him how one gets experience, and, not least of which, a school system that had failed to find successful ways to teach him. I believe he needed to develop a strategy and to know that others (such as the lawyer who visited our classroom) have succeeded in overcoming the obstacles that face African Americans from the inner city.

By allowing students to imagine themselves in new roles, Sweet Cakes Town was, I like to think, a dream that we as a class dreamed together. The power of dreams to transform a life is explained by Ernst Bloch:

> Dreams come in the day as well as at night. And both kinds of dreaming are motivated by wishes they seek to fulfill. But daydreams differ from night dreams; for the day dreaming "I" persists throughout, consciously, privately, envisaging the circumstances and images of the desired, better life. The content of the daydream is not, like that of the night dream, a journey back into repressed experiences and their associations. It is concerned with an, as far as possible, unrestricted journey forward, so that instead of reconstituting that which is no longer conscious, the images of that which is not yet can be phantasied into life and into the world. (quoted in Simon & Dippo, 1987, p. 102)

Derek, Shawntay, William, and most other children in the class proved eminently successful at daydreaming new futures — as a banker, the owner of a hair styling salon, or an entrepreneur.

— Helping students to divorce academic success from "acting White"

As has been observed by Fordham and Ogbu (1986), success in school is often perceived by African American children as "acting White," which makes having a positive racial identity and succeeding in school seem mutually exclusive. Erickson (1987) has pointed out that this perception can be exacerbated or ameliorated depending on the behaviors of teachers and school personnel. He cites a comparative study of two classrooms: in one, the teacher frequently corrected the students for using "Black English"; in the other, the teacher did not correct students' language (Erickson, 1987, p. 346, citing Piestrup). At the end of the year, students who had frequently been corrected were speaking a *more* pronounced dialect in the classroom. Students who were *not* corrected were using language that was closer to "Standard English."

Erickson explains this data using contrasting metaphors of a "boundary" and a "border" (used first by Barth, 1969). In the classroom where Black English was stigmatized, a boundary was created between the world of the student and the world of the teacher. With each correction, the students' *defense* of their own cultural style grew, raising the wall a bit higher. The ultimate impact of this boundary was a sacrifice of the mutual trust that is needed for a student to risk attempting new academic tasks. In contrast, in the classroom where Black English was not stigmatized, this boundary became a border that the students could cross in both directions without threat of giving up an aspect of their cultural identity (Erickson, 1987, p. 350).

Whereas Fordham and Ogbu (1986) have shown the effects of a closed labor market on African Americans' attitudes about education, Erickson's (1987) analysis shows how the actions of people in schools can affect these attitudes. In our classroom, one way we incorporated the observations of Fordham and Ogbu and Erickson into the neighborhood study was in the treatment of language difference. I presented both Black English and Standard English as options that were appropriate and useful in certain contexts (Ladson-Billings, 1992). More generally, I attempted to show that academic skills are tools in the ongoing struggle for equality (Freire, 1993; Ladson-Billings, 1990). As educators, we need to find new ways to show students that achieving academic success can be "acting Black."

— *Allowing students to take pro-active stances in relation to those in power*

In Sweet Cakes Town, the students not only had the chance to imagine themselves as grown-ups in roles of power, they also had power right then and there to influence the classroom study, each other, and me as their teacher. In the drama of the classroom economy, they experimented with strategies for using power: as workers who sue a corrupt boss, as exploited union members who strike for a fair wage, or as constituents who rally for a new mayor. In other words, as modern-day Davids, they found that the Goliaths of their day were within their range.

But beyond these chosen roles, Sweet Cakes Town also gave students a chance to experience new relationships between themselves and the authority figure with whose power they are most familiar: their teacher. Writers discussing such diverse topics as social reproduction, critical pedagogy, the hidden curriculum, process consultation, and education for empowerment have observed that having a passive role in educational institutions prepares students for taking a passive role vis-à-vis authority figures later in life: that is, a role as object rather than subject (Bowles & Gintis, 1976, p. 56; Freire, 1982, p. 59; Giroux, 1977, 1978, pp. 148–151; Schein, 1988, p. 9; Sleeter, 1991, p. 15). In contrast, problem-posing education replaces this vertical relationship between teachers and students with a horizontal one, a dialogue (Freire, 1982). In the case of Sweet Cakes Town, students were part of the process of guiding the course of study.

In our classroom, as students created a model of the neighborhood, they were *encoding* aspects of their culture (Freire, 1986). Derek's character Kool Homie was a code packed with elements of the situation faced by some African American men. Derek had an understanding of how one might portray himself as an African American male in a closed economy. I shared with Derek my belief that he could make it in the mainstream economy. In our daily discussion of Kool Homie, jobs, and strategies for getting jobs, the two of us came to a new understanding of his relationship to street corner life, as well as to how he could envision a different relationship.

Problem-posing education provides an opportunity to prepare the next generation for relationships qualitatively different than those we know between authorities and subordinates, such as bosses and workers or government leaders and constituents. Such changes are well-suited to current innovations in management practices, as U.S. corporations begin to realize the loss inherent in treating human beings like machines and move to less hierarchical, more team-oriented approaches to management (Byrne, 1993; Stewart, 1992, 1993).

For my students to play a role in changing their relationships to authority figures, they had to learn how to get, keep, and use power to participate in defining these relationships. The need for such practice will be developed below in my next-to-last recommendation.

— Creating curricula that treats reality as something to be questioned and analyzed (Giroux, 1979)

When teachers change their students' role in acquiring knowledge, I believe they also change the nature of the students' relationship to that knowledge. In more traditional forms of education, knowledge is deposited into the minds of uncritical students (Freire, 1982). Henry Giroux has pointed out that in such "banking" pedagogy, knowledge is treated as a set of objective "facts" (Giroux, 1979). He says that

> knowledge is divorced from human meaning and inter subjective exchange. It no longer is seen as something to be questioned, analyzed and negotiated. Instead, it becomes something to be managed and mastered. In this case, knowledge is removed from the self-formative process of generating one's own set of meanings, a process that involves an interpretive relationship between knower and known. (Giroux, 1979, p. 250)

Such "banking" instruction has been contrasted with a "mining" pedagogy, where teachers view their task as drawing knowledge *out* of the student, rather than depositing it within (Ladson-Billings, 1990, p. 340). Ira Shor (1980) says that when students are allowed to bring their experience into the classroom, teachers are able to help students see the familiar and accept it in a new light: "By identifying, abstracting and problematizing the most important themes of student experience, the teacher detaches students from their reality and then re-presents the material for systematic scrutiny" (1980, p. 100).

For example, when two students taunted each other, saying, "Your mother's homeless," I believed that the students had internalized the popular ideology of blaming the victim. Consequently, I related that example to their experience in Sweet Cakes Town, showing that factors outside of an individual's control sometimes interfere with a person's ability to pay the rent.

Similarly, as students in Sweet Cakes Town studied their environment, they created their own understanding of how their community works and where its hope lies. The structures of knowledge that they created were not isolated, abstract, and theoretical, but interrelated, concrete, and practical. To borrow terms from Lev Vygotsky (1978), the informal knowledge of their experience was organically connected to the formal knowledge of school learning. Or, from Pierre Bourdieu's (1977) perspective, the students used the "cultural capital" *from* their community to create "dividends" to *take back* to their community.

— Creating opportunities for students to develop strategies and hope for overcoming barriers to economic success in the mainstream

So far in this discussion, I have talked about aspects of my curriculum aimed at changing conditions internal to the students: their perceptions about their role in the world, their perceived relations both to those in power and to knowledge itself. But urban, African American children of lower socioeconomic status also face obstacles to success that are external to them, obstacles that they will need to understand if they are to stand a chance (Sleeter & Grant, 1986). First, there are those obstacles Black people have always faced in the United States: prejudice, residential ghettoization, poor education, lack of capital, and lack of networks to obtain capital, to name a few. Secondly, postindustrial changes in the economy have constructed new obstacles to economic success for those isolated in the inner cities: lack of jobs, jobs moving further out of the city where there is no public transportation, lack of access to job information networks, jobs that require higher skills, or, I would add here, that require them to speak differently than they do at home.[8] In the face of these obstacles to economic success, there are new self-destructive alternatives, such as crack cocaine, which also threaten to pull them down. As teachers, we want to say to our students, "If you try, you

---

[8] The split between low-wage (goods producing) and high-wage (service producing) sectors of the economy was not addressed in the curriculum, but would be wisely included in future neighborhood studies.

will make it," but we know that it's not that simple, and to say it is that simple is to imply falsely that those who did not make it did not try.

This brings me to the second of the two questions with which I began: *How do we avoid the twin pitfalls of a) stressing the obstacles to economic success, thereby encouraging defeatism, and b) stressing the possibilities for economic success, thereby encouraging the view that those who did not make it have only themselves to blame?* Some might argue that it is better to teach the bootstraps "myth," believing that a false hope is better than none. This, of course, would ultimately leave students unprepared for the obstacles ahead. Our students face the stark realities of the inner cities every day. As teachers we must face our responsibility to abandon the innocuous social studies curricula that do not take into account the abandoned buildings and crack vials that students pass on any walking trip to the fire station. We must help our students cope with their present problems, and prepare them to overcome future obstacles. I believe that children who are economically isolated in U.S. inner cities need to be educated about the structural obstacles to their success, while also being taught that with strategic planning and collective effort these obstacles are surmountable.

— *Offering opportunities for students to experience social structures as impermanent and changeable for the sake of those people who live within them (Freire, 1993)*

In the students' creation of Sweet Cakes Town, they had the opportunity to question why certain conditions exist, and to try out new approaches in such areas as legislation, taxation, social services, and labor/management relations. Here the importance of the imagination in social change becomes clear. I would like to explain this connection with a passage written by Northrop Frye (1964) about the literary imagination. What Frye says about the literary imagination I find equally applicable to the social imagination exhibited by my students in the creation of Sweet Cakes Town. While he wrote this in 1964, referring to the imagination of Canadians, I have taken the liberty of inserting the United States of our time:

> Just as [the material world] looks real, so this ideal world that our imaginations develop inside us looks like a dream that came out of nowhere, and has no reality except that we put into it. But it isn't. It's the real world, the real form of human society hidden behind the one we see. It's the world of what humanity has done, and therefore can do, the world revealed to us in the arts and sciences. This is the world that won't go away, the world out of which we built the [United States of 1964], are now building the [United States of 1994], and will be building the quite different [United States of 2004]. (Frye, 1964, p. 152)

My students found that they could change their roles in Sweet Cakes Town, as well as alter its social structures. Thus we see that the template for the society of the future need not be what the students have seen, but what they can imagine.

REFERENCES

Barth, F. (1969). *Ethnic groups and boundaries: The social organization of culture difference.* Boston: Little, Brown.

Bowles, S., & Gintis, H. (1976) *Schooling in capitalist America.* New York: Basic Books.

Bourdieu, P. (1977). *Reproduction in education, society, and culture.* London: Sage.

Byrne, J. (1993, December). The horizontal corporation. *Business Week,* pp. 76–81.

Davidson, M. (1986). *I have a dream.* New York: Scholastic.

Donnan, C. (1988). Following our forebears' footsteps: From expedition to understanding. In V. Rogers, A. D. Roberts, & T. P. Weinland (Eds.), *Teaching social studies: Portraits from the classroom* (pp. 3–11). Washington, DC: National Council for the Social Studies.

Erickson, F. (1987). Transformation and school success: The politics and culture of educational achievement. *Anthropology and Education Quarterly, 18,* 335–356.

Freire, P. (1982). *Pedagogy of the oppressed.* New York: Continuum.

Freire, P. (1986). *Education for critical consciousness.* New York: Continuum.

Freire, P. (1993). *Pedagogy of the city.* New York: Continuum.

Frye, N. (1964). *The educated imagination.* Bloomington: Indiana University Press.

Fordham, S., & Ogbu, J. (1986). Black students' school success: Coping with the "Burden of 'acting White.'" *Urban Review, 18,* 176–206.

Gans, H. J. (1990). Deconstructing the underclass: The term's danger as a planning concept. *Journal of the American Planning Association, 56,* 271–277.

Giroux, H. A. (1977). The politics of the hidden curriculum. *Independent School, 37,* 42–43.

Giroux, H. A. (1978, December). Developing educational programs: Overcoming the hidden curriculum. *Clearing House,* pp. 148–151.

Giroux, H. A. (1979, December) Toward a new sociology of curriculum. *Educational Leadership,* pp. 248–253.

Katz, M. B. (1986). *In the shadow of the poorhouse: A social history of welfare in America.* New York: Basic Books.

Ladson-Billings, G. (1990). Like lightning in a bottle: Attempting to capture the pedagogical excellence of successful teachers of black students. *Qualitative Studies in Education, 3,* 335–344.

Ladson-Billings, G. (1992). Reading between the lines and beyond the pages: A culturally appropriate approach to literacy teaching. *Theory Into Practice, 31,* 312–320.

Lukas, J. A. (1986). *Common ground: A turbulent decade in the lives of three American families.* New York: Vintage Books.

McCarthy, L. P., & Braffman, E. J. (1985). Creating Victorian Philadelphia: Children reading and writing their world. *Curriculum Inquiry, 15,* 121–151.

Mickelson, R. A. (1984). *Race, class, and gender differences in adolescent academic achievement attitudes and behaviors.* Unpublished doctoral dissertation, University of California, Los Angeles.

Ogbu, J. (1978). *Minority education and caste.* New York: Academic Press.

Ogbu, J. (1988). Variability in minority school performance: A problem in search of an explanation. *Anthropology and Education Quarterly, 18,* 312–335.

Richmond, G. (1989). The future school: Is Lowell pointing us toward a revolution in education? *Phi Delta Kappan, 71,* 232–236.

Schein, E. H. (1988) *Process consultation: Vol. 1. Its role in organizational development.* Reading, MA: Addison Wesley.

School District of Philadelphia. (1989). *Social studies grade three.* Philadelphia: Office of Curriculum.

School District of Philadelphia. (1991). *Superintendent's management information center, 1990-1991.* Philadelphia: School District of Philadelphia, Office of Assessment.

Shor, I. (1980). *Critical teaching and everyday life.* Boston: South End Press.

Sleeter, C. E. (1991). Multicultural education and empowerment. In C. E. Sleeter (Ed.), *Empowerment through multicultural education* (p. 15). Albany: State University of New York Press.

Sleeter, C. E., & Grant, C. A. (1986). Success for all students. *Phi Delta Kappan, 68,* 297–299.

Simon, R., & Dippo, D. (1987). What schools can do: Designing programs for work education that challenge the wisdom of experience. *Boston University Journal of Education, 169*(3), 101–117.

Sticht, T. (1987). *Cast off youth: Policy and training methods from the military experience.* New York: Praeger.

Stewart, T. (1992, May). The search for the organization of tomorrow. *Fortune,* pp. 92–99.

Stewart, T. (1993, December). Welcome to the revolution. *Fortune,* pp. 66–77.

Vygotsky, L. S. (1978). *Mind in society.* Cambridge, MA: Harvard University Press.

Wigginton, E. (1989) Foxfire grows up. *Harvard Educational Review, 59,* 24–49.

Wilson, W. J. (1987). *The truly disadvantaged.* Chicago: University of Chicago Press.

Wilson, W. J. (1990, February) Studying inner city dislocations: The challenge of public agenda research. 1990 Presidential address. *American Sociological Review,* pp. 1–14.

Those who know my teaching know that it has been a wildly uneven road to any success. As any teacher, I am indebted to the wisdom and generosity of others. Credit and thanks must first go to my students, and the many members of the community who supported us. For reasons of confidentiality, all of the above must go unnamed. I am also indebted to the wisdom of my mentors: Scott Tiley, my fifth-grade teacher; Virginia Miller of Bank Street College; Fran Motola of PS 87; Joan Billen, formerly of the Bank Street School for Children; Ewa Pytowska, of the Intercultural Training Resource Center; Barbara Moore Williams of the School District of Philadelphia; the principal of my school. Lastly, I am indebted to the many people who patiently helped me with the preparation of this manuscript: Nancy Brooks, Frederick Erickson, David Kinney, Michael B. Katz, Karl Otto, Ellen Skilton Sylvester, and my family.

Living with the Pendulum: The Complex World of Teaching

JEANETTE THRONE

As a classroom teacher, every time the educational pendulum swings from one opposing ideology to another, I feel that once again I have been hit by a moving object. Schools are either going back to basics or going beyond them, with little examination as to why these either/or choices have not been more effective. One side of the pendulum has teachers imparting knowledge to students through direct, systematic instruction with an emphasis on skills and content. The other side encourages children to take a more active role in constructing their own knowledge with less explicit teaching of skills. In math, the opposing sides may be computation versus problem-solving; in science, they may be content versus process; and in the reading/language arts area, they may be phonics versus whole language. In this article, I look at this problem from two perspectives: that of history and that of my kindergarten language arts program. Curriculum reforms examined through a historical lens provide a reference point for analyzing current reform promises and challenge educators not to repeat the excesses of the past. Analyzing these reforms from my classroom practice, I have found that these either/or choices conflict with the complex nature of the classroom, where different needs exist simultaneously.

These reform movements create a great deal of controversy in the language arts curriculum, especially in the primary grades (kindergarten through second grade), where learning to read is the main focus. In the primary grades, "the basics" usually refers to the skills needed to use the alphabetic code and the conventions of print (i.e., letters of the alphabet, sound-symbol relationships, decoding, spelling, handwriting, punctuation,

Harvard Educational Review Vol. 64 No. 2 Summer 1994, 195–208

and grammar). Current educational research on teaching young children to read places those educators who believe that the alphabetic code and the conventions of print should be directly taught into one ideological camp (Chall, 1989; Delpit, 1988; Stanovich, 1993/1994). In the other camp are whole language proponents, who believe children will naturally acquire these skills within the contexts of language and literacy experiences that focus primarily on meaning, process, problem-solving, creativity, and the interests of each child (Goodman, 1992; Watson, 1989). Classroom teachers may try to resolve these ideological differences by adopting an eclectic approach — a little bit of one method and a little bit of another — without always understanding that there is a complementary relationship between the theories and practices represented by opposing viewpoints. The paradox is that no one approach works for all children — which is why the pendulum never stops swinging.

Debating an issue by standing firmly on one side causes polarization, which prevents educators from seeing the whole picture. Educators therefore see the solution as an either/or decision rather than one in which both approaches have the potential to complement one another. Many educators find accepting both ideologies difficult. Such polarization is not a new problem for educational reform. In 1938, John Dewey, concerned about the excesses he saw in both traditional practices and the progressive movement, wrote:

> It is the business of an intellectual theory of education to ascertain the causes for the conflicts that exist, and then, instead of taking one side or the other, to indicate a plan of operations proceeding from a level deeper and more inclusive than is represented by the practices of the contending parties. (Dewey, 1938/1963, p. 5)

When theory does not reflect the realities of the classroom, classroom teachers working directly with children have difficulty finding common ground from which to discuss these conflicts with educators whose main responsibilities lie outside the classroom. Dewey (1929) attributed this difficulty to theory's quest for certainty when, in fact, "uncertainty is primarily a practical matter" (p. 223). In practice, theory's quest for certainty often leads to unfulfilled promises.

Children's literature and a language-experience approach (Van Allen & Allen, 1969) have been an important part of my curriculum since the beginning of my teaching career.[1] At various times in my career, I have also been responsible for teaching commercial reading programs that relied on a sys-

---

[1] The current whole language philosophy has some similarities to the language-experience approach. Important components of both are the integration of all language experiences (speaking, listening, writing, and reading) and teaching skills within the context of these experiences. Another similarity is the reading aloud of children's books and poetry and integrating children's literature into units that focus on a common theme. One of the fundamental differences between the two is the methods and the materials used for teaching writing and reading. The language-experience approach

tematic phonics approach (Boston Educational Research Company, 1971; Lindamood & Lindamood, 1975). When I taught these commercial programs, I had students who easily learned to read and students who struggled. When I was introduced to big books (Holdaway, 1979), process writing (Graves, 1983), and invented spelling (Temple, Nathan, & Burris, 1982) through the educational literature, I integrated them into my curriculum. I minimized the amount of phonics I taught and no longer used a commercial reading program. Again, I had students who learned easily and students who struggled. I found that the promise made by proponents of all of these approaches — that is, that all children will become successful readers and writers — did not hold true. I stopped believing in the certainty of this promise and began to see that no one program or approach held all the answers for all children.

THE QUEST FOR CERTAINTY

Currently, teachers are criticized when they rely too much on basal readers and the step-by-step lesson plans provided in most teachers' manuals.[2] Basals were originally advocated, however, as a way of improving reading instruction. In the 1920s, reading experts promoted the use of basals and teachers' manuals in order to render reading instruction more standard and scientific. In his book, *Broken Promises*, Patrick Shannon (1989) writes of this history:

> The problem facing these and other reading experts since the late 1920s was how to induce teachers, who were already using textbooks according to their own ideas, to follow the scientific directions included in the teacher's guidebooks. . . . And over the next sixty years, the control of reading instruction passed from teachers' hands to those of the reading experts and commercial publishers as basal use became more and more prevalent in elementary schools across America — so prevalent, in fact, that it often seems that the materials are using teachers rather than teachers using the materials. (p. 29)

Knowing where the promises of the past have led gives teachers a reference point from which to examine today's promises. When they analyze and articulate the uncertainties, struggles, and triumphs that reflect their daily experiences and philosophies, they add another dimension to the debates that challenge all educators. The role of a classroom teacher thus expands from one who implements theory to one who also creates, tests, questions,

---

uses children's dictation, written down by the teacher, as the primary method for teaching writing and reading. Language-experience charts, class books, and individual stories and books are generated by children's personal and classroom experiences. The whole language philosophy puts more emphasis on children doing their own writing and using trade books for teaching reading.

[2] A basal reading program is a series of graded readers organized by reading levels, starting with a kindergarten readiness program or a first-grade preprimer and extending to the middle school grades.

and informs theory within the context of his or her classroom. Teachers are able to move beyond what they have often done to cope with bureaucratic certainty — that is, to quietly shut their doors and teach.

By entering into the educational dialogue as active participants, teachers construct a deeper understanding of what they do and why. This dialogue begins among colleagues. Exchanging activities and procedures is part of the traditional dialogue among classroom teachers, but conversations that clarify a teacher's thinking and generate new knowledge can also be part of this exchange. Knowledge generated from inside the classroom is not only useful for teachers, it also challenges the assumption that knowledge about teaching and learning should be generated only by theorists working outside the classroom (Cochran-Smith & Lytle, 1993). If the classroom door is to be kept open, teacher inquiry should challenge and inform theory just as theory challenges and informs practice.

In the following sections of this article, I take a closer look at my own classroom. A teacher since the late 1960s, I currently teach all-day, every-day kindergarten in an integrated, suburban school district. I have no glorious success stories to tell — stories of how I or a particular instructional program achieved success while all others failed. Instead I offer an in-depth look at the strengths and needs of one child's learning within the broader context of my classroom. I also focus on my language arts curriculum and how it facilitates each student's need to comprehend the meaning and the conventions of print. Woven throughout is an examination of my role as teacher and as learner. Although these stories are told from the perspective of a kindergarten language arts teacher, I hope other teachers will see themselves in my stories and make connections that help them analyze and articulate their experiences, concerns, and insights. Perhaps as teachers look more closely at their own classrooms, all educators — those working inside and outside the classroom — will see that the quest is not one for certainty or single answers, but a quest for understanding the many influences that bear upon a child's learning and a teacher's teaching.

MATTHEW: INSIGHTS INTO ONE CHILD'S LEARNING

Whenever I think I have found "The Answer" (the one that solves every problem, every dilemma), I meet a child who reminds me to keep looking. Matthew was one of these children. Matthew entered my kindergarten with special needs in both written language and math. Matthew spent two years in my classroom because both his mother and I felt that he would benefit from a second year in kindergarten in order to give him more time to develop a better understanding of written language and mathematics. Matthew was a young kindergartner; he had a September birthday where, in Ohio, the cut-off date for school entrance is October 1. In addition to being young relative to his peers, Matthew needed more individual help than could be provided in the regular classroom. Thus, during his first year in my classroom, he received additional language support from the speech and language teacher, and he received help in the areas of reading and math from the basic skills tutor. In January of Matthew's second year in kindergarten he was placed in an afternoon kindergarten class specifically designed for children with special needs, while he remained in my classroom in the morning.

Matthew's greatest success was drawing. The first pictures he drew consisted of a mass of circles and lines. These circles and lines, however, gradually changed into people drawn with two eyes placed in a circle with two lines protruding from the bottom for legs. Crayons and markers were his favorite media, green was his favorite color, and people were his favorite subject. Matthew was a quiet child and, unlike some other children, did not verbally communicate what his pictures represented unless I asked him to dictate a story about his drawing. His first drawings were generally about his mom or himself. These pictures held meaning for Matthew, but neither I nor the other children knew what they represented unless Matthew told us.

In the two years Matthew was in my kindergarten classroom, he added more detail to his people until everyone had arms, hands, fingers, legs, feet, and hair. Faces had eyes and mouths but no noses; the males in his pictures wore shirts and pants, and the females wore dresses. Matthew spent a lot of time on these pictures, and the pages were always full; he drew wherever there was empty space. His progress with drawing continued and his pictures became more organized (Gardner, 1980). In the spring of his second year in kindergarten, Matthew began to arrange the people in his drawings into rows, and the meaning of his pictures could be better understood by others. A picture depicting Matthew's preference for drawing people in rows showed ten of his cousins and friends riding skateboards with a car drawn among them. They were skateboarding in two rows across consecutive pages in his writing book. Each boy was wearing sunglasses, and all had numbers written on their shirts. This was one of my favorite pictures.

Although Matthew's use of symbolic representation grew through his drawing, he struggled to learn the symbols of written language. Learning to write his name was difficult for Matthew. Teaching him to write his name was difficult for me. I felt Matthew wanted to learn to write his name, but he resisted because neither he nor I could find a way to begin. Both letter formation and putting letters in the correct sequence were a challenge for him. My biggest challenge was teaching him to write the first letter in his name. No matter how many times he traced over or copied the letters in his name using a variety of media such as plastic letters, sandpaper letters, clay, markers, crayons, chalk, or pencils, he could not retrieve the letters from memory. Nothing worked until I brought in a paper bag from a McDonald's restaurant, and we talked about how the golden arches represented the letter M. I am not sure if Matthew understood that the golden arches were intended to represent the first letter in the McDonald name and could also represent the first letter in his name, but the familiar shape of the arches seemed to help him to remember how the M is formed. This seemed an important breakthrough, but every letter in this name continued to be a struggle for him. Matthew's success in writing the letter M gave him more confidence in his ability to learn how to write his name. This confidence led to less resistance from Matthew, and the activities and materials that I introduced previously were more effective in helping him attend to and remember the visual features of print.

As Matthew began to write the letters in his name, he still was unable to write them in the correct sequence. This difficulty persisted into his second year of kindergarten. We both persevered, however, and by the end of that year he was able to write his first and last names, recognize letters, and use seemingly random letters in the stories he wrote. Although Matthew could write his name and use letters in this writing, he had not yet internalized the abstract nature of an alphabetic writing system and how it is organized to represent thoughts and speech. This came later. For Matthew, progress with symbolic representation in one area did not naturally lead to use and understanding in another. His progress using pictorial symbols came from his own initiative and motivation. His progress with written symbols came from the direct instruction he received from others and me.

I had to let Matthew teach me so I could learn how best to teach him. What I learned from Matthew enriched my teaching for all children. Watching him struggle with written language and flourish with drawing helped me to better understand the symbolic nature of art and to see how different symbol systems (oral language, written language, the arts, mathematics, etc.) are vehicles through which humans create and communicate meaning (Gardner, 1982). From Matthew's difficulty with putting the letters in his name in the correct sequence, I learned that serial order is important to young children's understanding of written language (Clay, 1991). I also came to see that my role as teacher was not just to provide my students with direct, explicit instruction or to provide opportunities for them to learn naturally; it was also to weave the two together to meet the strengths and needs of each child.

A COMMUNITY OF LEARNERS

Children learn and acquire knowledge long before they enter kindergarten. They are not empty vessels to be filled with equal amounts of knowledge. The complexity of teaching — working with young children and deciding how to guide and support them in their language learning — confronts me from the first day my kindergartners enter my classroom. Giving each child a writing book filled with empty sheets of paper elicits a diverse range of responses that emerge from each child's individual understanding of how humans use language and symbol systems to create meaning.

Some children enter kindergarten reading, and others are learning to write their names. Some enjoy expressing ideas through writing, and others prefer to express themselves through play or the arts. Some write or dictate stories with a narrative style, and others label each picture with a sentence beginning with "This is" or "There's a." Some talk their way through a story with friends nearby, some make running commentaries to themselves, and others work quietly.

One child writes independently using invented spellings, another fills the page by copying friends' names from their name cards, and yet another dictates long stories to me. Some children who already have a good knowledge of print can spell words phonetically and put space between words, but they write only limited stories without encouragement. For them, invented spelling is not "real spelling," and they want to use only words they can spell correctly. Other children may have a limited knowledge of print, but confidently start to write. One child draws elaborate, detailed pictures, but struggles with understanding how print works, and another child has original ideas but struggles with the physical aspects of using crayons or holding a pencil. And, there are some children who can put it all together — their ability to draw, write, and create stories challenges me to build on all their strengths.

Teaching would be easier for me if I adopted an either/or perspective — to teach letters and sounds or to encourage self-expression. Viewing my role from the first perspective, my job would be to impart the conventions of print that our society uses; the application of these skills would come later. From the second, more creative perspective, my role would be to provide encouragement and materials for my students to express their ideas through talking, drawing, and writing.

This either/or position is not a comfortable one for me. I have always enjoyed teaching the alphabet and introducing young children to its power to make sense of written language. This interest has been balanced with my love of children's art, children's play, and literature for children. I want my students to explore and begin to understand how books, poetry, the arts, mathematics, science, and play can expand their worlds and take them into new ones. Children who come to me with different strengths, needs, interests, behaviors, and backgrounds challenge me to see beyond these either/or choices.

THE CHILD, THE BOOK, THE TEACHER

Reading aloud to my kindergartners is an important part of my language arts curriculum. It provides the best way I know to enhance young children's enjoyment and comprehension of literature before they become readers themselves. The interaction between the child, the book, and the teacher is influenced by many factors, such as a child's interest, the difficulty of a book, or how a teacher chooses to use it. Children bring their own experiences (both literary and life) to their understanding of text, and these experiences are part of the transaction between them and the text (Rosenblatt, 1938/1976). When I read aloud with a child, three voices interact to bring meaning to the text — the author's, the child's, and mine — and the illustrations provide a visual interpretation of the story. Meaning is shaped and reshaped as the child and I build on each other's understanding of the book. Our conversations help me to understand a child's thinking about a story as well as my own. Without this exchange of ideas, further understanding of the story would be limited for both the children and me. We learn from the book and from each other. Practices that emphasize one part of this reciprocal relationship over another (such as if only the teacher asks the questions) limit what a child learns and how a teacher teaches.

My kindergartners select books to read with friends, to read alone, and to read with me. They make their choices during book choosing times and during free-choice times when other choices are available, such as puzzles, math, blocks, sand, paints, or computer. I choose books to read with the class during story times or to have a child read with me during our free-choice times. When a child reads with me, we may read the book together or the child may choose to read alone, which involves retelling a story, reciting the memorized text while pointing to the words on a page, or reading in the conventional sense. Repetition, rhyme, predictable language patterns, or a controlled vocabulary support beginning readers, but it is the story that engages their feelings and imaginations.

Knock Knock Who's There? (1988), written by Sally Grindley and illustrated by Anthony Browne, evoked lots of "ooo's" and "eee's" as I read it to my class. In this story, a little girl is in bed when she hears a knock at her door. When the door is first opened, the reader is introduced to a gorilla standing in the doorway. The refrain "Knock Knock Who's There?" is repeated throughout the story, when a witch, a ghost, a dragon, and a giant knock at her door. She does not let anyone in until her daddy knocks with a story to tell and a mug of hot chocolate. She tells him about the previous visitors and how she knew it was him all along . . . "really." The drawings show that each character who knocks on the door is wearing the same bedroom slippers.

The slippers sparked a lively discussion among my kindergartners. Some children wondered, were they the gorilla's shoes or daddy's shoes? The gorilla-shaped shadow drawn behind the father added more fuel to their debate. This book stretched my children's imaginations just as the knock on the door stretched the little girl's imagination. Their questions and comments reflected their feelings, perceptions, and search for meaning as they tried to answer the question of who was at the door. This question did not have the same answer for every child — some were convinced it was the gorilla and others were convinced it was the daddy. No one proposed that it could have been any of the other characters pictured knocking at the door. Several children suggested it was the little girl's daddy because she recognized his voice, but this hypothesis did not provide the proof needed for everyone to agree.

When Carmella chose to read this book with me, she questioned whether the main character was a girl or a boy. When I asked her what she thought, she answered, "I think the kid is a girl." She also thought the witch was the girl who married the gorilla and said, "Then she got all the children. All these children in these books." She looked through the book showing me the ghost, the dragon, and the giant. Her interpretation did not hold up when we got to the page showing the daddy. I realized this when she looked at me and said, "Daddy's not the children. He turned into a gorilla." When I asked her how he turned into a gorilla, she told me she thought he had a costume. Carmella's questions and comments indicated to me that the imaginative play taking place during the little girl's game of "knock knock" was not always clear to her. I am not sure it was clear to the other children either, but Carmella questioned it more as she tried to distinguish real from make-believe and to use both to explain the book to herself. I tried to give her support by asking questions, answering her questions, or by helping her answer her own.

When I first read this book to my class, I did not realize how important the bedroom slippers would be to the children's understanding of the story. Their response to these slippers strengthened my belief that the child, the book, and the teacher work together to enhance children's enjoyment and comprehension of literature. Focusing on the debate over the superiority of a child-centered versus a teacher-directed curriculum or a content-based curriculum (knowing children's literature is knowing content) blocks educators from seeing how each complements the other.

THE CHALLENGE OF EMBRACING BOTH SIDES OF THE DEBATE

Learning the alphabet and the phonetic structure of print are key parts of learning to read and write, but these skills are the object of great controversy when educators debate how and when to teach them. Much of the extensive research in this debate is confusing because the researchers' points of view are positioned oppositionally and rarely integrated. There are many questions in this debate, but the ones that most affect me as a kindergarten teacher are 1) what is the optimum age to introduce children to these skills? and 2) should these skills be directly taught in isolation from meaningful contexts, or should children learn them naturally within a print-rich environment?

Observing my students has shown me that the alphabetic code is important for children to learn. Children who struggle to understand the relationship between speech sounds and the letters they represent struggle with learning to read. Most children who understand sound-symbol relationships and use them to spell words phonetically (the letters a child writes closely match the sounds in a word) learn to read successfully. Although I feel the alphabetic code is important for children to learn, how to teach it so all children are successful is not an easy question to answer. Many basal reading readiness programs adopted by school districts focus primarily on teaching sound-symbol relationships and phonics. These programs conflict with educational organizations' recommendation for a whole language philosophy that focuses mainly on language development, children's literature, and children's writing (Bredekamp, 1987; Early Childhood and Literacy Development Committee, 1985; Strickland & Morrow, 1989). Both approaches have limitations. In my experience, the first approach focuses too much on teaching phonetic skills in isolation and not enough on the contexts in which they are used. The second approach may not focus enough on phonetic skills for children who need more direct, explicit instruction in order to apply these skills to their reading and writing.

Finding ways to incorporate the alphabet and phonetic skills into a balanced language arts curriculum in order to meet the strengths and needs of every child is a question I still work toward answering. My goal is to provide my kindergartners with a variety of literacy experiences so they will attend to print, talk about it, and use it. Each week I introduce a new letter and its sound to the whole class. I provide objects that correspond to the weekly sound, along with related pictures and words, a children's letter book for each sound (Randell, 1970), plastic letters, and environmental print (for example, McDonald's and M&M bags for "M" week). I place these materials on a table along with markers, colored pencils, and paper for the children to look at and use throughout the week. I also display self-portraits of those children whose first or last names start with the letter being highlighted. This area is a popular choice during our free- choice periods. Another popular activity is substituting the first sound of each child's name with the weekly letter-sound. Other phonetic-related activities that may not always relate to the weekly letter are clapping the syllables in our names and other words, reading alphabet and rhyming books, playing alphabet and letter-sound games, or analyzing the sequence of sounds we hear in words as the children or I write down the corresponding letters.

Even though the "sound-of-the-week" activities to which I refer focus primarily on teaching letters and sound-symbol relationships, I use this format because it gives me an organized structure to introduce letters and sounds. This structure, in turn, allows for an openness that fosters many spontaneous discoveries as children investigate and talk about print. Furthermore, this provides me with opportunities to expand my understanding of how my students are thinking about print. I listen to children's questions and comments to build on their thinking and clarify my own. Their observations move into new directions as they build on the ideas and information that I have presented to them. For example, while sharing pictures for "D" week, Jacqueline insisted I remove the picture of a dress because the word dress started with "jr" not "d," which is how she heard the /dr/ blend. This observation led to a discussion of how the sounds heard in words are sometimes different from the letters seen. There may be a time when I eliminate the sound-of-the-week, but not until I find another approach that gives me both the structure and the flexibility to meet different needs, both the children's and mine.

In over twenty-five years of teaching, I have yet to find one single approach that meets all children's needs. What I have learned, however, is that whatever method or approach I use, its problems must be examined along with its advantages. For this reason, I use the sound-of-the-week approach with caution. Just as any method or theory can be misused, so can this one. Because this approach focuses primarily on phonetic skills, I integrate it into my language arts curriculum that provides children with many opportunities to talk about and apply this knowledge within the context of stories, poetry, big books, writing, and other meaningful experiences with print. I am careful that the total curriculum does not center around the weekly letter and that worksheets are not used as the primary means for introducing my students to letter-names and letter-sound relationships. Just as important, I try to be aware of the times when a word or a word activity is confusing to a child. Understanding Jacqueline's confusion with the word "dress" from her perspective enabled me to help her try to resolve it. There may also be times when children who learn English as a second language may have difficulty hearing or saying sounds that are not in their native language, and children with cultural or regional dialects may also experience difficulty with particular sounds.

Examining both the advantages and the problems of different approaches helps teachers to critique and evaluate how the programs they create and those they are required to implement affect children's learning. Searching for the single, correct answer that has no problems or limitations takes classroom teachers from one curriculum reform to another and back again. A dialogue between teachers and theorists that reflects the advantages, problems, and limitations of different approaches and theories would benefit teachers more than a dialogue that pushes the pendulum from one opposing viewpoint to another. When the role of classroom teachers becomes more than the implementation of curriculum, teachers may find themselves questioning the experts. Such repositioning can lead to a deeper understanding of what teachers do and why, and it brings the teacher's voice into the dialogue that challenges all educators.

BUILDING ON CHILDREN'S THINKING

Research into the phonetic bases of nonstandard spellings by young children (Bissex, 1980; Read, 1975; Temple et al., 1982) has given educators many insights into children's thinking about print. My kindergartners apply their phonetic knowledge more readily to writing than to reading. Just as children construct and use their own system of rules when they first learn to speak (Brown, 1973), they construct and use a system of rules for writing that is different from conventional writing. My students form and test new hypotheses as they adapt their theories of how print works to the information and language (both oral and written) that others and I have shared with them.

I build on my kindergartners' understanding of how the alphabetic code works by helping them work out the discrepancies between their hypotheses and conventional print. I give support during whole class sessions as we discuss the letters and sounds we see and hear in words. I may sit with a small group of children working in their writing books, answering their questions about letter formation, letter-sounds, or words. When I transcribe children's stories, I work with them individually on a variety of writing skills. For example, I help the child who uses letter-like marks or writes only the letters she knows in her name to form letters and to learn the alphabet. I encourage the child who hears beginning consonants in words to use more letter-sounds in his writing. Some children may need guidance hearing the sequence of sounds in words, while others are encouraged to write left-to-right across the page or to put space between words. I introduce the spellings of high-frequency words to children who mix conventional spelling with invented spelling. I also help them to understand the use of silent letters or when a word does not "play fair" phonetically.

Writing gives children many opportunities to experiment with print, and it gives me a better sense of their thinking about written language. Meaning, however, often gets lost to children's intense concentration in putting letters, sounds, and words down on paper. Because these skills are not yet automatic for kindergartners, the conscious attention they must give to the mechanics of writing as they write makes it difficult for them to give their full attention to meaning. Therefore, I encourage my students to write what they can independently (or with my support to write more than they think they can) and to dictate the rest to me. Dictation fosters self-expression and extends children's writing. As I write what they tell me, we talk and think our way through a story together. I ask questions and offer suggestions to encourage them to clarify an idea, expand an imaginative thought, tell the reader more about an experience, or to pursue a new idea.

As teachers try to understand all that is involved in learning to read and write and how they can best help children become confident readers and writers, they must also look at how children perceive and respond to their teaching practices. To know when a child may need direct, explicit instruction or when a child would benefit from exploration and discovery, a teacher relies on his or her knowledge of a child's thinking and learning, knowledge of the curriculum, and knowledge of his or her own teaching.

SEEING BEYOND "EITHER/OR" CHOICES

I used to believe educators could stop the swinging pendulum; now I am not sure it can be stopped, or even if it should be. Curriculum reforms that put educators into opposing camps, such as direct teaching versus discovery learning, phonics versus whole language, or a child-centered curriculum versus a content-based or teacher-directed curriculum, move the field of education back and forth to the extreme ends of the pendulum. The educational debates that often ensue promote one ideology or the other and prevent educators from engaging in the back-and-forth dialectic that could help them better understand teaching and learning. The question educators should be asking is not how to stop the pendulum, but how to stop the ideological wars that block the effectiveness of the reforms represented by the different ideologies. These debates inhibit communication and too often take on a critical, patronizing, or elitist tone based primarily on the ideology being opposed or promoted. Mandates, policies, standards, and curricula based on either/or choices often rectify one problem and create another, thereby moving educators from one opposing reform to another. The power to mandate change (regardless of which side of the pendulum it is on) is not the same as the power to be effective.

Teachers are often caught in the middle of these changes. Teachers' voices as authorities are heard when they agree with or accept the changes; their voices are less likely to be heard by administrators, theorists, researchers, or policymakers when they question changes or express concern based on their knowledge and experience. Teachers do not have all the answers, nor can they do their job without support from the entire education community. Further, the exclusion of classroom voices (children's and teachers') pushes teachers from one opposing reform to another with little inquiry into understanding where they have been, where they are, or the consequences of where they are going. Communication based on a reciprocal relationship among teachers, parents, administrators, curriculum specialists, researchers, theorists, teacher educators, commercial publishers, and policymakers, rather than a hierarchical relationship, allows educators to see teaching and learning in new ways and gives them a more comprehensive view.

When I look at a child like Matthew, I see a child who not only challenges me, his teacher, but a child who challenges all educators to work together to see beyond either/or choices. Such choices limit the support teachers give to children, and they limit the support educators give to each other. Understanding children's strengths and needs, their difficulties and triumphs; designing a curriculum that focuses on meaning and the conventions of print; and teaching both directly and indirectly requires a vision that may encompass opinions on both sides of the pendulum. It is this perspective that enables educators to learn from each other to seek effective interventions.

Devising a language arts program for kindergartners is only one of the many issues that currently challenge teachers. Teachers are also challenged by issues inherent in subject areas that affect students differently at different grade levels. They are challenged by assessment, standards, mainstreaming, discipline, class size, at-risk students, and many other demands on their time. These challenges face all educators — those who work primarily with children as well as those who work with teachers. If educators are to meet these challenges, they must look beyond either/or choices in order to see solutions that reflect the realities of the classroom.

This article began with the image of a swinging pendulum; I would like to end with the metaphor of my grandmother's stereoscope. As a child in an age of television and movies, I was enchanted by the stereoscope's simplicity. A postcard-size picture with two photographs of the same scene taken from slightly different viewpoints was placed into the front slot, and when I peered through both lenses, I could see up close a three-dimensional world of faraway places. The realism and depth of these photographic scenes were recreated by looking through both lenses simultaneously, and my mind fused the two pictures into one.

When teachers look at what is in front of them with both eyes, the depth and breadth of their vision is clearer. When they look at the questions and the answers — the possibilities and the limitations — they see new opportunities for themselves and the children they teach. These opportunities merge with their beliefs, knowledge, experiences, and concerns as they begin to create a vision of learning and teaching as a multidimensional world that connects the values and needs of a democratic society, the interactive nature of a diverse classroom community, and the uniqueness of each child. This is the complex world of teaching.

REFERENCES

Bissex, G. (1980). *Gnys at wrk: A child learns to read and write.* Cambridge, MA: Harvard University Press.

Boston Educational Research Company. (1971). *Beginning to read, write and listen.* Philadelphia: J. B. Lippincott.

Bredekamp, S. (Ed.). (1987). *Developmentally appropriate practice in early childhood programs serving children from birth through age 8.* Washington, DC: National Association for the Education of Young Children.

Brown, R. (1973). *A first language: The early stages.* Cambridge, MA: Harvard University Press.

Chall, J. S. (1989). Learning to read: The great debate 20 years later – A response to debunking the great phonics myth. *Phi Delta Kappan, 70,* 521–538.

Clay, M. M. (1991). *Becoming literate: The construction of inner control.* Portsmouth, NH: Heinemann.

Cochran-Smith, M., & Lytle, S. L. (1993). *Inside/outside: Teacher research and knowledge.* New York: Teachers College Press.

Delpit, L. (1988). The silenced dialogue: Power and pedagogy in educating other people's children. *Harvard Educational Review, 58,* 280–298.

Dewey, J. (1929). *The quest for certainty: A study of the relation of knowledge and action.* New York: Minton Balch.

Dewey, J. (1963). *Experience and education.* New York: Macmillan. (Original work published 1938)

Early Childhood and Literacy Development Committee. (1985). *Literacy development and pre-first grade* [pamphlet]. Newark, DE: International Reading Association.

Gardner, H. (1980). *Artful scribbles: The significance of children's drawings.* New York: Basic Books.

Gardner, H. (1982). *Art, mind, and brain: A cognitive approach to creativity.* New York: Basic Books.

Goodman, K. S. (1992). I didn't found whole language. *Reading Teacher, 46,* 188–199.

Graves, D. H. (1983). *Writing: Teachers and children at work.* Portsmouth, NH: Heinemann.

Grindley, S. (1988). *Knock knock who's there?* London: Methuen Children's Books.

Holdaway, D. (1979). *The foundations of literacy.* Sydney, Australia: Ashton Scholastic.

Lindamood, C. H., & Lindamood, P. C. (1975). *The A.D.D. program: Auditory discrimination in depth.* Boston: Teaching Resources.

Randell, B. (1970). *PM listening skillbuilders.* Wellington, New Zealand: Price Milburn.

Read, C. (1975). *Children's categorization of speech sounds in English.* Urbana, IL: National Council of Teachers of English.

Rosenblatt, L. (1976). *Literature as exploration.* New York: Noble and Noble. (Original work published 1938)

Shannon, P. (1989). *Broken promises: Reading instruction in twentieth-century America.* New York: Bergin & Garvey.

Stanovich, K. E. (1993/1994). Romance and reality. *Reading Teacher, 47,* 280–291.

Strickland, D. S., & Morrow, L. M. (Eds.). (1989). *Emerging literacy: Young children learn to read and write.* Newark, DE: International Reading Association.

Temple, C., Nathan, R., & Burris, N. (1982). *The beginnings of writing.* Boston: Allyn & Bacon.

Van Allen, R., & Allen, C. (1969). *Language experiences in early childhood: A teacher's resource book.* Chicago: Encyclopedia Britannica.

Watson, D. J. (1989). Defining and describing whole language. *Elementary School Journal, 40,* 129–141.

About the Contributors

DEBORAH LOEWENBERG BALL is Professor of Education at the University of Michigan. Her professional interests include teacher learning and teacher education; the role of subject matter knowledge in teaching and learning to teach; and the relations of policy and practice in instructional reform. Her recent publications include "Integrity in Teaching: Recognizing the Fusion of the Moral and the Intellectual" in *American Educational Research Journal* (with S. Wilson, 1996) and "Teacher Learning and the Mathematics Reforms: What Do We Think We Know and What Do We Need to Learn?" in *Phi Delta Kappan* (1996).

CYNTHIA BALLENGER is a researcher at the Chèchen Konnen Center for Science Education Reform, an early childhood specialist at the Stephen Bennet School in Brighton, Massachusetts, and a member of the Brookline Teacher-Researcher Seminar. Her professional interests center around linguistic minority children and teacher research. She is author of "Approaches to Literacy in a Haitian Preschool" in *Teacher Research* (1996) and "Social Identities, Moral Narratives, Scientific Argumentation: Science Talk in a Bilingual Classroom" in *Language and Education* (forthcoming).

PATRICIA CLIFFORD teaches second grade at Banded Peak School in Bragg Creek, Alberta, Canada. Previously a team teacher at the junior high level, she is now involved in the development of the Galileo Project, a center for innovative practice, research, and teacher development. Her publications include "Whole Language, Edgy Literacy and the Work of the World" in *Applying Research to the Classroom* (with D. Jardine and S. Friesen, 1995) and *The Transgressive Energy of Mythic Wives and Willful Children: Old Stories for New Times* (with S. Friesen, in press).

MARILYN COCHRAN-SMITH is Professor of Education and Director of Programs in Teacher Education at Boston College School of Education. She is interested in teacher education, teacher research, and teaching for social change. Her publications include *The Making of a Reader* (1984), *Learning to Write Differently* (with C. Paris and J. Kahn, 1991), and *Inside/Outside: Teacher Research and Knowledge* (with S. Lytle, 1993).

JOAN KERNAN CONE is a teacher at El Cerrito (California) High School, a doctoral student at the University of California at Berkeley, and a consultant to the Bay Area Writing Project. Her major professional interest is teaching high school English. She is author of "The Key to Untracking: Learning to Teach an Untracked Class" in *College Board Review* (1993) and "Teaching *The Autobiography of Malcolm X* in an Untracked Class: The Urgency of Choice" in *Teaching Tolerance* (1993).

SHARON L. FRIESEN is a teacher at Banded Peak School in Bragg Creek, Alberta, Canada. Previously a junior high teacher, she is currently involved in the development of the Galileo Project, a center for innovative practice, research, and teacher development. Her publications include *Hard Fun: Teaching and Learning for the Twenty-First Century* (with P. Clifford, 1995) and "Great Explorations" in *Applying Research to the Classroom* (with M. G. Stone, 1996).

KAREN GALLAS is an elementary teacher in the Brookline, Massachusetts, public schools. She is interested in teacher research, with a focus on language, literacy, and culture. Her publications include *The Languages of Learning: How Children Talk, Write, Dance, Draw, and Sing Their Understanding of the World* (1994) and *Talking Their Way Into Science: Hearing Children's Questions and Theories, Responding with Curricula* (1995).

J. ALLEYNE JOHNSON (Jennifer E. Obidah) is Assistant Professor at Emory University's Division of Education Studies. Her professional interests focus on urban education and teacher development, specifically on the social and cultural dynamics within urban public schools serving minority students from low-income neighborhoods. She is author of "'Black-Mystory': Literate Currency in Everyday Schooling" in *Reconceptualizing Adolescent Literacy*, edited by D. Alvermann (1996).

TIMOTHY J. LENSMIRE is Assistant Professor of Education at Washington University in St. Louis, Missouri. His major professional interest is literacy studies. He is author of *When Children Write: Critical Re-Visions of the Writing Workshop* (1994) and coauthor of "Appropriating Others' Words: Traces of Literature and Peer Culture in a Third Grader's Writing" in *Language in Society* (with D. Beals, 1994).

SUSAN L. LYTLE, Joseph L. Calihan Associate Professor of Education at the University of Pennsylvania Graduate School of Education, is also Director of the Program in Reading/Writing/Literacy and The Philadelphia Writing Project. Her research centers on literacy education, teacher inquiry, professional development, and the literacies of adolescence and adulthood. She is coauthor of *Inside/Outside: Teacher Research and Knowledge* (with M. Cochran-Smith, 1993) and other publications related to literacy teaching and learning.

JOHN PRYOR is Lecturer in Education at the Institute of Education, University of Sussex, Brighton, England. His professional interests include classroom interaction and classroom assessment. He is author of "Assessment Ticksheets: Don't Throw Out the Baby!" in *British Journal of Curriculum and Assessment* (1995) and coauthor of "Teacher-Pupil Interaction in Formative Assessment: Assessing the Work or Protecting the Child?" in *The Curriculum Journal* (with H. Torrance, 1996).

GINNY SEABROOK is Student Teacher Supervisor at Kean College of New Jersey in Union, and Basic Reading and Writing Teacher at Union County College in Cranford, New Jersey. She is presently researching a book on a nineteenth-century woman who was an entomologist, missionary, and suffragist. Her publications include "Pagoda Shadows: The Life of Adele Marion Fielde, Missionary to China 1865-1889" in *America Baptist Quarterly* (1993).

PAUL SKILTON SYLVESTER is a doctoral candidate at the University of Pennsylvania, where he is Adjunct Professor and an educational action researcher with the Center for Urban Ethnography. His current work involves comparing organizational change in an inner-city school and a Fortune 500 company, in order to understand the changing dynamics of social reproduction in the informational economy. He is author of "Beyond the Bootstraps: African American Students Envisioning Strategies for Economic Success" in *Making Justice Our Project: Critical Whole Language Teachers Talk about Their Work*, edited by C. Edelsky (forthcoming).

JEANETTE THRONE teaches all-day kindergarten at the Mercer School in Shaker Heights, Ohio. Her current area of interest is examining why the field of education is so susceptible to reforms that fail to produce the promised results. She is author of "Becoming a Kindergarten of Readers" in *Young Children* (1988).

About the Editors

CAROLYN H. CAMPBELL is a doctoral candidate in the Language and Literacy Program in Human Development and Psychology at the Harvard Graduate School of Education. She has taught third- and fourth-grade students in public and private schools. Her current research interests include the development of written language and genre understanding in elementary school children.

IRENE HALL is a doctoral candidate in Teaching, Curriculum, and Learning Environments at the Harvard Graduate School of Education. An elementary school teacher for over fifteen years, she is currently Associate Director of Kids In Business®, a creative learning program for urban youth. She is also writing a biography of Alice Dewey, cofounder (with husband John Dewey) of the Laboratory School at the University of Chicago.

EDWARD J. MIECH is a doctoral candidate in Administration, Planning, and Social Policy at the Harvard Graduate School of Education. He has taught English, math, and English as a Second Language in public high schools. His current research interests include the politics and history of education reform and federal aid to schools.